(DIS)EMBODYING MYTHS
IN ANCIEN RÉGIME OPERA

(Dis)embodying Myths in Ancien Régime Opera

Multidisciplinary Perspectives

Edited by Bruno Forment

Leuven University Press

Published with support of Universitaire Stichting van België

ISBN 978 90 5867 900 0

D / 2012 / 1869 / 12

NUR: 662 - 694

Cover Design: Jurgen Leemans
Cover Illustration: *Ifigenia* (2006), rehearsal photograph by Matthias Schellens

CONTENTS

MUSIC EXAMPLES AND ILLUSTRATIONS

Music examples

Illustrations

PREFACE

Recent decades have seen a remarkable upsurge of interest in what was long declared the "dark ages"[1] of opera: the massive repertoire composed between Claudio Monteverdi's demise (1643) and Christoph Gluck's *Orfeo ed Euridice* (1762). Numerous Baroque operas are currently being rediscovered, recorded, and (re)staged, renowned conductors are investing their time and energy in unperformed (or 'unperformable') works, and singers of high caliber assemble record-selling recitals from arias by such forgotten composers as Antonio Caldara or Nicola Porpora. Now that seventeenth- and eighteenth-century opera have returned sound and safe from the library to the theater, where they belong, it seems that even the most conservative spectator is ready to adapt his (post-)romantic expectations to embrace, say, simple recitative and da capo arias.

Surfing this wave of enthusiasm, the editor of the present volume was given the rare opportunity to witness students and alumni from the Brussels Conservatoire revive one and a half hour of music from his doctoral dissertation on *opera seria*.[2] On 7 December 2006, seven talented singers and twenty instrumentalists breathed new life into two so-called 'cut & paste operas,' *Ifigenia* and *Ipermestra*, which were stitched together from excerpts in unpublished manuscripts (see the cover picture and Illustration 1).[3] As the titles of both one-acters betray, mythological narratives provided the binding agent between the selected excerpts. The choice of Iphigenia in Aulis and the Danaids was at once both deliberate and daring. In their focus on superstition and religious fanaticism, both stories – Iphigenia must be sacrificed for the patriotic cause; Hypermnestra is to kill her bridegroom on paternal order – fit twenty-first-century sensibilities like a straightjacket. Still, it is a challenge to confront an audience accustomed to the gimmicks and gadgets of the modern stage

1. Kerman 1988, 39.
2. Forment 2007a.
3. They were performed using period vocal techniques, instruments, gestures, and costumes. Paul Dombrecht was the conductor on duty, while Sigrid T'Hooft instructed the singers in historically informed stage performance.

with *eighteenth-century* re-embodiments of these tales and characters. The experiment was refreshing, to say the least, and led to the conclusion that *opera seria* lacked a standard formula to represent even a specific myth – for instance, we found three composers endorsing as many different dramaturgical solutions to conclude the Iphigenia in Aulis, despite their libretti being adapted from the same tragedy, Jean Racine's *Iphigénie* (1674).[4]

Illustration 1. Soprano Soetkin Elbers rehearsing Clytemnestra in *Ifigenia* (Brussels, December 2006). Photograph by Matthias Schellens.

4. *Ifigenia* contained excerpts from Antonio Caldara's *Ifigenia in Aulide* (Vienna, 1718; libretto by Apostolo Zeno), Carl Heinrich Graun's *Ifigenia in Aulide* (Berlin, 1748; libretto by Leopoldo de' Villati after a scenario by Frederick the Great and Francesco Algarotti), and Niccolò Jommelli's *L'Ifigenìa* (Rome, 1751; anonymous libretto). On their various conclusions, see Reinhard Strohm's chapter.

(Dis)embodying myths in Ancien Régime opera seeks to shed new light on the chameleonic appearance of mythology in musical drama between c. 1600 and 1800.[5] Indeed, opera in this period capitalized on the scenic potential of myth to no mean degree. At its inception, in late Renaissance Florence, the *favola in musica* (literally: 'fable in music') was almost uniquely built upon the crystal palace of Ovidian mythology. With the 'rediscovered' monody (*recitar cantando*) seen as a genuine equivalent to Orphic song,[6] the magical and healing powers of which were ascribed to extraordinary men, early opera staged the "ancient deities, such as Apollo, Thetis, Neptune, and other respected gods," but also the "demigods and ancient heroes," and in particular those "perfect musicians" like Orpheus himself, Amphion, or David – the words are drawn from the anonymous tract *Il Corago* (see Jean-François Lattarico's chapter).[7]

But the presence of myth in Ancien Régime opera was anything but uninterrupted or unproblematic. Difficulties arose from the very concept of 'myth' itself, which we today could define, with Mircea Eliade, as a "story of the deeds of supernatural beings" that "concerns a creation" and is considered "absolutely true" and "sacred" by its users.[8] When applied to seventeenth- or eighteenth-century opera, however, this definition proves unstable, if not inadequate. For instance, Pietro Metastasio's *Didone abbandonata* (1724), the most popular libretto ever to deal with the legend of Dido and Aeneas, introduces the supernatural in only an indirect, invisible sense (as Bruno Forment's chapter points out). Granted, the libretto alludes to two creations (Carthage by Dido and Rome by Aeneas and his offspring), the latter of which must have borne 'sacred' implications for Metastasio, Roman-born and a lifelong representative of *romanitas*. All the same, the poet cannot have considered the Vergilian story "absolutely true," for in his foreword, Metastasio acknowledged the concurrence of Aeneas' wanderings after the Trojan War (thirteenth century BC) and the

5. The term 'Ancien Régime' was chosen for the sake of comprehensiveness: alternative labels (e.g., 'Baroque' or 'classicism') simply fail to encompass the stylistic breadth of the two centuries of operatic history dealt with in this book.
6. See Tomlinson 1999, 17.
7. Anonymous 1983, 63: "Per cominciare da personaggi o interloquitori che la rapresentazione armonica pare che più convenevolmente abbracci, sembrano molto a proposito per le azioni profane le deità antiche come Apollo, Teti, Nettuno et altri stimati numi, come anche i semidei et eroi vetusti ... e sopra tutti quei personaggi che stimiamo essere stati perfetti musici, come Orfeo, Anfione e simili."
8. Eliade 1991, 5.

establishment of Carthage (814 BC) to imply a "fortunate anachronism" – hardly a claim for veracity.[9]

The entire Ancien Régime was prone to riddling the status of myth versus history. In the absence of archeological evidence, mythographic method was dictated chiefly by historical, literary, or linguistic criteria. The tone for discussion was set by such studies as Abbé Banier's *Explication historique des fables, où l'on découvre leur origine et leur conformité avec l'histoire ancienne* (1711). And while confusion reigned supreme, the epics of Homer and Vergil were read as (semi-)historical narratives. In 1755, Gluck's future librettist Ranieri de' Calzabigi effectively considered Hercules, Theseus, and Ulysses as *personaggi istorici* whose persona equalled the status of "modern historical characters," such as Alexander the Great or Cyrus of Persia.[10] In 1793, the Italian translation of André de Claustre's *Dictionnaire de mythologie* (1745) continued to uphold the existence of "historical fables," that is, "ancient stories mixed with many fictions" about the "principal deities and heroes, of Jupiter, Apollo, Bacchus, Hercules, Jason, [and] Achilles, the historical background of which" was "derived from the truth."[11]

Did the epoch then regard mythology as a narrative corpus comprising *any* 'story that mattered to the community,'[12] regardless of ontological and phenomenological premises? If so, did it retain Aristotle's notion of *mythos* as a "plot" or "action" that could be either true or not, but at least accorded with opinion?[13] At any rate, seventeenth- and eighteenth-century notions of *favola* in Italian – the words *mito*

9. Metastasio 2002-4, I, 69: "Tutto ciò [of the plot] si ha da Virgilio, il quale con un felice anacronismo unisce il tempo della fondazion di Cartagine agli errori di Enea."
10. Calzabigi 1994, 114: "certamente Agamennone, Achille, Teseo, Clitennestra, Ifigenia, Tieste, Ercole, Ecuba, Aiace, Ulisse, Polissena, personaggi istorici piú antichi, non sono piú cantanti di Ciro, di Didone, di Alessandro, di Semiramide e di Enea, personaggi istorici piú moderni."
11. Claustre 1793, 174, with emphasis added: "FAVOLE Storiche, sono le antiche Storie mescolate con molte finzioni [...] Tali sono quelle, che parlano degli Dei principali, e degli Eroi, di Giove, di Apollo, di Bacco, di Ercole, Giasone, Achille, *il fondo della storia de' quali è preso della verità*."
12. The expression is Thomas P. Wiseman's, here cited from Ketterer 2009, 2.
13. In *Poetics*, 1460^{b}36-1461^{a}2, Aristotle noted that "The tales about gods ... may be as wrong as Xenophanes [sixth-century philosopher who identified polytheism as the anthropomorphic projection of scandalous deeds] thinks, neither true nor the better thing to say; but they are certainly in accordance with opinion." See also Sommerstein 2005, 163, where it is argued that "the distinction between "myth" and "history" was, for an ancient Greek, far from clear-cut"; or Aristotle 1972, 122, where D. W. Lucas pointed out that Aristotle "believed that Greek myth, or much of it, was basically historical, or at least that names like Heracles or Achilles belonged to the class of *genomenoi*, real people, but that he distinguished between legends such as those of Troy or Thebes, and history of recent events like the Persian Wars."

and *mitologia* were less common – left veracity aside. In 1612, the Crusca Academy's authoritative *Vocabolario* described *favola* in terms of "what is found to be untrue, but [is] sometimes verisimilar, sometimes not."[14] In seventeenth-century France, by contrast, the words 'myth' and 'fable' were disambiguated and split into two semantic compounds: a neutral, structural denotation (*plot*) and a vilified object of reference (*invented, fictitious tale*). Thus, Hippolyte-Jules Pilet de La Mesnardière's *La poëtique* (1639) held that the term *fable* pertained to the "Composition of the Subject matter" rather than,

> as some ignorant Poets imagine, to one of those ridiculous and incredible actions of the Gods of the Metamorphosis [sic] and of the Iliad, which the Latins referred to by the name *Fabulæ* and which we call Fables: far from providing substance to the Tragedy, such [actions] are more apt to incite laughter than provoke pity.[15]

In keeping with other detractors of mythology (or 'pagan' antiquity by extension), La Mesnardière of course wrote against the background of religious persecutions and the emerging rationalist philosophy.[16] His statement should alert us to the fact that myths did much more than just 'matter' to readers and spectators, and that because of this their presence in opera merits re-assessment according to the sensibilities of the Ancien Régime.

14. Various 1612, "Favola": "Dal latino *fabula*, trovato non vero, ma talora verisimile, talora nò ...". Almost a century later, the Modenese rationalist Ludovico Antonio Muratori defined *favola* in his *Delle riflessioni sopra il buon gusto nelle scienze e nelle arti* (1708) as "che si dice, e racconta di qualche cosa; e la stessa cosa raccontata, e detta, tanto vera, come falsa, viene anch'essa nominata presso i Latini *Fabula* dal Verbo *fari*, e *mythos* presso ai Greci. Con parecchi esempj si potrebbe quì dimostrare, se occorresse, come da' gravi Autori sono state chiamate *mythos*, o *Fabulæ*, anche le cose e verità Istoriche." (Muratori 1767-73, VIII, 242)
15. La Mesnardière 1639, 14: "la Composition du Sujet, où la constitution des choses ... & non pas comme s'imaginent quelques Poëtes ignorans, l'une de ces actions ridicules & incroyables des Dieux de la Metamorphose, & de ceux de l'Iliade, exprimées chez les Latins par le nom de *Fabula*, & que nous appellons *des Fables*, puis que bien loin de servir de matiére à la Tragédie, elles sont beaucoup plus propres à exciter la risée, qu'à provoquer la pitié." See also page 42, where La Mesnardière contended that "la pluspart des Tragédies dont les Grecs & les Latins ont enrichi leurs Théatres, sont tirées de l'Iliade, où bien de la Thebaïde, meres du Poëme tragique; bien que nous n'ignorions pas que Troye ne fut qu'une bicoque qui ne merita jamais qu'on s'arrestât à l'assiéger, que ses deux Fleuves célébres, Xanthe & Simoïs, ne sont que deux petits ruisseaux. D'ailleurs l'Histoire de Thébes est si manifestement fausse en la pluspart des Avantures qu'elle nous fait passer pour vrayes, qu'il est fort aisé de juger que les plus belles Tragédies que les Anciens ayent admirées, ont des fondemens fabuleux, inventez, & mesme incroyables."
16. For a more comprehensive treatment of this subject, see Bruno Forment's chapter and Forment 2010a.

Assuming a multidisciplinary but historically informed perspective on the issue, the six essays gathered here address manifold questions. Through what ideological lens, first of all, did librettists and composers perceive the ancient gods? What dramaturgies did they devise to represent – or modify – individual characters, tales, and themes? Were classic precepts obeyed, or precisely overridden? And how could myths be made to fit changing modes of spectatorship? Confident that no single discipline can cover the full spectrum of either myth or opera, we have invited contributions from an international cast of scholars active in – and if necessary transgressing – the fields of music, literature, theater, and cultural studies. Our selection, arbitrary as it must be, is focused on Italian *dramma per musica* and French *tragédie en musique*. It is subdivided into three thematic sections.

The first, opened by Jean-François Lattarico, is devoted to the interrelatedness of opera, myth, and literature. In "*Lo scherno degli dei*: myth and derision in the *dramma per musica* of the seventeenth century," Professor Lattarico discusses the appropriation of the Greco-Roman pantheon by the Italian Baroque novel and libretto. He agrees that mythology initially monopolized operatic poetics, yet reveals how the hermeneutic treasure-trove of myth was rapidly transformed into a storehouse for poetic manipulation and parody, in keeping with the stylistic idioms of *barocchismo* or *concettismo*. Drawing comparisons between the writings of Andreini, Bracciolini, and the Accademia degli Incogniti on the one hand, and the libretti of Busenello, Aureli, Sbarra, and Corradi on the other, the author explains how Italian novelists and librettists embroidered the same myths and metaphors to represent the perceived decadence of mankind and to voice libertarianism on the writer's part.

Robert Ketterer's contribution "Helpings from the great banquets of epic: Handel's *Teseo* and *Arianna in Creta*" digs all the deeper into the meanderings of literary history to show that neither of Handel's two "Greek-like" operas starring Theseus actually derives from tragedy or epic; rather, their sources must be found in a variety of models known to Handel's audience in London. *Teseo* (1713) is in fact modelled on Quinault's 'Euripidean' libretto *Thésée*,[17] yet its plot and dramaturgy focus consistently on Medea's melodramatic traits as portrayed by Seneca. *Arianna in Creta* (1734) in turn blends ingredients from Plutarchan historiography and, surprisingly, from the chivalric legacy of Chaucer, Shakespeare, and Spenser; against all presumptions, then, it constitutes a vital chain in the series of Handel's romanesque operas from the 1730s (*Orlando*, *Ariodante*, and *Alcina*).

17. See Kimbell 1963.

Dramaturgy transects cultural history in the second section. GEOFFREY BURGESS' essay "Envoicing the divine: oracles in lyric and spoken drama in seventeenth-century France" examines a trope inherent in the mythological machinery of the Grand Siècle. Combining readings from La Fontaine and Racine, next to other authors, Professor Burgess reveals the poetic and typographic conventions through which oracular pronunciations were distinguished from ordinary theatrical 'speeches.' Literary and operatic oracles shared a number of characteristics, such as a certain semantic opacity (if not incompleteness) and brevity,[18] yet from Lully's era onwards, musical oracles began to be uttered offstage by a disembodied voice exemplifying their irrational nature.

Professor Burgess' chapter is paired with "Addressing the divine: the 'numinous' accompagnato in *opera seria*," in which BRUNO FORMENT analyzes a brand of accompanied recitative that was deployed to underscore invocations, oracles, and divine utterances. Easily recognizable by its 'halo' of homophonic strings, the topos would remain intact from the 1680s throughout the eighteenth century. All the same, its appearance in *opera seria* is at odds with the rationalist and religious discourse in which the genre was inscribed. That numinous accompagnati allowed composers to evoke Christian and pagan deities with the same degree of solemnity is striking even in light of the recorded hostility towards representations of idolatry and superstition. It is no coincidence that a growing number of instantiations of 'heathen fantasy' were apologized for in disclaimers distancing the operatic fiction from the author's 'true' beliefs.

Iphigenia's body appears in the footlight of the third and last section, whose majestic overture is provided by REINHARD STROHM's "Iphigenia's curious *ménage à trois* in myth, drama, and opera." Against the ingrained habit of regarding opera as a 'mythical' spectacle, Professor Strohm questions the distinctions that continue to be made between myth, history, and poetry on the one hand, and musical and spoken drama on the other. He scrutinizes no fewer than nineteen representations of the Iphigenia legend, conceived between 1640 and 1737 in four different languages, to highlight the fundamentally eclectic attitude towards Iphigenia's theatrical 'past.' With authors recycling, enhancing, or rejecting previous options at will, regardless

18. The enduring validity of brevity as a dramaturgical criterium for oracles is testified to by Mozart's decision to curtail the third-act 'Oracolo' in *Idomeneo* (Munich, 1781) – "If the Ghost in *Hamlet* were not so long-winded," the composer explained to his father on 29 November 1780, "he would be more effective." (Cited from Heartz & Bauman 1990, 29)

of generic and linguistic contexts, artificial categories do not seem to apply; rather, we notice various supranational traditions at work.

Bram van Oostveldt's closing chapter "Spectatorship and involvement in Gluck's *Iphigénie en Tauride*" zooms in on the late eighteenth century and its salient preoccupation with the Iphigenia in Tauris. Opera reformers, he explains, took an active interest in the myth's constituent motifs, most notably the shipwreck and the maiden's audacity, to express modern views on the emancipation of man and the existential position of the spectator vis-à-vis the (theatrical) catastrophe. Using references to a wide palette of philosophical writings, Professor van Oostveldt shows Gluck's *Iphigénie en Tauride* (1779) to mark a vital shift from distanced to involved spectatorship, thus exemplifying a central concern of Enlightenment esthetics.

LO SCHERNO DEGLI DEI

Myth and derision in the dramma per musica of the seventeenth century

Jean-François Lattarico

At its creation, near the close of the sixteenth century, opera maintained a narrow and privileged relationship with the realm of mythology. The theory of operatic practice, which was sparked by the experiments of Bardi's Camerata and aimed at reviving the ideal of Greek tragedy (whether or not sung in its entirety), associated the lyric theater exclusively with characters of 'musical' essence. Accordingly, poet-musicians like Orpheus, Arion, and David emerged as the perfect symbols of the artistic union[1] envisaged by the *favola in musica*,[2] and the earliest treatises dealing with opera put the accent precisely on the need to convene the gods of Antiquity or, conversely, on the incongruity of singing characters that did not originate from the timeless, ahistorical universe of myth. In this respect, the anonymous author of *Il Corago* (c. 1628-37) argued, in a chapter dedicated to the "characters or interlocutors" ("personaggi o interlocutori"), that "the ancient deities, such as Apollo, Thetis, Neptune and other similar gods, seem entirely appropriate for secular actions ... and above all those characters that we consider perfect musicians, such as Orpheus,

1. Significantly, the prologue of Giulio Rospigliosi's *Il palazzo incantato d'Atlante* (1642; score by Luigi Rossi) calls for the allegorical characters Painting, Poetry, and Music, who after a confrontation are reconciled through the intervention of Magic, the symbol of the *meraviglia* that the seventeenth century hoped to instill in the spectator.
2. According to Galilei 1581, the very first – unfortunately lost – experiments in monody, Galilei's own *Lamento del Conte Ugolino* and *Lamentazioni di Geremia* (both 1582), were composed "secondo l'uso degli antichi Greci, che ... era di far ragionare un solo cantando et non tanti altri nell'istesso tempo come oggi (contro ogni dovere) si costuma."

Amphion, and many others."[3] Operatic action built around contemporary figures, by contrast, was believed to verge on the ridiculous.[4]

The – *a priori* relatively clear – argument pro mythology sprang from the unheard, extraordinary practice of *recitar cantando*, which was to be reserved for "superhuman characters" rather than "ordinary men,"[5] the latter lacking the recorded habit of conversing through song. For more than one and a half centuries, the potential 'inverisimilitude' inherent in dramatic singing lingered above the heads of theorists, composers, and dramatists alike, only disappearing in the midst of Enlightenment via the treatises of Francesco Algarotti (*Saggio sopra l'opera in musica*, 1755-63)[6] and Pietro Metastasio (*Estratto dell'arte poetica di Aristotile*, 1783).[7] The ancient divinities provided a refuge from criticism by reason of their spatial-temporal distance, which forewent blasphemous interpretation in light of the neoplatonic doctrines of the time, but also because of the supreme feeling of *meraviglia* they inspired in the spectator.

On deriving their material from myth and pastoral, however, the first operatic poets excluded comic elements from their plots so as to avoid the lower register and contemporaneity of regular spoken comedy. Before 1637 and the opening of the first public opera house in Venice (the Teatro San Cassiano), degrading realities could simply not be associated with a "spectacle worthy of a Prince" – to borrow Marco da Gagliano's notorious expression.[8] To be sure, timid instantiations of comedy are present in Guidiccioni and Cavalieri's *La disperazione di Fileno* (1590), in the satyrs of Salvadori and Gagliano's *Flora* (1628), or even in Titon's lament appearing in

3. Anonymous 1983, 63: "sembrano molto a proposito per le azioni profane le deità antiche come Apollo, Teti, Nettuno et altri stimati numi ... e sopra tutti quei personaggi che stimiamo essere stati perfetti musici, come Orfeo, Anfione et simili." Unless indicated otherwise, all translations in this volume are the authors'.
4. Anonymous 1983, 63-4: "Similmente nelle azioni sacre i personaggi più a proposito per questa poesia pare che siano quelli che per antichità di tempo e diversità di costumi sono più lontani dalle cose presenti, quali sono i patriarchi antichi, massime quelli che hanno concetto di essere stati musici, come Davide e simili. Imperocché se noi prendiamo per interlocutori le persone vicine ai nostri tempi e di costumi più manifestamente simili ai nostri, troppo apertamente ci si appresenta subito improbabile et inverisimile quel modo di parlar cantando, massime se quelle persone fussero state conosciute da qualche spettatore, onde in simil caso è occorso che qualche auditore non poteva tener le risa ancorché l'azione per altro fusse molto seria, vedendo cantigolar ragionando quelli che lui sapeva esser stati et ignoranti afatto di musica, et uomini di parlar commune."
5. Anonymous 1983, 63: "personaggi sopra umani ... uomini ordinari".
6. Algarotti 1763, 25: "se ... la musica fosse scritta come si conviene, non vi sarebbe maggior disconvenienza, che uno morisse cantando, che recitando versi."
7. Metastasio 1998, in particular 39-73.
8. Gagliano 1608, "Ai lettori," s.n.: "spettacolo veramente da principi".

Chiabrera and Caccini's *Il rapimento di Cefalo* (1600); yet the Florentine *favola in musica* aimed at an inverse reflection of everyday reality, to the glory of the prince, who was its exclusive commissioner.

Initially, the Venetian operatic stage, too, rehearsed the mythical, or more generally those ingredients that had hitherto guaranteed the renown of court spectacle. Not by chance, the first operas of Ferrari and Cavalli, *Andromeda* (1637) and *Le nozze di Teti e Peleo* (1639), and the repertoire of the short-lived Teatro Novissimo (1641-5),[9] the first public venue to be entirely devoted to opera, bristled with mythological intrigues and figures. *Mutatis mutandis*, the Novissimo's underlying policy – the glorification of the Venetian Republic – was linked in its allegorical and encomiastic finality to Florentine court opera.

Quite rapidly, though, and in line with the acceptance of historical subjects (which annulled a former proscription),[10] myths began to be treated solely from the angle of derision, in favor of a poetic that enshrined the mixture of registers as its creed.[11] How does one explain this remarkable evolution, and what role was played in it by mythological mockery?

The burden of the Roman model

Rome was the first city to have the tragic cohabit with the comic in its opera – witness the original synthesis of comedy and hagiography in Giulio Rospigliosi's *melodrammi*. It was also the Roman branch of musical drama that revealed the earliest signs of mythological derision, and such on essentially ideological grounds: namely, as a limpid, devious way of worshipping the God of Christianity. It begins

9. The operas given at the Novissimo are *La finta pazza* by Strozzi and Sacrati (1641), *Il Bellerofonte* by Nolfi and Sacrati (1642), *L'Alcate* by Tirabosco and Manelli (1642), *La Venere gelosa* by Bartolini and Sacrati (1643), *La Deidamia* by Errico and Cavalli (1644), and *Ercole in Lidia* by Bisaccioni and Rovetta (1645).
10. *Il Corago* (Anonymous 1983, 64), while insisting on the difficulty of representing non-mythological characters, nonetheless seems to anticipate the development of both the opera genre and public taste towards historical, if not contemporary, reality: "Non si nega però che anche nelle azioni gravi non si sia per poter prendere qualche personaggio vicino ai nostri tempi, se massime si frequentassero le rappresentazioni armoniche, perché con il tempo il popolo s'avvezzarebbe a gustar ogni cosa rappresentata in musica...".
11. See Chiarelli & Pompilio 2004 for a panorama of Venetian opera poetics as evidenced by declarations in libretto prefaces.

with Giacomo Francesco Parisani and Giacinto Cornacchioli's *La Diana schernita*, which was performed in 1629 at the residence of Johann Rudolph, Baron von Hohen Rechberg. Definitely more interesting for its poetry than for its music, the opera adopts a deliberate stance against the Florentine *favola* in its transformation of a structurally orthodox fable into some sort of a mythological pleasantry, with respect to which Romain Rolland did not hesitate to declare that "the opera buffa makes its entry under the auspices of Prince Taddeo Barberini [1603-1647, the dedicatee of *Diana schernita*]."[12]

As outrageous as Rolland's statement may sound today, it cannot be denied that *Diana schernita* does initiate a tradition of buffoonery that would be exploited until the closing decades of the seventeenth century. Its plot is as follows: Diana banished Cupid to the grotto of the nymph Egeria, the seat of sorrow and misery. Endymion, who is secretly in love with Diana, pays the price for Cupid's rage to the benefit of Pan, who is equally enamored with Diana. After being metamorphosed into a deer as punishment for his eavesdropping on Diana's nude bathing (a passing wink at the myth of Actæon), Endymion is chased and torn apart by dogs, which incident then provokes Diana's inconsolable grief. *Diana schernita* thus makes a first assault on the traditional image of Diana as the emblem of chastity, representing the goddess as an immortal person who in her imperfection and infatuation is far removed from the Diana in Filippo Vitali's *Aretusa* (1620) – the latter has the protagonist escape the advances of the shepherd Alleo by transforming Arethusa into a river, in keeping with the edifying model of Ovid so dear to the Counter-Reformation.[13]

From myth to *commedia dell'arte*

If the mixture of registers makes its forceful entry in Rospigliosi's libretti via Lope de Vega's *Arte nuevo de hacer comedias en este tiempo* (1609),[14] whose influence is undeniable,

12. Rolland 1931, 158: "l'opéra bouffe fait son entrée sous les auspices du Prince Taddeo Barberini."
13. Tronsarelli's *La catena d'Adone* (1626) is equally permeated by Christian morality, as its preface (Tronsarelli 1626, "Al lettore," s.n.) suggests: "Adone poi, che lontano dalla deità di Venere patisce incontri di vani travagli, è l'Uomo che lontano da Dio incorre in molti errori."
14. See Lope de Vega 2006, 174-80, especially 141: "Lo tràgico y lo còmico mezclado, / y Terencio con Séneca, aunque sea / como otro Minotauro de Pasife, / haràn grave una parte, otra ridìcula, / que

the rendez-vous between myth and its parodical reversal finds a principal source in the contemporaneous literature with which opera entertained a narrow, all too often neglected relationship. For instance, the derision of Diana already constitutes the main theme of *Capitan Spavento inganna Diana dea delle selve*, one of the numerous irreverent dialogues in Francesco Andreini's *Le bravure del Capitan Spavento* (1607).[15] While Olympus assumes a preponderant role in the relevant dialogue, it is reduced to some sort of a carnivalesque machine that puts the gods on a par with the *camerati* of old comedy. Andreini's most arresting novelty, however, lies in his introduction – for the sake of "upsetting everything with mischief"[16] – of a comical aspect to the four customary modes of mythological interpretation: the historical, physical, ethical, and political – the latter being of most recent date and inspired by court culture and *raison d'état*. In an Italy dominated by the coercive measures of the Counter-Reformation, Andreini's statement on the falseness of the ancient characters rings as an ideological argument, a true leitmotif of the coming decades (see Bruno Forment's chapter):

> And so that my effort be more readily accepted by the Very Reverent Fathers of the Inquisition, I have conceived it in a poetic mode, availing myself of what is being printed daily, and in poetic pleasantries that treat the untrue and false deities of bygone times, simply to demonstrate how untrue and false all these gods were, and how untrue [and] false everything thought and written about them is.[17]

Natale Conti's *Mythologiæ* (1551), the direct source for Andreini, Vincenzo Cartari's *Le imagini de i dei de gli antichi* (1556) and Cesare Ripa's *Iconologia* (1593) would henceforth be deployed as monumental compendia of the gods, thus clearing the path to their very undoing. The most relevant contribution in this respect, if only for being the first of its kind in the seventeenth century, is Francesco Bracciolini's

aquesta variedad deleita mucho; / buen ejemplo nos de naturaleza, / que por tal variedad tiene belleza". On Lope de Vega's influence on seventeenth-century opera, see Tedesco 2003 and 2006.

15. Andreini's protagonist would deliver the model to the bragging Capitani found in cloak-and-dagger operas such as Rospigliosi's *Dal male il bene* (1654; set by Abbatini and Marazzoli) and *L'armi e gli amori* (1656; Marazzoli).
16. Andreini 1987, "Al lettore," 9: "disordinar il tutto con malizia".
17. Andreini 1987, 9: "E perché più facilmente potesse esser ammessa questa mia fatica dalli Molti Reverendi Padri Inquisitori, sono andato scrivendo poeticamente, valendomi di quello che giornalmente si vede alle stampe, e con poetici scherzi, trattando di quelle deità false e bugiarde degli andati tempi, solo per dimostrare che sì come falsi e bugiardi erano tutti quei numi, così falso [e] bugiardo, è tutto quello che di loro si ragiona e scrive."

'heroic-comic poem' *Lo scherno degli dei* (1618).[18] The crux of Bracciolini's work again consists in a mélange of registers. This is already apparent from its preliminary dialogue, between Thalia and Urania, in which the author pondered the stakes and legitimacy of generic contamination: whereas the one Muse can only conjure up divine plots and characters, the other responds with "pleasantries and derisions" ("beffe e scherni"), thus turning the poem's subject into the derision of the gods.[19] The cooperation between Thalia and Urania is furthermore advanced as a means towards rehearsing the Horatian and Jesuit maxims of "blending the useful with the pleasurable" (*utile dulci miscere*) and of "delighting and enlightening" (*delectare et prodesse*). The "fabulous and false Gods" ("favolosi e falsi Dei") of pagan Antiquity, on the other hand, are perceived from the angle of Counter-Reformation, as Bracciolini's disclaimer makes clear: "the rejection of the false Gods will largely be the same as acknowledging the One who incarnates Truth itself".[20]

The plot of *Lo scherno degli dei* revolves round the opposed loves of Venus, Mars and Vulcan, a trio that will be re-encountered with slight variations in a fair number of novels and *drammi per musica*. Venus experiences such disgust for her disfigured, crippled husband Vulcan that she succumbs to the favors of Mars. Vulcan takes revenge for his wife's escapades by weaving an extremely fine net that makes him almost invisible and allows him to catch the guilty lovers. It is in the intricate metaphor of the woven canvas, to which various additional episodes are tied,[21] that mythology intersects comedy. Once more, the terrible humanity of the Olympian gods sets the overall tone, reiterated at various instances, as if pushing the deities one by one from their fragile pedestals: "On earth, Jupiter, Mars, and Neptune were people like us, made from flesh and bones; like us, they were born in an obscure world, breathing this humid and pressing air."[22] Further in the same strophe, one reads: "The poets have sung that he [Jupiter, Mars, or Neptune] was a God, while he

18. The original *Scherno degli dei*, in thirteen cantos, was followed in 1628 by a more complete version in twenty cantos. Bracciolini, who belonged to the powerful Barberini clan, disputed the paternity of the *poema eroico-comico* with Alessandro Tassoni, whose *La secchia rapita* (1614) is today considered one of the Baroque's most original literary creations.
19. Bracciolini 1628, s.n.: "altro che materie e personaggi divini intrometter non si possono, e per la parte mia altro che beffe e scherni non ho io nel mio fondaco, onde acciocché ben composto riesca il mescolato nostro, è mestiere, che 'l soggetto da prendersi sia lo Schernire gli Dei."
20. Bracciolini 1628, s.n.: "il riprovar gli Dei falsi sarà un approvare maggiormente quell'uno che è l'istessa verità".
21. E.g., the inconstancy of Apollo, who is infatuated with both Daphne and Hyacinth.
22. Bracciolini 1628, XIV.XXXIX: "Giove, Marte, e Nettuno in terra furo / Huomini come noi, di carne, e d'ossa; / Nacquero come noi nel mondo oscuro, / E spiraron quest'aria umida, e grossa".

was a human species, as I am."[23] The same desacralization is maintained throughout the poem, and the ultimate canto gives the moral conclusion without blast: "The gods are appearances, and not the effect [i.e., cause]".[24]

The influence of the Academy: the literature of the Incogniti

In the literary genealogy of parodical deconstruction, pride of place is occupied by the Accademia degli Incogniti, the libertine society whose role in the development and diffusion of popular (or "mercenary"[25]) opera is hardly to be overstated. Interestingly, no fewer than three of the Incogniti's principal representatives, its founder Giovan Francesco Loredano,[26] the burlesque Giovanni Battista Lalli, and the virulent Ferrante Pallavicino, created mythological travesties that left their mark on the operatic field. Loredano is today best remembered for his *Iliade giocosa* (1653), a spoof on the first six cantos of Homer's epic. In its dedication to Pietro Michiel, Loredano's future accomplice in *Il cimiterio* (1634), the reader is asked to "Prepare [him]self to the raucous sound of my verses, for in my humble and low verses you will see a Trumpet metamorphosed into a Long-necked lute and the divine Homer made buffoon."[27] Lalli authored various satirical poems, such as *La moscheide* (1624) and *La Franceide* (1629),[28] next to a parody of Petrarch's *Canzoniere*. His Virgilian parody *L'Eneide travestita* (1633) would set the model for Paul Scarron's *Virgile travesty* (1652). Pallavicino's proteiform output, finally, does not include theatrical works, but otherwise embraces every literary genre, from the biblical, heroic, mythological, historical, and epistolary novel to academic discourse and the pamphlet (one of which would cause his decapitation for having insulted the Barberini). The work by

23. Bracciolini 1628, XIV.XXXIX: "I poeti cantar che gl'era un Dio, / Et era un pezzo d'uom, come son io."
24. Bracciolini 1628, XX.LV: "Gli dei sono apparenze, e non effetto".
25. The phrase appears in Ottonelli 1652, 519.
26. On this great Venetian intellectual, see Morini 1994. For a bibliographic deepening of this subject the reader will profit from the remarkable work of Menegatti (2000).
27. Loredano 1654, I.II: "Attendi al rauco suon de le mie rime, / Che vedrai ne i miei versi humili, e bassi / Una Tromba cangiata in Colascione, / Et Homero divin fatto buffone."
28. See, respectively, Lattarico 2008 and Cabani 2002.

Pallavicino that deserves to be singled out here, if only for being both related to and distant from Bracciolini's *Scherno degli dei*, is *La rete di Vulcano* (1640).[29]

Like many parodical novels, *La rete di Vulcano* reveals both a strong autobiographical basis and references to contemporary reality. In virtually the same way as Roman history would do for his novel *Le due Agrippine* (1643), mythology provided Pallavicino with a transparent screen behind which to denounce the wanderings of his era. Venus' adultery, for instance, symbolizes a Venetian society that made infidelity the norm: "if death and blood were necessary to punish adulterers, all the households would be turned to carnage, and the world would become quickly deserted."[30] By representing Venus' erotic liaison with Mars in a style combining metaphorical hyperbole with aposiopesis[31] (think of the phrase "They [Venus and Vulcan] held a few gracious games among themselves that ended in sleep"[32]), Pallavicino mused on the meanderings of amorous sentiment in a purely Baroque idiom complete with Bracciolini's motif of the net: "The net is a labyrinth of stretched string in which the holes for escape are more numerous than the knots for entwinement; things are not different in love".[33] From peripeteia to peripeteia, however, there emerges a stark picture of the goddess of love, Venus, whose inconstancy and attraction to Adonis are advanced as the causes behind Mars' jealousy. The third part closes on a moralistic note which rehabilitates Vulcan's vengeance using rhetorical tropes:

> not being satisfied with this lover [Vulcan], she [Venus] pointed out how the deformity of her own morals, not Vulcan's, had pushed her to such debaucheries; this is how her illicit loves explain themselves on account of her impure soul, instead of that of her contemptuous husband.[34]

29. See Pallavicino 1640, "L'Autore a chi vuol leggere," 12, where the author claims: "Ho fuggito di competere con Monsig. Bracciolini soggetto gloriosissimo, il quale nel suo Scherno degli dei, uscendo dalla carciera delle antiche favole, m'havrebbe dato occasione d'imitarlo."
30. Pallavicino 1640, 73: "se con la morte e col sangue fosse di mestieri punire gli adulteri, tutte le case sarebbero macelli; e si disertarebbe tantosto spopolato il mondo."
31. An elliptical type of discourse that is to be completed by the reader.
32. Pallavicino 1640, 101: "Passarono alcuni gratiosi scherzi, terminati coll'addormentarsi".
33. Pallavicino 1640, 105: "La rete è un laberinto d'ordite fila, nel quale sono più numerosi i fori per uscire che i lacci per stringere; non altrimenti in amore".
34. Pallavicino 1640, 146: Così nel non appagarsi di questo amante diede a vedere qualmente la deformità de' costumi, non quella di Vulcano l'havea sollecitata alle impudicitie; onde i suoi illeciti amori vedeansi radicati nell'haver un animo impuro, non un marito sprezzabile."

From novel to dramma per musica

Each of the themes outlined above would resurface in the *dramma per musica* appearing at the theaters of Venice at the very moment at which the Incogniti produced their literary efforts, beginning with the preface to *La Delia, o sia la Sera sposa del Sole* (1639) by Giulio Strozzi, a member of the Incogniti, which rehearses the legitimacy of mythological mockery: "In the end, fables are only fables and the deities of the Pagans but follies, which is why one may happily deride them."[35] In keeping with Bracciolini, mythological allegory allowed Strozzi to communicate a moral intention from which the spectator and – at a later stage – the reader could draw potential benefits. This idea also crops up in another opera from the Teatro Novissimo repertoire: Nicolò Enea Bartolini's *La Venere gelosa* (1643), whose address claims the work to "entertain and instruct our life with the verisimilar and the marvelous".[36] On the premise that the "poet's profession is difficult,"[37] the literary legitimacy of the *dramma per musica* vis-à-vis the more prestigious genre of spoken theater is thus apologized for: "there are so many complications in the plot of this Work, which is made to be sung, that it does not shrink from comparison with those that are only made to be recited."[38] A comparable apology is found in Giacomo Badoaro's foreword to *Ulisse errante* (1644; set by Francesco Sacrati), which alludes to the heroic-comic poetry of Alessandro Tassoni in order to legitimize, if only implicitly, the literary qualities of the *opera musicale*: "in another genre, which reunites the Comic and Heroic in an admirable way, Tassoni composed a Monster worthy of praise and fully meeting the favor of Men of Letters."[39]

Another illustration demonstrating the strong links between the *belles-lettres* and the operatic libretto is the *Deidamia* (1644) of the Incognito poet Scipione Errico, which was given at the Novissimo with Cavalli's (lost) music and a substantial

35. Strozzi 1639, "Lettori", 8: "Le favole finalmente son favole, e le divinità de' Gentili tute sciocchezze, onde ci si può scherzare sopra allegramente."
36. Bartolini 1643, s.n.: "col verisimile, e 'l maraviglioso diletta, e ammaestra la nostra vita".
37. Bartolini 1643, s.n.: "difficile è 'l mestiere del poetare".
38. Bartolini 1643, s.n.: "è tanto nodo, e intrecciamento in quest'Opera fatta per cantare, che non teme il concorso di quelle che solamente si recitano."
39. Badoaro 1644, 13: "Il Tassoni in altro genere unendo mirabilmente il Comico con l'Heroico ha composto un lodabile Mostro, che ne porta appresso molti i Letterati gli applausi." A modern edition of this work and its scenario is available in Zardini & Zardini Lana 2007, on 218-313 and 315-29, respectively.

œuvre which comprises, among others, *La Babilonia distrutta* (1623) and *Le guerre di Parnaso* (1643). While the former heroic epos narrates the destruction of Baghdad by the Westerners (!) after the model of Torquato Tasso's *La Gerusalemme liberata*, the latter parodical novel tackles the quarrel between the ancients and moderns by paralleling it with a revolt on Mount Parnassus led by the poet Marino against Apollo (who demands that Aristotle's precepts be imposed on all writers).[40] The latter expedient, at once aloof and efficient, allowed Errico to ponder the issues of literary genre and – under Lope de Vega's wings[41] – absolute liberty, which was the 'modern' poet's prerogative.

All the more interesting to our line of inquiry is Errico's *Le liti di Pindo* (1634), a so-called *comedia tragicomedia in comedia* which, as its generic designation suggests, flirts with the utterly Baroque topos of the 'theater-within-the-theater.' Within one impressive *mise en abyme*, the piece indeed inserts a comedy and a tragedy into the middle of yet another comedy, *Del maritaggio di Venere*, which in turn reunites the Venus, Vulcan, and Mars of Bracciolini's *Scherno degli dei* and Pallavicino's *Rete di Vulcano*, but situates the action right before the union of Venus and Vulcan, as if turning it into both an antecedent to the latter texts and a prolegomenon to the multiple disappointments of the mythical couple that will follow shortly. The chief quality of Errico's work is not confined to this ingenious structure, though, but rather in its emphasis on the humanity of the gods, conform with their Baroque reputation. The prologue opens with Mars complaining about Venus' promiscuity to his sister Bellona in a prose lament that evokes the eternal jealousy of Juno, who for her part reproaches Jupiter for his escapades with Semele, Diana, Europa, and even with Jupiter's own daughter Venus. The ultimate palm for linguistic originality is carried off by Vulcan who, unique for the epoch, expresses himself throughout in Sicilian dialect.

All the same, Errico's comedy appears not too far removed from the character comedies of the Renaissance and the works of Giovan Battista Andreini (who is not to be confused with the *commedia dell'arte* author Francesco).[42] Thus, Juno tellingly offers Venus' (i.e., her daughter's) hand to Mars, while Bellona acts as the matchmaker for her brother Mars, whose virtues she extols in order to dispel Venus' fear

40. See the critical edition established by the late Gino Rizzi, Errico 2004.
41. Errico 2004, 27.
42. Witness most particularly Andreini's *La Ferinda* (1622), which was partly set to music; *Le due commedie in commedie* (1623), which also adopts a *mise en abyme* structure; or even *La Centaura* (1622), a monster of theatrical hybridity (see the modern edition, Andreini 2004). On Giovan Battista Andreini, see Rebaudengo 1995 and Fiaschini 2006.

for the conjugal violence provoked by Mars' status as god of war: "But I have heard say that this brother of yours is excessively hot-tempered and so I'm afraid he will beat me every day; also, they tell me he hasn't taken a wife until now since no one wants him for husband."[43] Vulcan's servant Momus, on the other hand, profits from Venus' categorical refusal to marry Mars ("No, no, no, I don't want it; they say he has a bad breath"[44]) in order to force himself on her. While singing the praise of his master, Momus disparages the bellicose god; even when the latter's temper explodes, the *servo faceto* does not appear to fear anything (for "[Mars] is rather the God of cowardice than of war"[45]). Pallas for her part recalls the divine injunction against a marriage between Mars and Venus in view of the fact that she is one of Jupiter's offspring (even though Jupiter had previously married his sister Juno).

The strayed pastoral

These literary elaborations of myth would define the Venetian operatic plot to no mean degree, often serving as a cogent pretext for blending registers, in keeping with the heroic-comic travesties of Bracciolini and the like. In fact, whenever the heroic was combined with the burlesque, librettists invoked such literary authorities as Guarino Guarini, whose *Pastor fido* (1590) had given tragicomedy its patent of nobility.[46] Although verisimilitude and Aristotelian poetics remained at stake, they brutally overrode the rules, becoming torchbearers of liberty on behalf of both themselves and their public, whose taste dictated all options. Numerous in the latter respect are the Venetian poets who availed themselves of mythological transformations for comic-heroic purposes.

43. Errico 1634, 51: "Però ho inteso dire, che questo vostro fratello è soverchio furioso, ed io ho paura che ogni giorno mi darà de' colpi, e mi dicono che esso ha preso moglie insino ad hora, perché niuna lo vuole per marito."
44. Errico 1634, 52: "No, no, no, non voglio. Dicono che gli puzza il fiato".
45. Errico 1634, 62: "[Mars] è piu tosto Dio delle poltronerie che delle guerre".
46. The term 'tragicomedy' was a modern variant of the Greek *hilaro-tragedy*, which Ottaviano Castelli had defended in his *Dialogo sopra la poesia dramatica, dove in un congresso di letterati si discorre sovra il drama della Sincerità trionfante: ventilandosi in esso l'opinioni non solo de gli antichi Greci, ma ancora de' Latini e de gl'Italiani* (1640; for a modern edition of the tract, see Di Ceglie 1997).

Arguably the pioneering effort is Giovan Francesco Busenello's *Gli amori di Apollo e Dafne* (1640), with which the author achieved an astonishing synthesis of Florentine fables – within its three acts, we encounter the subjects of Ottavio Rinuccini's *Dafne*, Gabriele Chiabrera's *Rapimento di Cefalo*, and Ridolfo Campeggi's *Aurora ingannata* – in a way that is resolutely ironic, not to say parodical. Cupid, for instance, has quite arrogant chats with Apollo, who also does not mince his words and treats the former as a "Soldier in petticoats," and as a "pygmy Divinity of idleness and God of Nothingness."[47] The emblematic presence of the nurses Cirilla and Filena, the one symbolizing platonic love, the other sensuality, furthermore makes the hieratic universe of the ancient deities tilt towards the imperfection and pathos of humanity.

Aurelio Aureli, Busenello's greatest disciple and the author of some fifty libretti for Venice, Parma, Piacenza, and many other cities on the Italian peninsula and elsewhere,[48] poured the 'Venetian sauce' of irreverence and derision over a dozen of mythological operas, beginning with *Antigona delusa da Alceste* (1660), which uses Euripides' tragedy as an excuse for *quiproquos* and masquerades – one of its most notable inventions is the sudden love experienced by Admetos for Antigone right before marrying Alcestis. *Le fatiche di Ercole per Dejanira* (1662) and *Gli amori di Apollo e di Leucotoe* (1663) bring utterly effeminate heroes to the stage, while *Il Perseo* (1665), *L'Orfeo* (1673), *Helena rapita da Paride* (1677), *Teseo tra le rivali* (1685) and *Diomede punito da Alcide* (1685) ravished the spectators of the Venetian theatres of Santi Giovanni e Paolo, Sant'Angelo, and San Salvatore with harsh portrayals of Perseus, Orpheus, Paris, Theseus, and Diomedes, respectively.

In Venice, history and myth were indeed distorted to delight an audience that, as many libretto prefaces and chronicles reveal,[49] constituted opera's sole patron. Even in the second half of the seventeenth century, when opera began to explore the bloody combats and assassinations of medieval history, mythological themes persisted with remarkably urgency and with an ideological adherence to earlier poetic prescriptions. Arguably the most representative example here is Giulio Cesare Corradi's *La divisione del mondo* (1675), which was staged at the Teatro San Salvatore with music by Giovanni Legrenzi. The opera's otherwise heroic theme, the division of the universe after the victory of the Olympian gods over the Titans, merely

47. Busenello 1656, 32: "Vanne, Amor, col tuo dardo / A' ferir l'ombre, à saettar i venti, / Nudo guerriero, / Soldato in fasce, / Marte bambino, / Campion lattante, / Gran Cavalier, che pargoleggia in culla, Nume pigmeo dell'otio, e Dio del Nulla." (Act II, scene 3)

48. See Chavannes 2004 for an overview of Aureli's career.

49. An example of the latter is Ivanovich 1681: see Cavallini 1994.

serves to depict the worst debaucheries, from which no god is proclaimed innocent, save for the patriarch Saturn. As the "lascivious goddess" ("dea lasciva"), Venus for instance stirs up trouble among the entire pantheon, provoking the lust of Neptune and Pluto alike – not even Apollo, who as the guardian of morality remains imperturbable throughout a great deal of the action, can resist her temptations.

Corradi's libretto is particularly noteworthy for its portrayal of chaos, which overturns a universal order based on the equal division of the world. All certainties are crushed to pieces and every pre-established relationship between the characters is undone, and so Venus becomes the sole driving force, abetted by her son Cupid who himself has been chased from heaven by Jupiter. Determined to avenge himself, Jupiter at the close of the first act summons Discord, the "Servant of Scorn" ("Ministra degli Sdegni"), to turn heaven into an uproar. Faithful to the Venetian esthetic of the *dramma per musica*, the opera unfolds a chain of relations which gives way to conflict from the very start: Diana is promised to Neptune but loves Pluto, who himself is enamored with Venus, the wife of Vulcan and love of both Mars and Neptune.[50] The inextricable meanderings of amorous sentiment lead to grotesque situations, for example when Diana and Neptune admit *not* to be made for one another and sing an 'anti-love' duet,[51] or when Venus, desired by all and yet unsatisfied, acknowledges her inveterate concupiscence: "I want to have more than one love ... A sole heart is not sufficient."[52] While Jupiter proves pretty well-behaved in this opera, especially in view of his notorious antics, he succumbs to the charms of the goddess of Cytherea, invoking the metaphor of the labyrinth: "Ah, those blond hairs of hers are the labyrinth of the soul."[53] The complex intrigue continues by piling the one peripeteia upon another and by proceeding with the typically Venetian technique of *liaison des scènes*, linking the individual scenes through the common presence of one or more characters so as to preserve coherence, yet at the cost of opacification. The thematic link with literary parody is assured, even by the characters themselves, by reference to Vulcan's net, which Juno seeks to get hold of (in Act III, scene 8) in order to accomplish her vengeance.

Venice would continue to deride the gods throughout the Seicento, even in operas exported to foreign climes. Francesco Sbarra and Pietro Antonio Cesti's *Le disgrazie*

50. The scheme is attested to in numerous operas, from Bisaccioni and Rovetta's *Ercole in Lidia* (1645) through Faustini and Cavalli's *Calisto* (1652) to Apolloni and Cesti's *Argia* (1655) and *Dori* (1663).
51. Corradi 1675, Act II, scene 3: "Voli il Destin ch'io non lo possi amar."
52. Corradi 1675, Act II, scene 6: "Voglio aver più d'un amante ... Un sol cor non è bastante."
53. Corradi 1675, Act II, scene 19: "Ah, che quel biondo crin laberinto è dell'alme."

d'Amore, which was staged in Vienna in 1667, offers a clear example. Significantly branded a *dramma giocosomorale*, the work provides the perfect musical illustration to *Lo scherno degli Dei* or *La rete di Vulcano*, thus indicating the seamless continuity between literature and musical drama. Sbarra advanced somewhat the same disclaimer as Strozzi's in the preface to *La Delia*: "on introducing some of the false Gods of the Pagans in this comic Drama, I had no other objective than to mock their stupidity".[54] His libretto itself opens with a domestic scene between Venus and Vulcan that is worthy of an *opéra bouffe* by Offenbach: the Cyclops profit from Vulcan's absence by surrendering themselves to the pleasures of gaming and of wine.

Yet, Sbarra had the moral dimension assume a more preponderant role than was the case in Venice, due to the overwhelming presence of four allegorical characters, typical of court opera: Deception (Inganno), Adulation (Adulazione), Greed (Avarizia) and Friendship (Amicizia). The opera furthermore elaborates the motif of money, the reprehensible importance of which was then believed to be ever-increasing, witness the phrase "This has become the habit; / Today, everything can be bought, / And he who spends can purchase everything,"[55] and an idea that the Venetians could not stop repeating: "in the end, he who knows how to flatter and deceive, obtains everything."[56] Focusing in particular on the ill-fated tribulations of Cupid, who is chased from all sides (including by his own mother), *Le disgrazie d'Amore* blends moral allegory with popular realism in a skilful way, though in a style that does not attain the refinement of a Rospigliosi or Busenello. As in spoken comedy, Greed for instance runs an inn (*Hostaria*) in which Deception appears disguised as bohemian charlatan, reading a good story to introduce himself to Friendship, whose favor he courts with the help of Cupid's darts. In sum, *Le disgrazie d'Amore* is a comedy of errors that turns love into a commodity, while at the same time denouncing it. The requisite of the *lieto fine* – to both delight and enlighten – re-establishes order and serenity between Venus and Vulcan, meaning that harmony triumphs wherever constancy rules.

54. Sbarra 1667, "L'Autore a chi legge", s.n.: "Sì come nell'introdurre in questo Dramma giocoso alcune delle false Deità de' Gentili, io non hebbi altr'oggetto, che il deridere la loro sciocchezza".
55. Sbarra 1667, Act II, scene 2: "Così è lo stile / Hoggi tutto si vende, / E può tutto ottener quegli, che spende".
56. Sbarra 1667, Act II, scene 2: "Che al fin chi sa bene / Adulare, e ingannare, il tutto ottiene."

The triumph of derision

The entire seventeenth century was inhabited and obsessed by the ancient divinities, whose traits were described, represented, analyzed, declared dead, and yet kept alive through a poetic strategy that consisted in resuscitation through derision. As we have seen, the moral and religious (Christian) premises governing their rebirth and survival were often no more than a pretext for authorizing liberties. In Venice, the triumphant atheism of the Incogniti, who associated themselves with the adventure of opera, renders this pretext ambiguous, not to say dubious. However, beyond the interpretation of myths as an artificial screen to escape censorship and to decry a contemporary society, we must see in the gods' portrayal the mirror of a humanity that was inconstant[57] and fragile above all, and whose existence was reflected in the ephemeral characters embodied on stage.

57. It is precisely under the sign of inconstancy that Morini 1994 places the work of Loredano, so characteristic of both the Incogniti and the Seicento, which placed doubt in the dead center of its reflections, before certainties returned to grace in the age of Enlightenment.

HELPINGS FROM THE GREAT BANQUETS OF EPIC

Handel's Teseo *and* Arianna in Creta

Robert C. Ketterer

The myths that Baroque opera embodied on stage were not abstract, slightly mystical stories transmitted orally from a dim past, nor were they static, codified equivalents of scripture. Early modern Europe had inherited the artistic and self-conscious mythography of Greco-Roman literature mutated by translations, retellings, and reinterpretations throughout the European Middle Ages and Renaissance. And although classical mythology provided the first creators of opera with a rich body of stories and images from which to make their selections and adaptations, these pioneers were less interested in myth-telling *per se* than they were in reproducing the emotive power of word and music that they perceived to have been the driving force of Greek tragedy. The cutting-edge research of the day suggested, as the poet Ottavio Rinuccini wrote in his dedication to *Euridice* (1600), that the "ancient Greeks and Romans on the stage sang their tragedies throughout."[1] The ancient combination of word and music had apparently been highly successful in producing emotional effects, effects that Giulio Caccini, Jacopo Peri, and Claudio Monteverdi attempted to reproduce with the so-called *stile rappresentativo*, in which music was to support and enhance the libretto.[2] Although these librettists and composers cited Greek and Roman tragedy as their model, the new *favola in musica* derived its structure from court celebration and pastoral tragicomedy, and then applied it not to Greek tragic themes, but to unhappy romantic episodes from Latin hexameter poetry: the

1. Solerti 1903, 40: "gli antichi Greci e Romani cantassero sulle scene le tragedie intere." Jacopo Peri's preface to the same opera (Solerti 1903, 45) spoke of the music's relation to that of "gli antichi Greci e Romani (i quali, secondo l'opinione di molti, cantavano su le scene le tragedie intere)".
2. See Fabbri 1984 for a collection and discussion of the relevant texts, particularly in regard to Monteverdi. Also Solerti 1903, 40 (Ottavio Rinuccini), 50 (Giulio Caccini), and 145-6 (Giovanni de' Bardi). For a lively and critical commentary on the attitudes of the first composers and librettists vis-à-vis Greek drama, see Weiss 1988, 1-9.

Aristæus episode concluding Vergil's *Georgics* combined with Ovid's *Metamorphoses* for the story of Orpheus and Eurydice; Catullus' Poem 64 and Ovid's *Heroides* for Ariadne and Theseus. By the mid-seventeenth century, Vergil's account of Dido and Aeneas would join the group of unhappy love stories – derived largely from Latin *epyllia*, or mini-epics – that showed remarkable power in defining the history of opera well into the twentieth century.[3]

Behind the diction, romantic pathos, and structure of these formative Latin hexameter poems lay a similarly complicated web of influences that included Hellenistic and Roman elegiac and pastoral poetry, epic, comedy, and – of course – tragedy.[4] For Vergil and Ovid, tragedy meant Latin tragedy as written and performed since the third century BC, but which now exists only in fragments. It also meant the Greek tragedies of the fifth century, and in particular those of Sophocles and Euripides. The classical Greek tragedies in turn were ultimately dependent on narratives from the heroic epic cycles of archaic Greece – Aeschylus is supposed to have called his tragedies 'helpings [*temache*] from the great banquets of Homer.'[5]

I offer this very brief reverse history of literary influence to emphasize the continual interplay of serious drama with epic poetry from the time when drama itself had been invented. This essay explores the continuation of that interplay in two Handelian operas written on the mythic history of the Athenian hero Theseus: *Teseo* (1713) and *Arianna in Creta* (1734). *Teseo*, an adaptation from Philippe Quinault's libretto *Thésée* (1675), is Handel's first collaboration with the librettist and polymath Nicolà Haym. The young Handel composed its score at a time when he was deciding that his future lay in London; with his adaptation of a French opera he was abetting Queen Anne's policy of rapprochement with France, while at the same time attempting to make up for his failure with the unpopular *Il pastor fido* in the previous season.[6] *Arianna in Creta*, by contrast, was composed on an Italian libretto

3. On the literary background and structure of the first operas, see Sternfeld 1993, 1-30 and 53-5; Pieri 2003, 240-9. On Hellenistic and Roman *epyllia*, see Crump 1931, especially 115-31 (Ariadne) and 178-94 (Aristaeus); Lyne 1978, 32-6. On the care with which the term *epyllion* should be used, see Allen 1940.
4. For the background of the Orpheus story, see Mynors' comments (in Vergil 1990), 314-5, note to lines 453-527 with bibliography. For Ariadne, see Gaisser 2007, especially 228-51; and Kroll (Catullus 1989), notes to poem 64, lines 50-264. For tragedy and the *Aeneid*, see the assessment in Hardie 1997; for the Dido story, see the introductory comments of Pease (in Vergil 1935, 5-21) and the notes *passim*, in Austin (Vergil 1963).
5. Athenæus, *Deipnosophistai*, 8.347e. *Temache* literally translates as 'slices of fish or meat.'
6. On the political scene, see Burrows 1994, 70-1. For the comparative lack of success of *Il pastor fido*, see Harris 1989, II, xvi-ii; Dean & Knapp 1995, 215-6.

by an unknown arranger from an original by Pietro Pariati (*Teseo in Creta*, 1715). It was produced in Handel's final season at the Haymarket theatre in the spring of 1734. In revival it served as a bridge for his move to Covent Garden in the autumn of the same year, and was mounted in competition with Porpora's *Arianna in Nasso* (libretto by Paolo Rolli), which was being produced at the rival Opera of the Nobility at the theater in Lincoln's Inn Fields.[7]

Hence, Handel created two operas with Theseus as the *primo uomo* at important moments in his career. Dramatically, both *Teseo* and *Arianna in Creta* are interesting challenges to the operatic embodiment of myth since there is no Theseus tragedy nor a Theseus epic surviving from antiquity on which to base their librettos directly, as happens to be the case for Handel's *Admeto* (1727), the pasticcio *Oreste* (1734), or the oratorio *Hercules* (1745), adapted respectively from Euripides' *Alcestis* and *Iphigenia in Tauris*, and Sophocles' *Women of Trachis*. Instead, the plots of Handel's Theseus operas had to be pieced together from a variety of sources, some of them prose, and then fitted into a poetic-dramatic structure. In this essay, I am interested in the versions and details of the Theseus myths that Handel and his librettists were employing, and in the relationship between the resulting operas and the story-telling genres of epic and tragedy. I will begin with a brief discussion of the nature of Greek myth and its embodiment in Greek tragedy, and by reviewing Theseus' story as it was told in antiquity and received by the eighteenth century. My discussion will center on a close reading of important scenes in each of these operas, demonstrating how Handel and his librettists adapted classical drama and epic to the genre of serious Italian opera. In conclusion, some observations will be made about the ways in which *Teseo* and *Arianna in Creta* reflect broader methods of adapting Greek literature, tragedy, and dramatic practice in Handel's works.

7. Suzanne Aspden (2001) has described ways in which it was possible for a contemporary Londoner to identify the rivalry between the *Ariannas* of Handel and Porpora as part of the rhetoric and imagery surrounding the wedding of Princess Anne with Willem IV of Orange.

Myth, tragedy, and moral instruction

One striking characteristic of Greek myth is the interconnectedness among its constituent stories and characters.[8] This has partly to do with the narratological fact that many of these myths can be reduced to a handful of story patterns, such as the conquest of death, in which most mythical heroes take part and which includes defeat of danger in the person of mythological monsters or powerful opponents, and usually an actual trip to the underworld; the war between generations, which informs both the Oedipus legend and the Greek creation myths; or the founding of a local cult or city, most often effected by a hero passing by on one of his death-defying missions. Another reason for the interconnectedness of myth's figures lies in the notable procreativity of its father god Zeus / Jupiter, who intrudes continually in mythological history to re-enact the primal union of sky god with a daughter of the earth and to produce yet another hero, who in turn founds cities and cults, and reproduces with the local maidens whose country he rescued from marauding monsters.

One way or another, Theseus, Jason, Hercules, Perseus, and even Orpheus and Odysseus fit into these patterns. Many of these figures are related to one another through the processes just described, while their exploits mirror each other's adventures. Athenian tragedy – there is no other kind of tragedy extant from the classical Greek world – dealt with the moments of extreme danger when these mythic patterns of societal creation or salvation were broken, or nearly so. Tragic heroes and their female counterparts fail to conquer death and even inflict it on themselves or others. The collateral damage of the epic exploits and quests may become central figures in tragic drama.

This first literary drama produced by western civilization that was the vehicle for the retelling of ancient myth bore a heavy weight of cultural expectations for the eighteenth century, much as it does for us. In particular, tragedy was then thought to be responsible for giving moral advice; as one English critic put it: "The aim and business of the *Greek tragedy* was by some fable or other, to teach and inculcate some moral

8. My approach here is influenced by formalist studies of traditional tales such as those of Raglan 1956, 173-85, especially 176; or Propp 1968. See the summaries in Scholes 1974, 59-69; Graf 1993, 49-50; Burkert 1979, 5-18. My purpose is to emphasize parallel mythic structures that appear in epic and tragedy.

passion."[9] André Dacier in his *Poétique d'Aristote* (1692) wrote: "Their theatre was a school, where virtue was generally better taught, than the schools of their philosophers, and at this very day, the reading of the pieces will inspire a hatred to vice, and a love to virtue."[10] Whether the contemporary Athenians supposed their drama to have such an instructional purpose is another question. Despite Dacier, the source of this eighteenth-century attitude to Greek drama is not from Aristotle, exactly; the *Poetics* implies a moral code with its description of the proper kinds of action and character to be depicted, but does not speak overtly of tragedy imparting moral lessons.[11] Aristotle was underplaying discussion of the moral question as part of his answer to Plato, who had suggested that poets *should* teach morals, but thought that epic and tragedy as the Greeks knew it did quite otherwise. Poetry, according to Plato, was such a potential cause of moral disintegration that, unless poets could be made to preach virtuous behavior and self-control, they ought to be banned from the ideal state.[12]

Plato as a young man could watch the late-fifth-century tragedies at their first performances, and according to a widely repeated tradition had even written tragedies before he met Socrates. But if that story is true, he abandoned his efforts precisely because poetry as he knew it lacked moral and rational force.[13] Both Plato and Aristotle were writing about tragedy a generation and more after the deaths of the great fifth-century tragedians, and for a fourth-century readership. The place in *fifth-century* Athenian literature where the didactic purpose of tragedy is overtly asserted, is Aristophanes' *Frogs*, which has the character Aeschylus state: "Just consider how beneficial the noble poets have been from the earliest times. ... For children the teacher is the one who instructs, but grownups have the poet. It's important that

9. [Charles Gildon] *The laws of poetry ... explained and illustrated* (1721), 149, as quoted and cited in Smith 1995, 56 and note 18. Smith further cites similar contemporary judgments on tragedy and poetry.
10. The translation of Dacier is from *Aristotle's art of poetry translated from the original Greek ... together with Mr. Dacier's notes translated from the French* (1705), xx, as quoted in Smith 1995, 63.
11. Janko 1992, 352 concludes that the concept of *catharsis* in the *Poetics* finally does provide a social benefit since it "habituates us to achieve and maintain the proper standard in our moral choices, leading toward the mean in emotional terms and hence to practical wisdom and virtue." See also the comments of Nussbaum 1992, 287, who feels that according to Aristotle's *Poetics*, "through pity and fear, indeed *in* those responses, spectators attain a deeper understanding of the world in which they must live, the obstacles their goodness faces, the needs each has for the help of others." Yet, both Janko and Nussbaum's conclusions (and others like them) have to be teased out of an inexplicit text.
12. The critiques of poetry in Plato are in *Apology* (22B-C), *Ion*, and *Republic* II-III (377A-398B) and X (595A-608B). See Aristotle 1987, x-ii, on Plato's critique of poetry. His final word in the *Republic* 607E is that we need to reject poetry "like a lover who renounces a passion that is doing him no good." (Aristotle 1987, xiii); for a brief analysis of Aristotle's reply to Plato, see Aristotle 1987, xii-iv.
13. For the sources of the tradition and the uncertainty of its reliability, see Riginos (1976) 44-51.

we tell them things that are good."[14] Ultimately, Dionysus does take Aeschylus back from the underworld with him as the poet who is mostly likely to serve a desperate Athens with his practical knowledge. This, at least, is the chorus' conclusion:

> Happy is the man who has
> keen intelligence [*ksunesin ekribomenen*]
> as is abundantly clear:
> this man, for his eminent good sense [*eu phronein*],
> is going back home again, a boon to his fellow citizens
> a boon as well to his family and friends, through being intelligent [*dia to sunetos einai*].[15]

But theories of tragedy and ethics should be handled carefully when they are presented in Aristophanic comedy: Aeschylus' solemn pronouncements on the use of tragedy are uttered in the context of a slapstick contest between him and Euripides at the end of which both poets look worse for wear; Aeschylus appears old-fashioned and at times incomprehensible. Moreover, the implication of the comedy is that Athens is in such a hopeless state that the only thing that will save it is the (impossible) resurrection of a dead tragedian.[16] One may assume that Aristophanes was playing on some generally held notion that tragedy had a didactic value, but that he, like Plato after him, depicted what he thought tragedy *ought to achieve*, rather than what in most cases it did achieve.[17]

The eighteenth-century, moralistic approach to tragedy comes therefore from idealizing theory rather than from the actual practice of tragedy. This idealization also derives from the Roman poet Horace's *Ars poetica*, which holds that "a man who has managed to blend profit with delight wins everyone's approbation, for he gives his reader pleasure at the same time as he instructs him."[18] Coupled with a percep-

14. Aristophanes 2002, 164 (*Frogs*, ll. 1030-1 and 1054-5).
15. Aristophanes 2002, 229 and 231 (ll. 1482-90).
16. The resolution of *Frogs* is on the same plane as Aristophanes' former proposals to safeguard Greece from war by means of a women's sex-strike in *Lysistrata*, or by bringing Peace from heaven by means of a flying dung beetle in the *Peace*.
17. On the ambiguous nature of the poetic criticism in *Frogs*, see for example Ford 2002, 280-2. Dover in his edition of Aristophanes' *Frogs* (1993), 10-37 offers a sober assessment of this notoriously difficult scene, concluding (on pages 22-4) that Aeschylus wins because he represents "the old days." But Dover is very clear about the dangers of taking the results of this poetic contest too seriously and points out that Aristophanes could also portray Right Argument (*Clouds*, ll. 889-1104) as a character with "considerable absurdity" to him (page 17).
18. Horace, *Ars poetica*, ll. 343-4: "omne tulit punctum qui miscuit utile dulci, / lectorem delectando pariterque monendo"

tion inherited from Aristotle's *Poetics* that Sophocles was the model tragedian, especially in his *Oedipus tyrannus*, Horace's dictum reinforced for the eighteenth century (and for us) the sense of high purpose that serious poetry, including tragedy, are supposed to have had.

But not all plays were like the *Oedipus*, not even all of Sophocles' plays. Furthermore, even if one does not look at the tragic plays themselves, between the contest in *Frogs* and Aristotle's tart criticism of the visually spectacular *mêchanê* (*deus ex machina* in Latin), whereby a god might descend from the heavens via stage machinery to intervene improbably in the action,[19] one gets a sense that there was more than one way to write a tragedy. Tragedies might end happily, for instance, indulge in verbal pyrotechnics, and appeal shamelessly and melodramatically to the emotions as much as the intellect. This might have little to do with teaching a moral or improving the audience beyond a catharsis effected through the kind of emotional excess that Plato deplored. Had they not usually done so, the criticisms of Aristophanes and Plato would have had no point. Euripides was famous and/or notorious in these respects, depending on one's point of view. It seems to me that Handel and his librettists were taking their cues from this second, more melodramatic type of tragedy, rather than from the soberer, moralistic vision of tragedy espoused by at least some theoreticians from Plato onward.[20]

Theseus in the ancient tradition

These reflections concerning the nature of tragedy will inform the concluding discussion of the relation of Handel's librettos to tragedy and epic. Let us turn now to the subject of Theseus and his myths.[21] Theseus was the son of Aethra, princess of

19. *Poetics*, ll. 1454b1-b7; compare Horace, *Ars poetica*, l. 191.
20. I continue to believe that the fundamental structure of opera was a celebration of social union won through vicissitude, inherited from the Renaissance encounter with Roman comedy adapted to festive court occasions and pastoral tragicomedy, see Ketterer 2003 and 2009, 3-6, *et passim*. However, Hoxby 2005 and Heller 2005 have made persuasive arguments about the ways in which the Euripidean mode of tragic writing informed the production of serious opera in the seventeenth and eighteenth centuries, and it is their line of inquiry I am following here.
21. For the narrative of Theseus' myths and their sources in literature and art, see Gantz 1993, I, 248-70 and 276-98; Mills 1997.

Troezen in the northeast Peloponnese. Sometimes he was called the son of Poseidon, a paternity that was in accord with Athens' historical identity as a naval power; yet Theseus' father is usually said to be Aegeus, King of Athens. Theseus himself was an Athenian analog to Hercules. His bones were discovered in the fifth century BC and relocated to Athens where he was revered as semi-divine. The parallel with Hercules was made explicit even in the ancient sources. Plutarch reports that Theseus

> had long since been secretly fired by the glory of *Hercules*, held him in the highest estimation, and was never more satisfy'd than in listening to any that gave an account of him ... in the Night his Dreams were all of that Hero's Actions, and in the Day a continual emulation stir'd him up to perform the like. Besides, they were nearly related, being born of cousin-Germans.[22]

Like Hercules, Theseus destroyed monsters: as a young man in Troezen, he lifted an enormous rock under which Aegeus had left sandals and a sword; his mother Aethra had instructions that when Theseus was grown to the point where he could lift the rock and retrieve the tokens of his paternity, it was time for him to make his way to Athens. Setting off across the dangerous Isthmus of Corinth towards Athens, he purged the countryside of ogres and noxious beasts as he went, including Procrustes, of the procrustean bed, Sinis, who split people apart using two pine trees, and the wrestler Cercyon, who killed the opponents he defeated. After arriving in Athens and being acknowledged by his father Aegeus, Theseus rescued his city from the power of Minos of Crete by killing the Minotaur of the labyrinth, united the district of Attica under the command of Athens, conquered the Amazons, and like any good hero made a trip to the underworld.

Theseus was a constant friend of Hercules, whom he so admired, but like that hero, got into a good deal of trouble over sex. As Heinrich Spoor recorded in his mythological emblem book: "Theseus left proof that the struggle with lust is harder than the struggle with hardship, since the poets tell us that after he overcame tyranny, he fell into the most serious difficulties on account of Helen and other women."[23] The "other women" included Helen, later of Troy, whom he kidnapped while she was still a girl; the daughters of Minos, Ariadne and Phaedra; and a lesser-known nymph called Aegle, who is featured as his beloved in Lully's *Thésée* (Aeglé)

22. Plutarch 1702-11, I, 9-10.
23. Spoor 1707, 87: "Difficilius tamen esse voluptatum, quam difficultatum certamen Theseus testatum reliquit. Cum superatis tyrannis, ob Helenam, aliasque fæminas in gravissimas ærumnas incidisse fabulentur poetæ."

and Handel's *Teseo* (Agilea). Theseus' requisite heroic trip to the underworld was an attempt to carry off Persephone herself, a misbegotten adventure from which he was rescued by Hercules and which caused him to leave part of his buttocks stuck to a bench in Hades.[24] Edmund Spenser's *Faerie queene* (1590) in consequence mentions him among the underworld's great sinners:

> There was *Ixion* turned on a wheele,
> For daring tempt the Queene of heaven to sin;
> And *Sisyphus* an huge round stone did reele
> Against an hill, ne might from labour lin;
> There thirsty *Tantalus* hong by the chin;
> And *Tityus* fed a vulture on his maw;
> *Typhoeus* joynts were stretched on a gin,
> *Theseus* condemnd to endlesse slouth by law,
> And fifty sisters water in leake vessels draw.[25]

Theseus is moreover a relative latecomer as a hero, claimed by the Athenians as a founder figure in imitation of other cities' heroes. No Theseus epic has survived from the archaic period, though one may have existed.[26] Bacchylides' *Dithyramb* 17 recounts an episode on Minos' ship during Theseus' voyage to Crete to destroy the Minotaur, and in *Dithyramb* 18, Aegeus briefly narrates Theseus' exploits on the Isthmus of Corinth to choral response. The most complete account left to us from the ancient world is not in a tragedy or epic, but in the rationalized biography by

24. Apollodorus 1921, II, 152-3 n. 4. A humorous version of the parallels between Theseus and Hercules was published in the 4 July 1722 issue of the Tory *Freeholder's journal* as a 'Dialogue of the dead' in the style of Lucian. The ghosts of Theseus and Hercules wrangle over which of them was the better hero by comparing their adventures and reciting each other's faults in respect to women. In the course of the dialogue, Theseus argues (at pages 167-8): "And I – have not I vanquished all the Robbers of *Greece*; drove away *Medea* from my *Father*; slain the *Minotaur*, and extricated my self out of the *Labyrinth*, on which Account the *Istmian* Games were instituted? They don't fall much short of the *Nemean* [Games, founded by and held in honor of Hercules]. Besides this I overthrew the *Amazons* upon their March to besiege Athens. To these Exploits you may add the Battle of the *Lapiths*, *Jason's* Voyage for the Golden Fleece, and the Hunting of the wild Boar of *Calydon*, in which I had no inconsiderable Part; and I dared, as well as you, to descend into *Hell*."
25. Book 1, Canto V, xxxv. Compare with Ariosto, *Orlando furioso* 34.14, where Theseus, in company with Jason and Aeneas, is allotted severe punishment in the underworld for deceiving women. It is this more negative view of Theseus on which Porpora's *Arianna in Nasso* chooses to play, depicting his dilemma over his obligations to thee Amazon Antiope, while Ariadne is championed first by Pirithous, and then by the god Bacchus.
26. For the evidence, see Mills 1997, 19-25, especially 19 with note 74.

Plutarch I have already quoted; it was written in the second century AD and made available in modern times through the editions of Amyot (1559) and Dryden (1683).[27]

This late arrival on the Athenian mythic scene, combined with the vicissitudes of textual survival, often made Theseus a secondary character in other people's stories. Sophocles and Euripides wrote tragedies about the events depicted in Handel's operas, but only a few, not very revealing fragments remain.[28] He appears in four extant tragedies: Sophocles' *Oedipus at Colonus*, and Euripides' *Suppliant women*, *Herakles*, and *Hippolytus*. In *Suppliant women* and *Herakles*, Theseus plays the role of magnanimous protector of the unfortunate and helpless; *Suppliant women* (to which I will make reference again at the end) describes the aftermath of the events portrayed in Sophocles' *Antigone*. Theseus is persuaded by grieving widows of the slain men to march on Thebes and to recover the bodies of those who have been left unburied, along with Antigone's brother Polynices, after a fratricidal battle between Oedipus' sons. Euripides' *Hippolytus* displays Theseus' darker side, an angry father figure who rashly believes the lying letter of the suicidal Phaedra and curses his son Hippolytus so that the young man is thrown from his chariot and dragged to his death. In addition to these, his son Demophon appears as magnanimous receiver of suppliants in Euripides' *Children of Herakles*, and his father Aegeus arrives in the middle of Euripides' *Medea* and innocently promises asylum in Athens to Medea, who is planning the murder of the Corinthian royalty. Aegeus then exits, as an Athenian audience would know, to travel to Troezen and beget Theseus.

If an author chose to ignore Theseus' less creditable behavior in respect to women, then one is left with a culture hero and magnanimous ruler of the kind that makes Theseus a better candidate for *tragédie en musique* and *opera seria* than he was for Greek tragedy. This was already true in fifth-century Athens where, as we have seen, with the exception of Euripides' *Hippolytus*, he was presented as a young, conquering hero and analog of Hercules, or else, as King of Athens, the generous defender of helpless suppliants.[29] Similarly, Chaucer (in *The knight's tale*), and Fletcher-Shakespeare (in *The two noble kinsmen*) were able to ignore Theseus' bad reputation with women when

27. For a brief description of the important early modern and eighteenth-century translations of the *Lives*, see Russell 2001, 141-63 and 175-6.

28. The tragedies with plots similar to *Teseo* were Sophocles' *Aegeus* (Sophocles 1996, 18-23) and Euripides' *Aegeus* (Euripides 1998-2003, I, 1-13; Euripides 2008, VII, 3-11); *Arianna in Creta* had a parallel in Euripides' *Theseus* (Euripides 1998-2003, II, 145-65; Euripides 2008, VII, 415-27). Sophocles may also have written a *Theseus* on the same subject (Sophocles 1996, 106 and 344-5). For these and other fragmentary plays in which Theseus was a character, see Mills 1997, 222-67.

29. Mills 1997, 222-3.

it suited them to create in Theseus an authority figure with sufficient moral standing to act as judge over the quarrels of his subjects.[30] It is this heroic Theseus that Handel depicted twice at crucial moments in his career as composer of operas.

Medea in Handel's Teseo

Teseo is based on the events of the young Theseus' arrival in Athens to claim his patrimony, as reported in Plutarch's *Life of Theseus*:

> [Theseus] found [Athenian] public affairs full of all Confusion, and divided into Parties and Factions, *Aegeus* also, and his whole private Family, labouring under the same Distemper; for *Medea*, having fled from *Corinth*, and promis'd *Aegeus* to make him, by her Art, capable of having Children, was entertain'd by him, and admitted to his Bed she had the first knowledge of *Theseus*, whom as yet *Aegeus* did not know; and he being in years, full of Jealousies and Suspicions, and fearing every thing by reason of the Faction that was then in the City, she easily persuaded [Aegeus] to poison *Theseus* at a Banquet, to be prepar'd for him as a Civility to a Stranger. He, coming to the Entertainment, thought it not fit to discover himself first, but willing to give his Father the occasion of first finding him out, the Meat being on the Table, he drew his Sword as if he designed to cut with it; *Aegeus*, upon the sudden perceiving the Token, threw down the Cup of Poison, and discovering his Son, embrac'd him; and having gathered together all his citizens, he own'd him publickly before them, who receiv'd him with great Satisfaction for the Fame of his Greatness and Bravery.[31]

The libretto's title page calls the opera a *dramma tragico*, a generic label that translates the *tragédie lyrique* of Quinault's *Thésée*. But despite the title, Theseus is not really the main character, just as was the case in many of the ancient sources. Rather, it is Medea, the subject of one of the most horrific tragedies by Euripides, who gets much of Handel's most striking music in the opera. Medea first appears in Act II, scene 1 singing a *largo* that in the vocal line seems to be leading to a sleep scene: "Sweet Repose and peaceful Innocence; / Happy that Breast that ye Possess."[32] But a disqui-

30. Donaldson 1985, 32-6.
31. Plutarch 1702-11, I, 14-5.
32. "Dolce riposo, ed innocente pace, / Ben' felice, è quel sen', che vi possiede." (All quotes from *Teseo* are taken from Quinault & Haym 1715). Here and elsewhere I give the English translation in the

eting marching rhythm in the strings underlies these apparently tranquil lyrics (see Example 1), and no sleep follows: it quickly emerges that she is not possessed by either repose or innocence.[33] Although she is engaged to be married to King Aegeus (Egeo), the passion of love that made her commit theft and murder in the past has now made her pine for the hero Theseus, not yet revealed to be Aegeus' son. That passion turns to vengeful rage when she discovers the love between Theseus and Agilea. In the fourth act, Medea conveys the lovers to a barren wasteland and calls up spirits to torment them, an episode suggested perhaps by the mythic Theseus' journey to the underworld. When her efforts fail, she tries to impress Theseus with her magnanimity; when that, too, fails, she resolves to kill him, and it is here that the story joins Plutarch's account once again, for she provides Aegeus with a cup of poison to give the young man, whom he still does not know to be his son. When Aegeus

Example 1. George Frideric Handel, *Teseo* (1713), Act II, scene 1 (aria, bars 1-4). Transcribed by the editor from Handel 1874, 30.

main text on the assumption that that is how most English spectators would have received the words of the drama.

33. This is more striking in *Teseo* than in *Thésée*. Quinault and Lully's Medea sings in dialogue with a maidservant Dorine, who interrupts her musings with advice about love. Haym gave Medea a solo scene that Handel set first with the arioso line, interrupted by Medea's own recitative, and finally an aria to an agitated unison violin accompaniment that expresses the discontent her love has brought to her.

at the last minute recognizes Theseus and dashes the cup from his hand, Medea flies away, only to reappear in a chariot drawn by flying dragons to set fire to the whole palace. Only Minerva's appearance in the *scena ultima* in response to the cast's cries for help saves the day. Thus Medea gets good spectacle as well as good music, surpassing even that of her Euripidean original, who with her escape to Athens in a dragon-drawn chariot had become her own *dea ex machina*.

The real debt of Handel's Medea to Euripides' cannot be direct, if only because Haym's immediate model is Quinault's *Thésée*. Her appearance in the flying chariot at the end of the opera might seem to be an most obvious reference to the Greek stage, but that spectacle was inherited from Quinault's Act V, scene 6 where, in addition, a celebratory banquet on stage metamorphoses into fearsome monsters ("animaux horribles").[34] Moreover, the dragon-chariot had already in Roman antiquity become Medea's signature vehicle: this is how she travels in Ovid's *Metamorphoses* (Book VII, lines 218-9, 234-7, 350-1, and 391-2) and how she makes her escape at the conclusion of Seneca's *Medea* (lines 1022-7).

There is, however, another, subtler adaptation of the ancient dramatic tradition that occurs at the opening of Handel's Act V, where Medea contemplates whether she can bring herself to kill Theseus, whom she loves: this is an echo of the excruciating moment in Euripides' play in which Medea agonizes over whether she really can kill her own children.[35] The events of that play take place in Corinth and precede her flight to Athens. At the moment in question, Medea has already killed Creusa, the princess of Corinth, her rival for Jason's love, and Creusa's father king Creon, by means of a poisonously pyrotechnic robe and crown. She has heard of her success and now turns to the problem of her children by Jason, whom she had resolved to kill as her final act of revenge. She looks at them and vacillates, suffering a natural mother's qualms at the thought, and then returns to an almost cold assessment that the die is cast and she must do it. The version that follows is the Latin translation from a 1703 Cambridge edition of the play:[36]

> Mulieres, quia vidi lætos oculos liberorum,
> Non possem facere quod statui. Valeant consilia
> Priora: abducam filios meos e terra.

34. Quinault 1999, 155-6.
35. *Medea*, ll. 1040-64.
36. The Latin preserves accurately the simplicity of the original Greek and was the most accessible means of reading Euripides at the beginning of the eighteenth century. It also provides a pointed contrast with Seneca's Latin as quoted below.

Quid opus est me patrem horum, horum malis
Cruciantem, mihi bis tanta mala accersere?
Nequaquam ego hoc faciam. Valeant ista consilia
Verum quid patior? An volo derideri,
Dimittens meos inimicos impunitos?
Audendum hoc est....
Heu, heu!
Nequaquam vero, mi anime, ne tu saltem hæc
Mitte eos, o miser; parce liberis:
Illic nobiscum viventes exhilarabunt te.
Non per dæmones infernos, qui sunt apud Plutonem,
Nunquam hoc fiet; ut ego inimicis
Filios meos relinquam injuria afficiendos.
Omnino actum est eos mori: & quoniam hoc oportet,
Nos occidemus eos, qui [sic] procreavimus eos.
Omnino actum est hoc, & non aliter fiet.[37]

The speech is direct, rhetorically understated, and all the more powerful for being so. In fact, the lines beginning "Nequaquam vero, mi anime" ("Oh, do not, my heart") to the end of the quotation have been suspected as a non-Euripidean addition, which would mean that Euripides' original was even less sensational than the received text makes appear.[38] Euripides' Medea is not a melodramatic witch. She is a woman pushed to her limits who, unfortunately for those who offend her, has a way with dangerous herbs, and a dragon-chariot at her disposal with which to escape after she has had her revenge. The melodramatic Medea, by contrast, is a later development from Apollonius' Hellenistic epic *Argonautica*, Books III and IV, and from the Roman authors, particularly Ovid (*Metamorphoses*, Book VII) and Seneca (*Medea*), all of whom emphasize her spectacular and often destructive magical powers. It was this aspect of her character that the European Renaissance chose to emphasize and

37. Euripides 1703, *Medea* 109 and 111, ll. 1043-51 and 1056-64. Rex Warner's English translation of the same lines (in Grene & Lattimore 1960, III, 95) reads: "I cannot bear to do it, I renounce the plans / I had before. I'll take my children away from / This land. Why should I hurt their father with the pain / They feel, and suffer twice as much pain myself? / No, no, I will not do it, I renounce my plans. / But oh, what is wrong with me? Do I want to / Let my enemies go unhurt and be laughed at for it? / I must face this thing. ... / Oh, do not, my heart, you must not do these things! / Poor heart, let them go, have pity on the children. / If they live with you in Athens, they will cheer you. / No! by Hades' avenging Furies it shall not be – / This shall never be that I should suffer my children / To be the prey of my enemies' insolence. / Every way is fixed."

38. Reeve 1972.

which is neatly summarized in a description by Pierre Gautruche in his compendium of classical literature:

> Medea was a famous enchantress ... She was the grandchild of the [Sun]. She was tutor'd and made acquainted with the secrets of her devilish art by Hecate, who taught her how to perform wonderful things by spels [sic] and enchantments. She was able to transport woods from one place to another, to cause the current of rivers to turn back towards their source, to bring down the moon and the other stars upon the earth and to give life to the dead.[39]

Compare, therefore, a passage from the equivalent speech in Seneca's *Medea*, which ends with her murder of one of the children. As in Euripides' play, Medea vacillates before making her final decision, then takes what is understated in Euripides and turns her horror and anger into a full-blown vision of the Furies who drive her. She is not worried about shame or the laughter of enemies; it is her sense of her own power and identity that demands this self-fulfilling revenge: "*now* I am Medea" ("nunc sum Medea"), she declares in the same speech.[40] Her diction is overwrought and ends in melodramatic hysteria that threatens mutilation and fire:

> Cor pepulit horror, membra torpescunt gelu
> pectusque tremuit. Ira discessit loco
> materque tota coniuge expulsa redit.
> Egone ut meorum liberum ac prolis meæ
> fundam cruorem? Melius, a, demens furor!
> incognitum istud facinus a dirum nefas
> a me quoque absit. Quod scelus miseri luent? ...
> urget exilium ac fuga:
> iam iam meo rapientur avulsi et sinu,
> flentes, gementes. Osculis pereant patris,
> periere matris. Rursus increscit dolor
> et fervet odium, repetit invitam manum
> antiqua Erinys. Ira, qua ducis, sequor....
>   Quonam ista tendit turba Furiarum impotens?
> Quem quærit aut quo flammeos ictus parat,
> aut cui cruentas agmen infernum faces
> intentat? Ingens anguis excusso sonat
> tortus flagello. Quem trabe infesta petit
> Megæra? Cuius umbra disperses venit

39. Gautruche 1701, 168.
40. At line 910. On this monologue and the power of its language, see Boyle 1997, 131-2.

incerta membris. Frater est, pœnas petit.
dabimus, sed omnes. Fige luminibus faces
lania, perure, pectus en Furiis patet.[41]

It is this Senecan Medea that Haym invoked in *Teseo*, first with the infernal spectacle of Act IV, adapted from Quinault's third and fourth acts, and now with the version of Medea's debate with herself at the opening of Act V.[42] First, in the recitative, she concentrates on herself: *her* soul, *her* self, *her* revenge. Second, it is heightened both in the recitative and aria by emphasis on Furies and revenge, and by the violent language of the dismemberment and slaughter, that she means to visit on Theseus and Aegle. The English text of the libretto reads:

Then now to gratify Revenge, must I
Destroy the Idol of my Soul?
Whither, whither does my Fury drive me?
To punish his ingrateful Heart,
Is to torment my self.
The Thought o'rewhelms my Soul with Grief:
But Agilea triumphs o're my Sufferings

41. Seneca 2002, I, *Medea*, ll. 926-32, 948-53, and 958-66: "Children once mine, you must pay the penalty for your father's crimes. My heart is struck with horror, my limbs freeze, my breast trembles. Anger retreats, and the mother returns, with the wife utterly banished. Could I shed the blood of my children, my own youngsters? Do not say so, mad rage! Let that unheard-of deed, that abomination be left untouched by me as well ... But exile and flight are close. At any moment they will be snatched and torn from my embrace, in tears, in distress. Let them be lost to their father's kisses, they are lost to their mother's. Once more my pain grows and my hatred burns, the Erinys demands my reluctant hand again. Anger, where you lead, I follow ... What is the target of this wild throng of Furies? Whom are they hunting, whom are they threatening with fiery blows? At whom is the hellish band pointing its bloody torches? A huge snake hisses, entwined in a lashing whip. Whom is Megaera seeking with her bludgeon? Whose shade approaches ill-defined with limbs dispersed? It is my brother, he seeks amends. We shall pay them, yes, every one. Drive torches into my eyes, mutilate me, burn me; see my breast is open to the Furies."
42. Quinault's underworld in his third and fourth acts embodies the vision of Seneca's Medea in that it torments the two lovers cruelly with its dances of specters holding knives and torches, while Medea calls for the flowing of innocent blood (Act IV, scene 2). Medea's recitative at Quinault's Act V, scene 1, however, is understated in an almost Euripidean fashion, for whereas Haym's Medea calls for blood and slaughter, Quinault (1999, 162-3) wrote more simply, "Quoi, laisser mon amour sans peine et sans danger?" (line 1001), and in a lyric passage (ll. 1011-21) contemplates a vengeance "horrible et barbare," that is, since she herself has killed her own children, to induce Aegeus to commit a similar act: "Contre un fils, inconnu, j'arme son propre père. / Je ne puis me venger / À moins d'un parricide." (ll. 1017 and 1020-21). It was therefore Haym's choice to return to the more violent, Senecan diction for the London audience, which Handel treated with appropriate musical violence.

Unmolested. Shall she enjoy my Love?
Can I without Concern
Behold her Satisfaction?
No, no. Now I'll hasten my Revenge:
Theseus shall dye, since he has forgot his Love.

I want to die, but avenged!
Avenged I shall die!
And before I die I shall see my rival,
Rent and slaughtered,
And the unfaithful one, too, who
So cruelly insulted me.[43]

Handel set these lines as a simple recitative followed by a rage aria. His music aptly emphasizes the near schizophrenia of the moment, beginning more gently with Medea's contemplation of her love for Theseus, and then suddenly changing – together with the harmony (from g to f minor in bars 10-1) – on the word "But" ("Ma") to the harsh refusal to let Agilea get the better of her (Example 2a). As she begins the aria with "I want to die" ("I will die" or "Morirò" in Handel's score, see Example 2b), the orchestra torments her with insistent, repeating g minor chords and a wailing oboe, reminiscent of "Pensieri, voi mi tormentate" in *Agrippina* (Act II, scene 13).[44] Rushing ascending and descending scales in strings and voice then press her forward as she contemplates her revenge (see bars 29 ff.). Insistent repetitions emphasize the brutality of the vivid and brutal "rent and slaughtered" ("lacerata, trucidata"). While a kernel of the original Euripidean passage remains visible in this Medea's nearly schizophrenic deliberation about whether she can kill the one she loves, in terms of diction and music Handel's character is more in the style of Seneca than Euripides. The important point here, however, is to observe how the librettists and composer have adapted a famous scene from the heritage of *Medea* tragedies, tangentially but not directly related to the story of Theseus' life, to create a scene and dramatic situation organic to this opera from the life of Theseus.

43. "Dunque per Vendicarmi, ora degg'jo / Dar Morte, all' Idol mio? / Dove, dove mi Spinge il mio furore? / Punir l'Ingrato Core, / E['] Un punire mè stessa; / L'alma in pensarvi, è già di duolo Oppressa. / Mà; trionfa Agilea al mio Martoro: / Non Contesa, havrà dunque il ben' ch'adoro! / Potrò senza tormento, / Mirare il suo Contento! / No', No'; che Vendicarmi ora degg'Jo; / Teseo Morrà, già ch'il suo Amore oblio. // Vuò Morir; mà vendicata / Vendicata Morirò; / E Vedrò pria di Morire/ Lacerata / Trucidata / La rivale, e l'infedele / Che crudele m'oltraggiò." The translation of the aria is my own, since the libretto only summarizes aria texts in English.

44. Both passages are in g minor and begin with a held note on the oboe followed by two eighth notes descending to another held note on the fifth below.

Example 2a. Handel, *Teseo* (1713), Act V, scene 1 (recitative). After Handel 1874, 89.

Example 2b. Handel, *Teseo* (1713), Act V, scene 1 (aria, bars 20-31). After Handel 1874, 90.

THESEUS AS MEDIEVAL KNIGHT IN *ARIANNA IN CRETA*

I would like to turn now to the figure of Theseus himself in *Arianna in Creta* to observe a different kind of literary and dramatic adaptation. Once again, Pierre Gautruche gives a succinct summary of the events on which the opera is based:

> The most famous and notable of all *Theseus'* exploits, was the Victory that he obtained of the *Minotaure*, who was half Man and half a Bull, whose Birth we have mentioned in the former Book, speaking of *Pasiphae*, the wife of *Minos*, who was the Mother of this Monster, begot by a Bull on her body. And that we may know how *Theseus* was engaged in this business, we must understand, that King *Minos* made War upon the People of Attica, to revenge the death of his son *Androgeus*, massacred by them in a treacherous manner. In this War he ... [overcame] the *Athenians*; so that he obliged them to send unto him as a Tribute, every year a certain number of young Men, whom he gave to this *Minotaurus* to be devoured. *Theseus* requested to be sent amongst the other young Men, that he might destroy this Monster, that had destroyed already so much of the Blood of his Citizens. The Labyrinth was the place where this *Minotaurus* was kept. This Edifice hath been built by *Daedalus*, in such a manner that there were in it so many Windings and Turnings, that it was a difficult matter for one within to find the way out again. *Theseus* wisely prevented this inconveniency, for he won the good liking of *Ariadne* the King's Daughter, and she delivered to him a Thread, by the assistance whereof he found a way out of the Labyrinth, after he had killed the *Minotaurus* in it, *Ariadne* he took with him, promising unto her wonderful advantages of his Kingdom of *Athens*.[45]

Plutarch's account of the matter adds:

> The Cretans will by no means allow the truth of this, but say that the Labyrinth was only an ordinary Prison, having no other Ill in it, than that it secur'd the Prisoners from escaping, and that *Minos*, having instituted the games in Honour of *Androgeus* gave as a Reward to the Victors those that till that time had been Prisoners in the Labyrinth. And that the first that overcame in those Games, was one of the greatest Power and Command among 'em, named *Taurus*, a Man of no merciful or sweet Disposition, but that carry'd himself towards the *Athenians*, that were made his Prize, in a proud and cruel manner.[46]

45. Gautruche 1701, 150-1.
46. Plutarch 1702-11, 18-9.

This Taurus (called 'Tauris' in the English text and 'Tauride' in the Italian), obviously a rationalization of the mythic Minotaur, becomes in Handel's *Arianna* a "Son of Vulcan" and "General of the Cretan Army,"[47] a double of the monster and a second obstacle for Theseus to conquer in single combat before he can unite with Ariadne and save Athens from Minos' power. The action of *Arianna in Creta* builds through its three acts to Theseus' confrontations, first with the Minotaur, and then with Taurus, who has of course been involved in some of the romantic complications of the plot, and whose defeat allows Theseus and Ariadne, as well as the secondary lovers named Alcestes and Carilda, to unite happily under the now-magnanimous gaze of King Minos in the *scena ultima*.

Unlike the scene of Medea's dilemma in *Teseo*, there is no extant corresponding tragic precedent for Theseus' combats in *Arianna in Creta*. Combats did not take place on stage in Greek tragedy at all. It is striking how the character of Theseus is instead presented throughout as a champion knight who follows a code of medieval chivalry rather than any ancient code of manly behavior. His efforts against the Minotaur and Taurus is cast in terms of a single combat for the safety and honor of the ladies. This is even more notable in the English translation of the libretto than it is in the Italian. It begins already in the argument, which explains that "[Minos'] fatal Law further bore, that it [the sacrifice of seven young men every seven years] should continue for ever, unless there came some *Champion*, who, to save the Victims, should offer himself to overthrow the Monster" [emphasis mine]. In Act I, scene 8, Minos in condemning the young woman Carilda to be devoured by the Minotaur, announces: "And if in a short Space no Champions come / To combat for Carilda, she must die."[48] The fact that Theseus and Alcestes vie with one another to be the champion fighting for Carilda's life is one of the dramatic complications that drive the second act, especially in scenes 3, 4, and 12, the last of which concludes with a somewhat irrelevant but show-stopping aria in which Alcestes contributes to the medieval feel of the piece by comparing himself to an exhausted pilgrim ("Son qual stanco Pellegrino"). Minos warns Taurus of the valor of Carilda's great champion in Act II, scene 6. Although we are in the world of Greek myth, Theseus is quite clearly being

47. All citations from *Arianna in Creta* are taken from Pariati & Rolli 1734.
48. "[E] se in brev'ora / Non vè [sic] chi alle due pugne / Si cimenti per lei, Carilda mora." There is a parallel situation in Act III of the overtly chivalric *Ariodante* (London, 1735), in which Ginevra, accused of adultery, is championed at a tournament, first by the hypocritical Polinesso and then by the disguised Ariodante.

cast as a medieval knight errant. He defends fair ladies from monsters and other evil knights, and fights for his own honor and glory while doing so.[49]

Act II, scenes 1 to 3 offer a good illustration of how the elements of classicism are resolved into medieval, chivalric behavior in the opera. The scene is "A Wood, at the Bottom of which is seen the Temple of Hercules, on one Side a dark Cave, opposite to it a Tower."[50] Theseus, singing an accompanied recitative in dialogue with the strings and oboes, is torn between the demands of love and glory:

> Oh my dear Country! hapless Citizens!
> Oh! Ariadne, my Delight and Treasure!
> Oh! pow'rful Love that combats in my Breast!
> Oh Glory! Oh my Faith! which shou'd I follow?
> ...
> How is my Heart perplex'd between my Doubts!
> Tell me ye Gods! on which shall I resolve?[51]

In a lullaby sung to himself, he summons Sleep (il Sonno) to resolve his dilemma. Sleep arrives "in the Form of a venerable old Man on a cloud," in turn singing: "Open ye Gates of most transparent Dreams."[52] The dreams appear from a gate of transparent horn, "of the kind the ancients made up," and bring him a vision in which he fights the Minotaur to "Shew him the future Triumphs of his Arms, / And Fame prepar'd for him by Fate."[53] Theseus then wakes as Alcestes enters. The two argue over which of them will fight the Minotaur and Taurus, and so champion the condemned Carilda. Theseus asserts his desire to be that champion; when Alcestes asks if loves Carilda, he denies it and reveals that he loves Ariadne, the long lost daughter

49. The medieval romantic qualities of Theseus' story are also present, though much less pronounced, in Porpora's *Arianna in Nasso*. In Act I, scene 3, Pirithous arrives to challenge Theseus, calling himself one "who has long been in search of the great Athenian champion, to make trial of him." Theseus answers: "But who art thou?" Pirithous: "I am Pirithous." Theseus: "I know the name, and with the proof of our courage. [*They fight*." (Rolli 1734). In Act I, scene 6, Pirithous briefly offers to champion the honor of the Amazon Antiope. But the story of the opera is about leaving a woman so Bacchus may have her, and Theseus' chivalrous knighthood is not to the point.

50. "Bosco, nel fondo di cui si vede il Tempio d'Ercole, da un lato, Caverna oscura, e di rimpetto a questa, una Torre."

51. "Oh! Patria! oh! Cittadini! / Oh! Arianna mio bene! / Oh! Amor che mi combatti! / Oh! Gloria! oh! Fede! E chi Seguir conviene? ... Agitato cor mio! / Dite, ditemi oh Dei! che far degg' Io?".

52. "Il SONNO sotto figura d'un vecchio venerando in una nuvola."; "Disseratevi o' Porte / De' più lucidi Sogni."

53. "Tù dimostra, O Morfeo, / Il futuro Trionfo al gran Teseo." The stage directions in the score are more specific about the nature of the gate than is the libretto: "Si vede la porta, di corno trasparente, da cui finsero li antichi, escono i sogni veridici." (Act II, scene 2, beginning measure 5.)

of Minos. His dream has resolved for him the apparent contradiction between the two: he wants to marry Ariadne, "But still I seek the Liberty of Athens: / A victory at once will save my Country, / And Crown my Wishes in the Fair I love."[54] When Alcestes asks for friendship's sake to be allowed to fight, Theseus answers: "My Friend, I cannot now, the Field is mine, / I have no Fear, but for the Combat burn."[55] He closes with an aria in which he compares himself to an oak tree:

The Forest Oak the Winter bears,
  And gathers Strength by being beat,
It's Head amidst the Tempest rears,
  And does its utmost Force defeat.[56]

Thus these scenes blend classical myth, philosophy, and epic with medieval chivalry.[57] The temple of Hercules on stage emphasizes the old link between Theseus and that hero. The visual reference to Hercules, combined with Theseus' anguish over his need to make a choice between his "Delight and Treasure" and his desire for Glory evokes the famous 'choice of Hercules,' in which the Greek hero chooses a life motivated by virtue rather than one of pleasure.[58] The references to a gate that brings true dreams, and the image of the tree standing firm in the face of a tempest are both adaptations of famous passages from Vergil's *Aeneid*.[59] The recitative dialogue between the two men, especially in the English translation in the libretto, casts the heroism in medieval and chivalric terms, with the *championing* of Carilda against the monster and Taurus as single 'Combat and Trial' (*Cimento*) on a 'Field' (*Campo*), which will win for Theseus both Liberty for his country and for the Fair he loves.

Consequently, where the scene for Medea in *Teseo* took its beginning from scenes in Euripidean and Senecan tragedy, this group of scenes in *Arianna in Creta* uses stage spectacle, references to Latin epic, and the conflict inherent in chivalric combat to build to a bright aria in D Major (see Example 3), in which driving ascending and descending sixteenth-note scales express Theseus' heroism, climaxing on a

54. "[M]a pure bramo / La libertà d'Atene; una vittoria / Può la Patria Salvar, darmi chi amo."
55. "Non posso; il Campo è mio nulla pavento."
56. "Salda Quercia, inerta balza / Quando il vento più l'incalza , / Hà più forza, e più valor."
57. The evocation of Sleep and the subsequent dream and ballet were added for the London libretto (Gronda 1990, 301); in consequence the analysis that follows applies specifically to this version of the opera and not to Pariati's original.
58. Xenophon, *Memorabilia*, 2.21-34; Cicero, *De officiis*, 1.32.118.
59. IV.441-9 (Aeneas as a steadfast oak) and VI.893-6 (the gates of dreams).

six-measure melisma on the word "valor."[60] Finally, the chivalry here, as elsewhere in Handel's operas for London, combines the chivalry with an appeal to patriotism and liberty that has political resonances.[61]

The 1734 *Arianna in Creta* was produced in a group with three Ariostan operas: *Orlando* (1733), *Ariodante* (1735), and *Alcina* (1735). It might appear from this that the decision of Handel and his arranger to portray Theseus as a medieval knight in *Arianna* was simply part of a newly acquired habit, a temporary convenience that suited the occasion.[62] But the literary and dramatic heritage is more interesting than that, at least for Handel's English audience, who received the opera partly through the translated words of the libretto. If they were at all inclined to read poetry, they would know that in their literary tradition Theseus was as much a medieval knight as he was an Athenian hero. In Geoffrey Chaucer's *The knight's tale*, for instance, he appears as the victorious King of Athens in a chivalric story about the brothers who are rivals for the love of a lady they have seen out of a prison window. Chaucer adapted his tale from Boccaccio's twelve-book epic *Teseida* (1340s). Shakespeare twice depicted Theseus in the role of a feudal Duke of Athens: in *Midsummer night's dream* (1594-6) and in the *Two noble kinsmen* (1613) he wrote with John Fletcher and which is, as its prologue acknowledges, a dramatization of Chaucer's *Knight's tale*.[63] In 1700, John Dryden published a modernized version of Chaucer's *Knight's tale* among his collection of *Fables* that praised Chaucer's poetry in the same category with the Homer and the Vergil:

60. The music was written in part to show off the talents of Handel's new singer Carestini. See the comments in Dean 2006, 261-2 and Burrows 1994, 219-20.
61. For the themes of chivalry and liberty on the contemporary London stage, see Ketterer 2001 and Ketterer 2009, 114 and 142.
62. The impulse for the following discussion came from Ellen Harris' observation (Harris 1989, vii) that Handel's operas of 1732-6 "are distinguished by their use of mythological or epic sources, which separates them from the operas Handel had composed between 1720 and 1732. In many ways the group forms a sequel to the early London operas of 1711-5; both groups use mythological, epic, and pastoral sources, both include magic and sorcery, and both emphasize the spectacular element through set design and stage machinery." These clusterings of operas that include spectacular supernatural effects may be what Gronda (1990, 301) had in mind when she says that the sleep scene in *Arianna in Creta* "caratterizza il gusto 'anglico' della drammaturgia handeliana e rinvia ad analoghe visioni di spiriti, streghe e folletti della poesia e del teatro inglese."
63. Shakespeare also drew on *The knight's tale* for *A midsummer night's dream*. See Donaldson 1985, 30-73 for the debt of both *Dream* and *Two noble kinsmen*, and especially 32-6 on Theseus' role as a medieval duke. For discussions of the Theban stories in medieval and Renaissance literature, see Fletcher & Shakespeare 1989, 26-9; Fletcher & Shakespeare 1997, 40-7.

Example 3. Handel, *Arianna in Creta* (1734), Act II, scene 3 (aria, bars 13-31). After Handel 1881, 48-9.

Example 3. (continued).

> I prefer in our Countryman [Chaucer], far above all his other Stories, the Noble Poem of *Palamon* and *Arcite*, which is of the *Epique* kind, and perhaps not much inferiour to the *Ilias* or the *Aeneis*: The Story is more pleasing than either of them, the Manners as perfect, the Diction as poetical, the Learning as deep and various; and the Disposition full as artful.

In 1737, moreover, Thomas Morell published a critical edition of Chaucer, in which he mentions Dryden's high assessment of the poem.[64] At least among literary circles, then, the image of Theseus as medieval knight and duke was a live one in early-eighteenth-century England.

The versions of Boccaccio and Chaucer begin with an account of how Theseus, returning from his conquest of the Amazons, was accosted by the widows of warriors killed in the expedition of the Seven against Thebes. They plead with him to take his army and force the Thebans to allow them to bury the bodies of their husbands who had been left exposed on the field. This, as we saw above, is the story told in Euripides' *Suppliant women*, one of the extant Euripidean tragedies featuring Theseus as a character. This might suggest a Greek tragic source for Chaucer and Boccaccio's depictions of Theseus, and that might also stand behind the characterization of his combats in *Arianna in Creta*, were there not one other twist. Chaucer and Boccaccio did not have Euripides available to them and could not read Greek; they were not getting the story from *Suppliant women* but rather from Book XII of Statius' *Thebaid*, a Latin epic that told the story of Theseus' rescue of the bodies from before the walls of Thebes. The *Thebaid* remained a model of classical epic throughout the Middle Ages and was the source used by Boccaccio to turn Theseus from an Athenian king into a medieval duke.[65] In consequence, Theseus' association with the chivalric tradition in the late Middle Ages and in English Renaissance also means that he belongs with the other knights errant of Handel's operas based on Ariosto and Tasso. *Arianna in Creta* with its strong flavor of medieval romance is therefore not a classical aberration in the midst of *Orlando*, *Ariodante*, and *Alcina*, but a perfectly logical part of the set.

64. Dryden 1713, s.n. In the same Preface, Dryden says: "As [Chaucer] is the Father of *English* Poetry, so I hold him in the same Degree of Veneration as the *Grecians* held *Homer*, or the *Romans* held *Virgil*." On Morell, see Anderson 1988, 193-4.

65. On the debt of Boccaccio's *Teseida* to Statius' *Thebaid*, see Anderson 1988, especially 38-191. Anderson goes on to find direct borrowing from Statius in Chaucer's poem (see pages 192-224). On the absorption of the Theban legends in to the medieval tradition see the comments of Michael Dewar (Statius 1991, xxxvii-xlviii: xlii), who says that by the late Middle Ages, "The tale of Thebes was now so firmly ensconced in the vernacular tradition that even nominal fidelity to Statius was no longer required."

Helpings from the banquet of epic

If we return to the text of *Teseo* with Theseus' medieval persona in mind, we find a similar association of subjects among Handel's first London operas. In it, Theseus is not so explicitly a knight and champion, but the ambience is nevertheless feudal. Throughout the opera Theseus insists that he does battle loyally for his king Aegeus (see Act II, scene 5; Act III, scene 3; and Act V, scene 3). While, as in the ancient myth, the sword with which he does battle is the visible token of his birth that brings about the recognition of his paternity, it is also, in the chivalric manner, the symbol of his prowess as a warrior and man. By means of her sorcery, Medea takes this symbolic object away in Act IV, and then returns it to him when he wins back his lady Aegle through his steadfast loyalty to her. Just at the climactic moment in the recognition scene (Act V, scene 3), in which Aegeus recognizes Theseus as his son, Theseus calls attention to his sword with a summary of its medieval and chivalric valences: "Here by this sword I swear, / Which has heap'd Laurels on my Arms, / That all they Foes are mine; / and that amongst your Vassals I promise to be most faithful."[66] Medea, too, is a sorceress from the medieval tradition, even though her scenes were derived from ancient tragedy and epic: the *dramatis personæ* call her a "Princess and Enchantress" ("Principessa Maga"), thus putting her in the same category with Armida ("a famous Enchantress" or "Incantatrice") in *Rinaldo* (1711) and Melissa ("an Enchantress" or "Maga amante") in *Amadigi* (1715). In consequence, *Teseo*, like *Arianna in Creta*, is not a mythic-tragic anomaly: its subject matter is in harmony with the operas based on chivalric epic that were performed in the years around it.

And yet, the Theseus operas remain an especially interesting demonstration of how the early eighteenth century might choose to make a Greek-like drama, even if their source materials and manner of presentation remained beholden to the Roman and medieval traditions. As we have seen, the Theseus operas have no original Greek dramatic model to follow for their plots. Handel, his librettists, and adapters were making serious dramas out of heroic narratives, that is, creating operas that Handel's contemporaries might have regarded as tragic: hence the monicker *dramma tragico* on the title page of *Teseo*. In these cases, Baroque librettists, like the Greek tragedians before them, were taking helpings from the banquets of

66. "Giuro per questo acciaro, / Che colmato hà di Gloria il braccio mio, / Che saran miei nemici, i tuoi nemici; / E che frà tuoi Vassalli / Il più fido m' havrai."

epic, although their epics were not Homeric but Italian and Spanish Renaissance romances, based in turn on Vergil and Statius. As the Greek and Roman authors had done in treating their own myths, so these eighteenth-century operatic mythographers capitalized on interrelated story patterns and character types from epic to depict questing knights like Orlando, Rinaldo, or Amadis, who saved fair maidens, operated on a chivalric code of honor, and defeated monsters or other warriors. In the case of *Teseo* or *Arianna in Creta*, the monster can be the Minotaur rather than a dragon. It can also be a fearsome sorceress: as Ruggiero and Rinaldo must overcome, respectively, Alcina and Armida, so Theseus must overcome Medea. In the taste of the day, those monsters, sorceresses, and battles did not stay remotely offstage, but intruded gloriously, like Athenian tragedy's gods from the machine, with verbal and musical pyrotechnics, and emotion of the kind associated more with melodramatic-tragic practice than Platonic or Horatian theory. If the sources through which these effects were embodied were Latin and medieval, the process of adapting Theseus' story to the stage was as old as Aeschylus.

ENVOICING THE DIVINE

Oracles in lyric and spoken drama in seventeenth-century France

Geoffrey Burgess

CAMILLE
Un oracle jamais ne se laisse comprendre,
On l'entend d'autant moins que plus on croit l'entendre,
Et loin de s'assurer sur un pareil arrêt,
Qui n'y voit rien d'obscur doit croire que tout l'est.

Pierre Corneille, *Horace* (1641) – Act III, scene 3[1]

Despite growing rationalist scepticism regarding the supernatural, divine revelations were not completely renounced in seventeenth-century French drama. The mingling of supernatural and mortal characters was justified to some extent by the favored setting in the mythical world of pagan Greece and Rome, but the dependence on gods was still treated judiciously: *deus ex machina* plot rescues were subjected to derisive criticism, and theatrical propriety proscribed supernatural apparitions in spoken tragedy.[2] In the place of their on-stage presence, gods were manifest in the form of oracular decrees whose impact was no less profound on the lives of the characters whose drama was being played out.

In the machine plays and operas that emerged in France in the middle of the century, change was much tardier. Here, restrictions on the representation of *le merveilleux* were more relaxed: divinities regularly intruded into the affairs of mortals as *deus ex machina*, and also made their wills known through oracular pronouncements.

1. Corneille 1963, 258: "An oracle never gives up its meaning. The less one understands it, the more one believes to understand it. And far from being comforted by such decrees, those who find nothing obscure about them must believe that everything is obscure."
2. The treatment of *le merveilleux* in spoken and lyric tragedies is theorized in Kintzler 1991, particularly 244-97.

Indeed, supernatural revelations were as essential to the operatic scenario as they were disdained in spoken tragedy. In the pantheon specific to French opera, a superior status was reserved for oracles. Voiced either directly by a divinity, through the mouthpiece of a medium, or quoted by a mortal character, oracular pronouncements represented ultimate, incontrovertible authority. More than in the case of physical manifestations where gods and goddesses were open to the vicissitudes of mortality, oracles preserved the detached, impartial, even unfathomable qualities of divinity and were consequently implicated with the earthly sovereign authority of the King.

In this chapter, I discuss the poetic and musical characteristics of oracles in literature and opera, focusing on works from the reign of Louis XIV. The primary question I wish to address is why French opera continued to hold onto oracles as pivotal ingredients, their veracity largely unchallenged up to the early years of the eighteenth century, and long after they had been debunked in intellectual debate and had all but vanished from spoken drama.

The debate opens

From the middle of the seventeenth century, the source and authenticity of oracles were subjected to intense scrutiny in French intellectual circles. Works such as Laurent Bouchet's *Oracles des sybilles* [sic] (1645),[3] which sought to legitimate the early Christian sibylline oracles, were met with censure from the Protestant David Blondel (1591-1655), who labeled the sibyls as impostors.[4] The debate very soon divided down religious lines, the Protestants taking the opportunity to demonstrate the Roman Church's falsification of history to bolster its own authority, the Catholics (e.g., Jean Crasset in his *Dissertation sur les oracles des Sibylles*, 1678) re-endorsing the authenticity of the sibyls' predictions to rebut the Protestant claims. The ensuing stream of writings taking one of these two antithetical positions included the *Discours sur l'histoire universelle* (written 1679) by the staunchly conservative, but equally

3. Bouchet 1645. Bouchard 1947 provides an extensive history of the debate on oracles in French literature up to the publication of Fontenelle's *Histoire* (see below).
4. See Blondel 1649.

influential Bossuet, who declared that at the birth of Jesus the oracles of false gods were miraculously silenced.[5]

The dispute was brought to a head in 1687 with Bernard Le Bovier de Fontenelle's *Histoire des oracles*.[6] This work, which enjoyed widespread popularity from its initial publication, was an adaptation of a Latin dissertation published three years prior by the Dutch scholar Antoine van Dale (1638-1708). Van Dale's *De oraculis ethnicorum* broadened the investigation to pagan as well as Christian oracles, while also bringing extensive evidence to disprove the long-standing belief that oracles were the work of the devil and were eliminated with the birth of Jesus. Belonging to the small Christian sect of Socinians,[7] van Dale's theology was radically anti-Catholic in its rejection of miracles. Accordingly, his dissertation maintained that oracles were devoid of supernatural agency – their putative miraculous qualities, he contended, were shams staged by charlatan priests. Fontenelle appropriated van Dale's basic argument and rejected the dependence of oracles on any form of divine or supernatural agency, but despite softening the Dutchman's more inflammatory religious views, *L'histoire des oracles* was nevertheless viewed by some as a veiled critique of the Catholic priesthood.[8]

Living at a time when superstition held sway and when the French Court nurtured an obsession for magic potions, poisonings, and prophesies administered by La Voisin among others, Fontenelle may have found it hard to resist being drawn into the study of divinations, occult practices, and oracles. For him, the widespread prevalence of oracles in ancient cultures arose from the basic human desire to foresee the future, while the rituals and oracular invocations served to obfuscate the charlatanism of those that fed off this instinct. What may appear perplexing is that this champion of rationalism also participated in operatic projects that made no apology for staging the divine.

Against the background of this debate, we might wonder whether anyone gave any credibility to the gods and oracles frequenting the stage. More than anything, these creatures provided splendid theatrical display, which was certainly part of their continued popular appeal. Oracles make early appearances in tragedies from the 1630s and 40s, but I will begin my enquiry with the hindsight of Jean de La Fontaine in the late 1660s.

5. Bossuet 1681.
6. Fontenelle 1908.
7. Dale 1683. Socinianism, which had its roots in the Protestant Reformation and is named after one of its prime theologians, Faustus Socinus (1539-1604), rejected accepted Catholic views on the omniscience of God, the Trinity, and the divinity of Christ.
8. See Bouchard 1947, 101; Niderst 1972, 293.

La Fontaine and the two essential qualities of oracles

A succinct evaluation of the conventions that informed the literary representation of oracles is found in La Fontaine's *Les amours de Psyché et de Cupidon* (1669), a work that also sets the stage for a discussion of opera. This unique and sadly maligned novel by a writer who was himself something of a maverick, an outcast from court, occupies a special place vis-à-vis the emergence of music theater in France and also provides a distanced perspective that registers some of the deeper implications of literary conventions.[9] Published on the eve of the establishment of the Académie Royale de Musique (28 June 1669), its innovative mixture of prose and poetry provided a model for a multi-media and mixed-genre esthetic that would achieve its most flamboyant expression in the productions of the Opéra. But the novel's relationship with the operatic stage was even closer as it most likely served as the inspiration for a *tragédie-ballet* and a *tragédie en musique* (see below).

In the preface to *Les amours de Psyché*, La Fontaine confessed to an inability to conform to two criteria essential to oracles: ambiguity and brevity.

I admit that, instead of emending the oracle he [Apuleius] makes use of at the beginning of Psyche's adventures and which is part of the crux of the tale, I augmented its deficiencies, by desisting from making this oracle ambiguous and short, which are the two essential qualities of the gods' responses, but which were impossible for me to observe.[10]

The passage refers to the oracle in the first part of the novel. Distressed by Venus' jealous curse on their daughter, Psyche's parents "were obliged to take recourse in the oracle. Here is the response that they were given, with the gloss added by the priests" ("Ses parents furent constraints de recourir à l'oracle. Voici la réponse que leur fut faite, avec la glose que les prêtres y ajoutèrent."):

L'époux que les Destins gardent à votre fille
Est un monstre cruel qui déchire les cœurs,
Qui trouble maint État, détruit mainte famille,
Se nourrit de soupirs, se baigne dans les pleurs.

9. Jean de La Fontaine's status as maverick and subversive critic of the Louis quartorzien state is the thesis of Marc Fumaroli's extensive study of the *fabuliste*'s output (Fumaroli 1997).
10. La Fontaine 1965, 405: "J'avoue qu'au lieu de rectifier l'oracle dont il [Apulée] se sert au commencement des aventures de Psyché, et qui fait en partie le nœud de la fable, j'en ai augmenté l'inconvénient, faute d'avoir rendu cet oracle ambigu et court, qui sont les deux qualités que les réponses des dieux doivent avoir et qu'il m'a été impossible de bien observer."

À l'univers entier il déclare la guerre,
  Courant de bout en bout un flambeau dans la main:
  On le craint dans les cieux, on le craint sur la terre;
  Le Styx n'a pu borner son pouvoir souverain;
C'est un empoisonneur, c'est un incendiaire,
  Un tyran qui de fers charge jeunes et vieux.
  Qu'on lui livre Psyché; qu'elle tâche à lui plaire:
  Tel est l'arrêt du Sort, de l'Amour, et des Dieux.
Menez-la sur un roc, au haut d'une montagne,
  En des lieux où l'attend le Monstre son époux;
  Qu'une pompe funèbre en ces lieux l'accompagne,
  Car elle doit mourir pour ses sœurs et pour vous.[11]

Although not obvious from the text, the two *qualités* that divine responses must meet, ambiguity and brevity, delineate the conventional treatment of oracles established by classical authors and emulated by La Fontaine's contemporaries. In *Horace* (1641), for instance, Pierre Corneille also cited ambiguous conciseness as essential to the elusive power of oracles: "On l'entend d'autant moins que plus on croit l'entendre," which can be interpreted loosely to read "The less they say, the more believable they seem."[12]

A comparison of La Fontaine's oracle with the corresponding model, a passage in the *Golden ass* or *Metamorphoses* of the second-century Latin writer Lucius Apuleius, immediately clarifies the point about brevity:

Montis in excelsi scopulo, rex, siste puellam
  ornatam mundo funerei thalami.
Nec speres generum mortali stirpe creatum,
  sed saevum atque ferum vipereumque malum,
quod pinnis volitans super aethera cuncta fatigat
  flammaque et ferro singula debilitat,
quod tremit ipse Iovis, quo numina terrificantur
  fluminaque horrescunt et Stygiæ tenebræ.[13]

11. La Fontaine 1965, 409: "The husband whom Destiny has reserved for your daughter is a cruel monster who tears apart hearts, disrupts many a State, destroys many a family, takes nourishment from sighs, and bathes in tears. He declares war on the entire universe, running from one end to the other with a torch in his hand: they fear him in heaven, they fear him on earth; the Styx cannot limit his sovereign power. He is a poisoner, an arson, a tyrant who holds young and old in bonds. That Psyche be offered up to him, that she try to please him: such is the decree of Fate, of Love, and the Gods. Lead her to a rock atop a mountain in the place where the Monster awaits her husband; may a funeral procession accompany her there, as she must die to her sisters and to you."
12. Corneille 1963, 258 (see also above).
13. Apuleius s.d., IV: "Let Psyches corps be clad in mourning weed, / And set on rock of yonder hill aloft: // Her husband is no wight of humane seed, / But Serpent dire and fierce as might be thought. // Who flies with wings above in starry skies, / And doth subdue each thing with firie flight. // The

Alongside the eight verses of Apuleius' oracle, La Fontaine's version is considerably longer, comprising four quatrains of *alexandrins* in so-called *rimes croisées* (*abab*). The poetic form of the oracle sets it off from the prose narrative. Throughout the novel, extraordinary phenomena – here the apparition of a goddess, there the words of the oracle, or a particularly evocative scene – are marked with similar shifts of register that La Fontaine (often through the mouthpiece of his narrator/protagonist Polyphile) justified as the result of subject matter that lay beyond the expressive resources of prose: "This is material appropriate for poetry ... I don't think that [this] can be expressed with ordinary discourse."[14]

The other *qualité* of oracles, ambiguity, is more difficult to discern from La Fontaine's text. His meaning seems to be that, even though obscurity was an essential ingredient of oracular proclamations, he was unable to render Apuleius' oracle more ambiguous or obscure in meaning. This was because obscurity did not suit his narratological purpose. For La Fontaine, the story's interest lay in the reader's ability to see through the artifice of the oracle and to observe the process by which Psyche came to realize the identity of her lover:

> The suspense [for the reader] and artistry of this tale do not consist in preventing the reader from perceiving the true character of the husband whom Psyche has been given; it suffices that Psyche remains unaware of whom she has married and that one should be eager to discover if she will ever see her husband, by what means she will see him, and what emotional state will be hers after she has seen him.[15]

La Fontaine hence worded the oracle so that it became obvious to the reader that Psyche's husband was in fact not a monster but Cupid, who "déchire les cœurs ... un flambeau dans la main".[16]

gods themselves, and powers that seem so wise, / With mighty Jove, be subject to his might, // The rivers blacke, and deadly flouds of paine / And darkness eke, as thrall to him remaine." (Translation cited from Apuleius 1566)

14. La Fontaine 1965, 408-9: "Ceci est proprement matière de poésie ... je ne pense pas qu'on pût exprimer avec le langage ordinaire."
15. La Fontaine 1965, 405: "La suspension des esprits & l'artifice de cette fable ne consistent pas à empêcher que le lecteur ne s'aperçoive de la véritable qualité du mari qu'on donne à Psyché; il suffit que Psyché ignore qui est celui qu'elle a epousé, et que l'on soit en attente de savoir si elle verra cet époux, par quels moyens elle le verra, et quelles seront les agitations de son âme après qu'elle l'aura vu."
16. An earlier discussion regarding the ambiguity of oracles appeared in the preface (*Examen*, 1660) to Pierre Corneille's machine play, *Andromède* (1650). For the purposes of his dramaturgy, Corneille contrived that the oracle be so ambiguous that its apparent and intended meanings were contradictory: "L'oracle de Vénus, au premier acte [scene 1], est inventé avec assez d'artifice pour

"Inventé avec artifice..."

In the tragedies of La Fontaine's contemporaries Pierre Corneille and Jean Racine, divine pronouncements are exceptionally rare and when they occur, they are never voiced directly by a divinity. What is heard, by contrast, are the echoes of divine utterances repeated by mortal characters. The revelations themselves take place beyond the temporal and spatial boundaries of the stage – usually before the action has begun, or less often during the progress of the drama, but always beyond the confines of the stage.[17] The prohibition on the physical presence of divinities focused the attention away from the production of sensational effects onto the impact of the oracle on the lives of the characters. As Pierre Corneille explained in his *Discours de la tragédie et des moyens de la traiter selon le vraisemblable ou le nécessaire* (1660), "it is good to hide the event from view, and to make it known by a *récit* which shocks less than the sight and affects us more easily."[18]

Although oracular pronouncements are infrequent in spoken theater, poets nonetheless developed distinctive poetic characteristics in order to distinguish them from mortal speech. In *Les amours de Psyché*, the shift of register from narrative to oracle was achieved by interrupting the prose with verses in alexandrines. In spoken theater, where alexandrines take the place of prose or blank verse as the normative and virtually uninterrupted mode of communication,[19] the extraordinary nature of oracles was marked with verses of different lengths and varied rhyme schemes. This disruption of the poetic form articulated the intrusion of the divine into the

porter les esprits dans un sens contraire à sa vraie intelligence ..." (Corneille 1963, 467). To this end, Corneille modified the oracle as transmitted in the classical sources so that it would only be realized in hindsight that Andromeda was to be sacrificed at the same time as she was to be married.

17. This is also the case with references to oracles in seventeenth-century pastorals. For instance, Dalla Valle 1982, 145-52, points out that, although in these plays oracles serve to give a sense of order in the midst of chaos from outside the drama's immediate frame, they are rarely the "moteur initial" of the drama as they are in tragedies, but instead serve a more decorative function.
18. Corneille 1963, 836: "il est bon de cacher l'événement à la vue, et de le faire savoir par un récit qui frappe moins que le spectacle, et nous impose plus aisément." This observation refers not only to divine apparitions and extraordinary phenomena, but also to events that were avoided for practical reasons, such as on-stage violence. Théramène's *récit* describing the destruction of Hippolyte in Racine's *Phèdre* (1677; Act V, scene 6) is perhaps the most famous example of this practice.
19. See Aubignac 1715, 241, where he argues that "Les grands vers de douze syllables, nommez *Communs* dans les premiers Auteurs de la Poësie Française, doivent être considerez au Théâtre comme de la prose."

seemingly autonomous space of human drama communicated through the closed poetic structure of alexandrines in rhyming couplets.

Only three oracles occur in Racine's tragedies.[20] The elements of this style of versification are seen in Act II, scene 2 of *La Thébaide* (1664) where Olympia reports the oracle as revealed to Eteocles:

	syllable count[21]	rhyme
OLYMPE		
Prince, pour en juger, écoutez leur réponse:	12+	
Thébains, pour n'avoir plus de guerres	8+	a
Il faut, par un ordre fatal,	8	b
Que le dernier du sang royal	8	b
Par son trépas ensanglante vos terres.[22]	10+	a

This oracle is made up exclusively of short lines. However, in the second instance of a quoted oracle in Racine's output, in Act I, scene 1 of *Iphigénie* (1674), two eight-syllable lines are interpolated among *alexandrins*, again with an irregular rhyme scheme:

AGAMEMNON		
Vous armez contre Troie une puissance vaine,	12+	a
Si, dans un sacrifice auguste et solennel,	12	b
Une fille du sang d'Hélène,	8+	a
De Diane, en ces lieux, n'ensanglante l'autel.	12	b
Pour obtenir les vents que le ciel vous dénie,	12+	c
Sacrifiez Iphigénie![23]	8+	c

The mixture of *alexandrins* and eight-syllable lines in *rimes croisées*, and the overall length of four to six verses, typical of oracles in spoken drama, became the model for lyric tragedy.[24]

20. Here, I am taking into consideration only the plays up to *Esther* (1689) and *Athalie* (1691), in which Racine breaks from the rule of the *alexandrin* to create lyric variety in his versification.
21. "+" indicates e *muet* endings.
22. Racine 1962, 72: "Prince, to judge [the gods], listen to their response: *Thebans, in order to avoid wars, by fatal order, the last of the royal blood must by its demise stain your lands.*"
23. Racine 1962, 227: "*You arm yourselves against Troy in vain if, in a solemn and august sacrifice, the blood of a daughter of Helen's line does not stain Diana's altar in this place. In order to benefit from the winds that the heavens deny you, sacrifice Iphigenia.*"
24. For the oracle in Act I, scene 2 of *Horace* (1640), Pierre Corneille used alexandrines in *rimes croisées*, which although representing the same verse structure of La Fontaine's *Les amours de Psyché*, is less typical for oracles in dramatic works. Hélène Baby (in Aubignac 2001, 386n337) cites examples in

Racine's third oracle, or rather prophecy, is voiced by Joad in Act III, scene 7 of *Athalie* (1691). Here, while the musicality of varied verse lengths of the oracle text is not as clearly distinguished from the remainder of the text as in other plays because, like other sections, it was composed with the lyrical qualities of musical setting in mind, the musicality of the passage is underscored by Racine's rubric calling for the preceding chorus to be sung "to the sound of the harmony of all the instruments."[25] This exceptional instruction for the combined harmony of voices and orchestra serves as a frame to Joad's divinely-inspired words.

What was also customary in both spoken and sung drama for the words of divine decrees was their appearance in italic script (see Illustration 2). This typographical convention not only had the effect of placing the words of the oracle between imaginary quotation marks, but also aligned them with the stage directions and other rubrics that were also conventionally printed in italics. Inscribing oracles, along with directions on machines, decorations, lighting, costumes, and the like associated them with a power beyond what the characters could themselves call upon: not only the power of the gods who controlled the lives of the characters, but the power that put the actors on the stage – the power of the patron who, particularly in the case of the Académie Royale de Musique, wielded the ultimate wordly authority of kingship.[26]

Verses that, like oracles, break the otherwise uninterrupted chain of *alexandrins* are discussed in d'Aubignac's *Pratique du théatre* (1657). Although what it terms *stances* refers specifically to poetry that emulates lyrics (such as where a character is meant to be singing, or quoting a letter, or the maxims and *petits airs* Quinault later devised for Lully's *tragédies en musique*), they share similar musical aspects with oracles:

> In a word, Stanzas are to be thought of as verses that a man would have been able to speak in the state in which he is placed on Stage, but also as Lyric verses, that is, verses sung with musical instruments, and which to that end are limited in their meter, have similar caesuræ and measured irregularities.[27]

tragi-comédies from 1635-45 by Colletet, Boisrobert, and Mairet that also feature oracles breaking the rule of the alexandrine.

25. Racine 1962, 296: "LE CHŒUR chante au son de toute la symphonie des instruments."
26. It was common to compare the King's wisdom and decrees to oracular pronouncements. See, for instance, Jean de Mairet's *Chryséide et Arimand* (1625), which reads: "La promesse d'un roy passe en force d'oracle." (Mairet 1925, 159)
27. Aubignac 1715, 241: "En un mot, les Stances sont considerées comme des vers qu'un homme auroit pu dire en l'état auquel on le met sur le Théatre, mais encore comme des vers Lyriques, c'est à dire, propres à chanter avec des instrumens de musique, et qui pour cet effet ont leur nombre limité, leur repos semblable, et leurs inégalitez mesurées." I am indebted to Buford Norman (private communication, 13 January 2010) for his advice in interpreting this and other passages from d'Aubignac.

TRAGEDIE.

AGAMEMNON.

Tu vois mon trouble. Appren ce qui le cause,
Et juge s'il est temps, Amy, que je repose.
Tu te souviens du jour qu'en Aulide assemblez
Nos vaisseaux par les vents sembloient estre appellez.
Nous partions. Et dé-ja par mille cris de joye
Nous menassions de loin les Rivages de Troye.
Un prodige estonnant fit taire ce transport.
Le vent qui nous flattoit nous laissa dans le Port.
Il fallut s'arrester, & la rame inutile
Fatigua vainement une mer immobile.
Ce miracle inoüi me fit tourner les yeux
Vers la Divinité, qu'on adore en ces lieux.
Suivi de Menelas, de Nestor, & d'Ulysse,
J'offris sur ses autels un secret sacrifice.
Quelle fut sa response! Et quel devins-je, Arcas;
Quand j'entendis ces mots, prononcez par Calchas!

Vous armez contre Troye une puissance vaine,
Si dans un sacrifice auguste & solennel
Une Fille du sang d'Helene
De Diane en ces lieux n'ensanglante l'autel.
Pour obtenir les vents que le ciel vous dénie,
Sacrifiez Iphigenie.

ARCAS.

Vostre Fille!

AGAMEMNON.

Surpris, comme tu peux penser,
Je sentis dans mon corps tout mon sang se glacer.
Je demeuray sans voix, & n'en repris l'usage,
Que par mille sanglots qui se firent passage.
Je condannay les Dieux, & sans plus rien oüir,
Fis vœu sur leurs autels de leur desobeïr.
Que n'en croyois-je alors ma tendresse allarmée?
Je voulois sur le champ congedier l'Armée.
Ulysse en apparence approuvant mes discours,

A ij

Illustration 2. Agamemnon's *récit* of the oracle in Jean Racine's *Iphigénie* (1674), Act II, scene 2. Reproduced from Racine 1675.

D'Aubignac's somewhat elliptical explanation can be interpreted to mean that the arrangement of words and syllables in *stances* had a restricted rhythmic profile ("nombre limité"[28]), regular caesuræ, and a balancing irregularity in their verse lengths.

D'Aubignac also cautioned that *stances* should conform to a sense of *vraisemblance*, and emphasized that characters needed time to compose these more elaborately developed verses. His discussion makes a passing but nonetheless pertinent reference to oracles:

> It is not that one cannot, in most instances, put Stanzas or verses in the mouth of the Actors without giving them the occasion to compose them, as long as it is credible that they are improvised on the spot, such as in the case of an Oracle for which the Divinity who pronounces it does not need time, indeed cannot take the time, to formulate its response.[29]

A mortal character can only be expected to extemporize verse and music in extraordinary circumstances; however, the more sophisticated compositional makeup of *stances* is suited to the speech of gods whose superior command over the resources of language allow them to speak spontaneously in 'musical' verse. Just as in verses that are intended to be sung, the metric qualities of oracles draws attention to their performativity – the musicality of the utterance.

The oracles considered so far are all highly crafted, representing a significant degree of mediation between the supposedly divinely inspired utterances and their literary transmission. La Fontaine justified the length of the oracle in *Les amours de Psyché* by the inclusion of gloss. The actual words of Apollo were quoted in the final stanza; the rest comprised the priests' exegetic preamble. According to the preface: "This oracle also includes the priests' gloss; as the priests do not hear what the god tells them: however, it could have inspired the paraphrase just as much as the text, and I excuse myself again with that."[30] It is clear from this passage that La Fontaine concurred with the view, expounded by van Dale and Fontenelle, that oracles were fabricated by impostors.

28. According to Furetière 1690, II, "Nombre" refers to "certaines mesures, proportions ou cadences qui rendent agréable à l'oreille un air, un vers, une periode."
29. Aubignac 1715, 243-4: "Ce n'est pas que l'on ne puisse en beaucoup de rencontres mettre des Stances, c'est à dire des vers en la bouche des Acteurs, sans leur donner aucun loisir de les faire, pourvu qu'il soit vraisemblable qu'ils ayent été faits sur le champ, comme un Oracle pour lequel la Divinité, qui le rend, n'a pas eu besoin de temps, comme elle n'en peut avoir pour répondre."
30. La Fontaine 1965, 405: "Cet oracle contenait aussi la glose des prêtres; car les prêtres n'entendent pas ce que le dieu leur fait dire: toutefois il peut leur avoir inspiré la paraphrase aussi bien qu'il leur a inspiré le texte, et je me sauverai encore par là."

Les amours de Psyché includes another oracle that evidences an awareness of the distance between inspired utterance and formulated oracle. The second oracle occurs in part two, after the narrator Polyphile has re-evaluated the generic monstrosity of his recitation, with its mixture of prose and poetry, and hybrid tragicomic tone, and establishes a style for his recitation that conforms more to conventional expectations.[31] The form of this oracle, which Psyche herself consults at a temple to Diana, is quite different from the first. Psyche is forbidden to enter the temple and must wait outside for the priestess to bring the oracle to her. The *ad hoc* nature of the invocation is reflected in the impromptu style of the pronouncement, which involves minimal mediation and no gloss: "Cease your wanderings: that which you search has wings; when you, like him [Cupid], will be able to walk in the air, you will be happy."[32]

This oracle is all that the first is not: it is both concise and cryptic. It is as if La Fontaine / Polyphile was no longer able to resist convention. But at the same time, its formalist elements most emphatically break from convention. Its disjointed clauses suggest a poetic formula that could be reparsed as verse, but the result would be verse with no discernible rhyme scheme, nor agreeable *nombre*:

> Cesse d'être errante:
> Ce que tu cherches a des ailes;
> Quand tu sauras comme lui marcher dans les airs
> Tu seras heureuse.

In short, this passage is devoid of the musicality associated with oracles, and lies somewhere between poetry and prose. La Fontaine seems to be creating the illusion that this is the priestess' "random utterances" delivered in a state of divine frenzy before they have been glossed or given poetic form.

The process of glossing together with the conventions associated with the literary transmission of oracles touched on the crucial question of the authority empowering oracular speech. Did Apollo, for example, actually speak through the mouthpiece of the Pythia in perfectly formed verses? To Fontenelle and La Fontaine, it was obvious that the wording of the oracles was fabricated by the attendant priests. This theory was becoming increasingly accepted and served as the basis of several studies, including the *Explication historique des fables* (1711) by the renowned mythographer Antoine Banier. His account of the Delphic oracle discredits its divine agency and exposes the corrupt priesthood's barbaric practices. It draws attention to the violent

31. This shift in tone is theorized in Birkerick 1998.

32. La Fontaine 1965, 440: "Cesse d'être errante: ce que tu cherches a des ailes; quand tu sauras comme lui marcher dans les airs tu seras heureuse."

and sexual implications of the ceremony in which a woman is held down by a coven of male priests for penetration by a male god – an act that with little exaggeration can be described as ritualized rape:

> The Priests, who were called Prophets, took the Pythia, led her into the Sanctuary, and placed her on the Tripod. As soon as the divine vapor started to agitate her, one saw the hairs on her head rise, her appearance become terrifying, her mouth foam, and a sudden and violent trembling seize her whole body. In this state, she tried to break loose from the Priests who held her down by force, and her cries and wailing reverberated in the Temple, filling those present with holy terror. Finally, no longer being able to resist the God who agitated her, she abandoned herself to him and proffered in spurts some poorly articulated words which the Prophets carefully collected, arranged, and by means of verse gave a coherence to that they did not have in the mouth of the Priestess.[33]

Unlike d'Aubignac, whose sense of verisimilitude allowed divinities to speak spontaneously in finely wrought verses, Banier expressed little doubt that oracles resulted from the priests' literary mediation.

Re-inscribing divine law in the operatic mode

The practice of 'composing out' the divinely inspired 'random utterances' can be seen in the reworkings of the oracle from part one of *Les amours de Psyché* in two music theater pieces both entitled *Psyché* and produced in the 1670s: the first with a text written by a team headed by Molière and music by Lully (1671), the second, an operatic adaptation of the first work by Thomas Corneille and Lully (1678). The cryptic

33. Banier 1715, I, 188: "Les Prêtres, qu'on nommoit les Prophétes, prenoient la Pythie, la conduisoient dans le Sanctuaire, & la plaçoient sur le Trépied. Dès que la vapeur divine commençoit à l'agiter, on voyoit ses cheveux se dresser sur la tête, son regard devenir farouche, sa bouche écumer, & un tremblement subit & violent s'emparer de tout son corps. Dans cet état elle tâchoit de s'arracher aux Prêtres qui la tenoient comme par force; & ses cris, & ses hurlemens faisoient retentir le Temple, & remplissoient les assistans d'une sainte fureur. Enfin ne pouvant plus résister au Dieu qui l'agitoit, elle s'abandonnoit à lui, & proféroit par intervalles quelques paroles mal articulées, que les Prophétes recueilloient avec soin, les arrangeoient, & leur donnoient avec la forme du vers, une liaison qu'elles n'avoient pas dans la bouche de la Prêtresse." Banier's encyclopedic study was well known in the eighteenth century and would almost certainly have served as a reference for poets working with mythological material, including librettists.

description of Psyche's husband is similar in these texts, but the oracles in both the machine play of 1671 and its reworking as a *tragédie en musique* seven years later are considerably more compressed than La Fontaine's.

For the oracle that Lychas quotes in Act I, scene 5 of the 1671 *tragédie-ballet*, Molière followed the practice adopted in spoken tragedies of alternating eight- and twelve-syllable verses in *rimes croisées*. Given the non-congruency between the verse lengths and the rhyme scheme, the rhymes connect verses of differing lengths, creating a poetic formula of particularly varied rhythm and meter. However, as can be seen in the verses at the beginning of Lychas' speech, the oracle is not the only part of the play set in *vers libres*, and so it is less distinguished from mortal speech as would have been the case in Racinian tragedy:

LYCHAS

Hélas! ce grand malheur dans la cour répandu,	12	
Voyez-le vous-même, Princesse,	8+	
Dans l'oracle qu'au Roi les Destins ont rendu.	12	
Voici ses propres mots, que la douleur, Madame,	12+	
A gravés au fond de mon âme:	8+	
Que l'on ne pense nullement	8	a
A vouloir de Psyché conclure l'hyménée	12+	b
Mais qu'au sommet d'un mont elle soit promptement	12	a
En pompe funèbre menée,	8+	b
Et que de tous abandonnée,	8+	b
Pour époux elle attende en ces lieux constamment	12	a
Un monstre dont on a la vue empoisonnée,	12+	b
Un serpent qui répand son venin en tous lieux,	12	c
Et trouble dans sa rage et la terre et les cieux.[34]	12	c

Seven years later, when Lully reworked *Psyché* as a *tragédie en musique*, he called on Thomas Corneille to transform Molière's spoken dialogue into recitative. As time was of the essence, Corneille called up his nephew Fontenelle, who helped him complete the task in just three weeks. How much of the *livret* can be eventually attributed

34. Molière 1962, 542: "Alas! hear for yourselves, Princess, the great misfortune which is known to the whole court. These are the very words which, through the oracle, Destiny has spoken to the King and which grief, Madam, has engraven on my heart: *No one must think to lead / Psyche to Hymen's shrine; / But all with earnest speed, / In pompous mournful line, / High to the mountain crest / Must take her; there to await, / Forlorn, in deep unrest, / A monster who envenoms all, / Decreed by fate her husband; / A serpent whose dark poisonous breath / And rage e'er hold the world in thrall, / Shaking the heavens high and realms of death.*" (Translation after Molière s.d.)

to Fontenelle is not known. Still, it seems noteworthy that, at the age of twenty, the author of the *Histoire des oracles* witnessed the creation of an opera that made no apology for displaying supernatural beings with all their trappings.[35]

LYCHAS		
Le Roy d'abord nous a caché l'oracle,	10+	a
Mais malgré luy le Grand Prestre a parlé.	10	b
Ah! pourquoy n'a-t'il pû se taire?	8+	c
Voicy ce qu'il a revelé,	8	b
Et l'arrest qui nous desespere.	8+	c
Vous allez voir augmenter les malheurs	10	d
Qui vous ont coûté tant de pleurs,	8	d
Si Psyché sur le Mont, pour expier son crime,	12+	e
N'attend que le Serpent la prenne pour victime.[36]	12+	e

Corneille and Fontenelle retained the overall *dessein* of Molière's work, and thus the oracle is again narrated by the servant Lychas. The process of transforming a play with musical interludes into an opera with continuous singing involved the reduction of long speeches into shorter units more suited to musical setting. Here, the oracle is compressed into a brief four lines, thus conforming to the second of La Fontaine's two *qualités*. As for the first, the speech entails a different degree of ambiguity to that of its precursors. Unlike both La Fontaine's novel and Molière's scenario, the *tragédie en musique* opens in a kingdom devastated by a fierce serpent sent by Venus. Consequently, to both the characters in the drama and the audience, the identity of the monster-spouse of the oracle is more obviously ambiguous.

Opera composers reinforced the lyrical elements of the verses used for oracles with specific musical techniques that imbued their oracular voices with superhuman qualities. The seeds are set in Lully's *Psyché*, which contains the earliest oracle in a *tragédie en musique*. The text reverses the versification practices encountered thus far. Whereas eight- and twelve-syllable lines would be short verses in spoken tragedy, in this *livret* they are amongst the longest. Furthermore, instead of the formula found in spoken tragedies whereby alexandrines in rhyming couplets give way to shorter

35. For more on the creation of the two versions of *Psyché*, see Powell 2004, 240.

36. Various 1703-45, II, 69: "The King initially hid the oracle from us, but in spite of him, the High Priest has spoken. Ah! Why could he not have kept silent? Here is what he revealed, and the judgment that causes our despair. *You will see your misfortunes, which have already caused you so many tears, increase if Psyche, to atone for her crime, does not wait on the Mountain for the Serpent to take her as victim.*"

Example 4. Jean-Baptiste Lully, *Psyché* (1678), Act I, scene 2. Reproduced from Lully 1720, 34-5.

verses in *rimes croisées*, this oracle uses shorter verses in rhyming couplets. A comparison with the texts of the *airs* in this opera can help to explain this treatment.[37] On the whole, the *airs* comprise verses of equal length and, as outlined by d'Aubignac, their lyricism involves regular rhymes and *nombre limité*. In the setting of the oracle (Example 4), Lully reinforces the rhymes by aligning the phrase endings with the metric pulses, requiring the shift to triple metre for the lines ending in the feminine rhyme *son crime / victime*.

Both its tonality and vocal delivery set the quoted oracle apart from the surrounding *récitatif*. The preceding music is in d minor; the quotation is tonally closed in g minor. There is a preponderance of repeated pitches in the vocal line. Alongside the rise and fall of the speech patterns of the *récitatif*, the static, chant-like intonation of the oracle helps to elevate it to the status of divinely inspired utterance.[38] By drawing the words out and prolonging each syllable with more equal emphasis, furthermore, the musical setting deflects attention from its syntactical elements onto the sonic qualities of the delivery. This declamatory vocal style is heard in numerous musical settings of oracles in later operas by Lully and his successors.[39]

The gods address the Opéra, with Fontenelle their speechwriter

Since, in French opera, the gods could speak for themselves, quoted oracles are exceptions rather than the rule. In fact, the example in *Psyché* is one of only three that I have identified out of the total of approximately seventy-five *tragédies en musique* staged by the Académie Royale de Musique up to the middle of the eighteenth

37. I use *air* here to refer to sections where a character moves from the sung-speech of *récitatif* to a closed lyrical form that is intended to be understood as song.
38. In a recent recording of *Psyché* (Lully 2008), the static nature of the oracle is underscored by a change in the style of continuo realization of continuo accompaniment: in contrast to the preceding dialogue, when Lychas quotes the oracle, the continuo players switch to sustained chords on organ and *lirone* with an added violin line. Although not part of Lully's original musical setting, this interpretation appropriates the style of accompaniment found in later works in this genre.
39. For a list, see Burgess 1998, 441.

century.[40] Intriguingly, of the remaining operas that contain oracles intoned either directly by a divinity or through a medium, Fontenelle worked on three. I will take these examples as a point of departure to discuss the emergence of oracles at the Paris Opéra.

In 1679, Fontenelle collaborated again with Lully and Thomas Corneille on *Bellérophon*.[41] This is the earliest opera to include an extensive oracular invocation informed by ethno-historic research into the ritualistic practices of classical Greece. Jobates, the King of Lydia, calls for an oracle to foretell the fate of his lands which are being destroyed by the monster Chimera. The high priest summons the Pythia, who becomes possessed by Apollo and acts as the vessel for the divine revelation. The Pythia's disheveled appearance and androgyny (she is performed by a male *haute-contre* dressed as a woman) mark 'her' as mediatrix between the human and supersensory realms. Her recitative enumerates the signs of the god's presence: each phrase is punctuated by short orchestral passages representing in turn the earthquake, rush of wind, thunder, and lightning.

> LA PYTHIE
> Gardez tous un silence extrême,
> Apollon vous entend, & va parler luy-même;
> Son approche déja fait briller les éclairs,
> Entendez raisonner le sifflement des airs,
> Ecoutez le bruit du Tonnerre,
> Voyez trembler & le Temple & la Terre.[42]

But instead of becoming possessed by Apollo and intoning his oracle herself, the Pythia "*bows to the earth while Apollo appears as a golden statue and intones the following Oracle*" ("*se penche vers la terre, tandis qu'Apollon paroît en statuë d'or, & prononce l'Oracle qui suit*") (Example 5):

40. The others occur in Act I, scene 7 of Duché de Vancy's *Cephale et Procris* (1694; music by Jacquet de la Guerre), and in Act I, scene 2 of La Serre and Pellegrin's *Polidore* (1720; Stuck).

41. Recent research (La Gorce 2002, 631) has shown that Fontenelle played a more important role in the composition of this libretto than was hitherto acknowledged. Thomas Corneille and Nicholas Boileau-Despréaux, who was also listed as one of the official authors of the *livret*, took advantage of their seniority by underplaying their debt to the twenty-year old Fontenelle. Although the exact distribution of work on this libretto remains unclear, it is still likely that Fontenelle was closely involved with establishing the details of the oracle scene.

42. Various 1703-45, II, 135: "Be totally silent, all of you, Apollo hears you and is himself about to speak. His approach already makes the lightning flash; hear the howling wind talk, listen to the sound of Thunder, see both the Temple and Earth shake."

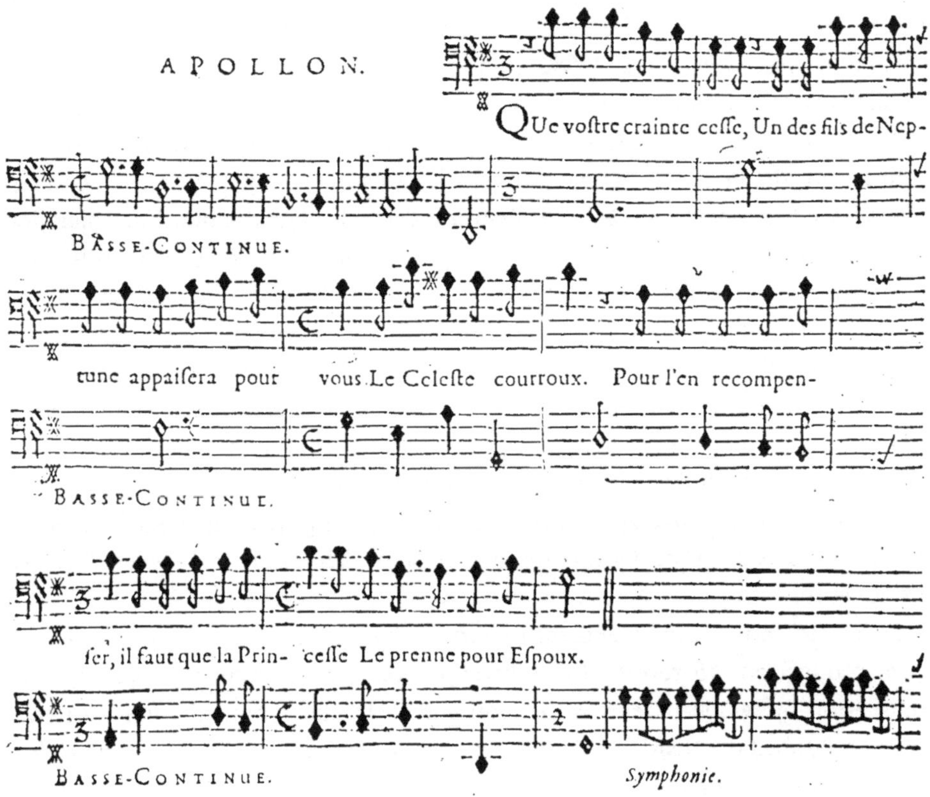

Example 5. Lully, *Bellérophon* (1679), Act III, scene 4. Reproduced from Lully 1697, 95-6. ["May your fears cease. One of the sons of Neptune will appease Heaven's wrath for you. In recompense, the Princess must take Him as Husband."]

Apollo's speech is introduced by a short *pont* played by the bass instruments, but otherwise there is little in the musical setting to distinguish it from mortal speech. Instead, the visual cue of the golden statue stepping forward signals that what is heard are the very words of Apollo. As well as providing an opportunity for an impressive stage effect and the means to differentiate human and divine characters, the physical embodiment of the divinity avoided the words of the oracle by being compromised by human mediation. This oracle represents a degree of confidence in the notion of absolute authority and divine presence that would become increasingly untenable over the course of the next decades.

About ten years after *Bellérophon* and just three years after he had written the *Histoire des oracles*, Fontenelle furnished another two opera libretti that included oracular scenes. *Thétis et Pélée* (1689) and *Énée et Lavinie* (1690), both set to music by Pascal Collasse and bearing Fontenelle's name as the sole author of the literary text, took a more critical stance towards the credibility of oracles. In Act III, scene 8 of *Thétis et Pélée*, the Priest of Destiny (Ministre du Destin) is suddenly seized by "a type of possessed frenzy" ("une espece d'enthousiasme"), but the oracular voice does not originate from his body. Instead of the god appearing on stage as in *Bellérophon*, Destiny remains invisible, heard as a voice emanating from the back of the temple.[43]

This oracle addressed to Neptune hints at the impossibility for the future to be faithfully revealed. It is exceptionally brief, comprising just the third and fourth verses ("*L'espoux de la belle Thétis / Doit être un jour moins grand, moins puissant que son fils*"), the remaining three verses being a call to attention and a reminder that the future can never be fully divulged. A harmonic accompaniment mimics the rhythm of the vocal part and envelops the voice of Destiny, amplifying its audible presence even in the absence of the deity's presence on stage. The short score gives a sense of this effect (Example 6).

From the end of the seventeenth century, it became increasingly frequent for opera productions to revert to this variation on the Racinian practice of divine obfuscation by which oracles were pronounced by disembodied voices penetrating from beyond the 'real' world of the stage. Whereas the gods continued to hear the entreaties of humans, they maintained a mysterious disengagement and their oracular responses consistently bore ill omens. This representation of divinity as an absent presence at odds with humanity corroborates Jean-Noël Laurenti's observation that, particularly in the period from 1690 to 1710, librettists exposed the injustice and absurdity of divine decisions by forging a decisive rift between humanity and the divine.[44] Laurenti proposes that this may have been in part a reflection of the growing disillusionment over the divine right exercised by Louis XIV in the last years of his reign. Disheartened by constant warfare, rising taxes, and a king who had retreated from public spectacle to become increasingly aloof and autocratic in his leadership, the French population was restless for change. Even the Académie Royale de Musique, which from its establishment fulfilled its charter to validate the

43. The *livret* gives the rubric: "*On entend une voix qui sort du fond du temple.*" ("*A voice is heard from the rear of the stage.*") Invisible oracles are more common in rituals where no medium is present, see Burgess 1998, 441, for a list of scenes in which oracles were heard from off stage.
44. Laurenti 2002, 267.

Example 6. Pascale Collasse, *Thétis et Pélée* (1689), Act III, scene 8. Reproduced from Collasse 1716, 119-20. ["Listen, God of the Waves, to what Destiny permits as a response. The Spouse of the beautiful Thetis must one day be less grand, less powerful than your son. The rest lies hidden in a profound night."]

Example 7. Collasse, *Énée et Lavinie* (1690), Act II, scene 3. Reproduced from Collasse 1690, 65. ["Cupids will soon restore amongst you the Peace that they had formerly banished. Heaven will second Lavinia in her choice of a Spouse."]

sovereign's power, became an arena for dissent. The unjust fate oracles invariably sentenced on innocent mortals in the operas of this period was doubtlessly seen by many as an allegory of the despotic measures to which France was being subjected by a monarch disinvested with the welfare of his subjects.

In *Énée et Lavinie* (1690), two otherworldly voices are heard in the space of a single scene in the second act. The first emanates from a sylvan god, the second is the proclamation of a clairvoyant ghost. Lavinia and her father Latinus summon Janus at his bucolic temple, and the deity offers optimistic advice in a bass-trio air accompanied by oboes – a texture suited to the pastoral setting, but inadequate to reinforce the authority of a divinity (Example 7).

Lavinia welcomes the news that she is free to choose a lover and, by so doing, save her lands from devastating war. But her plans to marry Aeneas are soon placed in doubt when the ghost of Dido visits to warns of Aeneas' treachery. The spirit's presence is announced with full string texture at "Écoute-moy," and then each phrase is punctuated by abrupt gestures played by the bass instruments. But when Dido explains how Aeneas' sudden departure drove her to suicide ("Mon desespoir extreme..."),[45] a soft five-part texture rises as the shade had itself risen from the "ténébreux empire." The tonality is f minor, with a preponderance of flat-wise progressions and frequent reiterations of flattened second and sixth degrees. The ghost is distinguished from her living counterpart by a chant-like monotone borrowed from oracles and supported by a five-part accompaniment. Lavinia's short phrases are wider-ranging; even more significantly, each time she sings, the five-part accompaniment dissolves into a single continuo line.

By virtue of her accompaniment, the presence and authority of Dido's words, while emanating from the ghost of a mortal, are invested with greater weight than those of the immortal Janus who sings in the less impressive three-part texture. By juxtaposing two numinous presences that virtually contradict each other, Fontenelle at once satisfied the popular demand for spectacle and exposed operatic deities as unreliable.

45. The designation for the *ombre* to take over at this point is missing in the full score.

Example 8. Collasse, *Énée et Lavinie* (1690), Act II, scene 5. Reproduced from Collasse 1690, 86-7.

["LAVINIA: Where am I? What frightens me? Just gods, what a terrible sight! Hide it from us, if it is possible. DIDO: Stop, Lavinia, [and listen to me]. I am Dido, I reigned in Carthage. A Stranger, washed ashore by currents and a storm received from my royal hand a thousand benefits. On his behalf, Cupid seduced my heart, by a feigned passion he added to my desire, and then abandoned me forever. LAVINIA: Ah, what treachery! DIDO: My extreme sorrow set my arm against myself and my death never touched my indignant conqueror. LAVINIA: The ungrateful traitor! DIDO: That ungrateful traitor is the same Trojan for whom love decides in the depth of your heart. LAVINIA: Aeneas! Oh, righteous Heaven! DIDO: I have no more to say. It is your decision to make, you must reflect on this. I am going to return to the dark empire, it recalls me, I must descend once more."]

Example 8. (continued).

Example 8. (continued).

Example 8. (continued).

Example 8. (continued).

Example 8. (continued).

The earliest example of a supernatural voice accompanied by a full, sonorous texture is found in Act III, scene 3 of Lully's *Amadis* (1684). Here, too, the voice from the beyond emanates not from a divinity, but from the ghost (*ombre*) of a deceased hero, Ardan Canile (Example 9).

Amadis belongs to the period when Lully was beginning to compose full orchestral accompaniments for solo voices. Up to this time, all characters – whether mortal or superhuman (with the exception of those sung by basses who were routinely accompanied by trio texture) – had been supported by the continuo section alone.[46] Their *airs* may be introduced by an orchestral ritornello, but they sang unobstructed by the instrumental interference. Lully still reserved full accompaniment for exceptional characters and/or circumstances in his late operas, but from this point on, the harmonic accompaniment became the most distinctive marker of *ombres* and oracles. By the 1690s, when Collasse composed *Thétis et Pélée* and *Énée et Lavinie*, it had become almost obligatory for a *tragédie en musique* to include either form of supernatural being, the musical treatments of both being virtually indistinguishable.[47]

The numinous accompaniments of oracles took on a more autonomous role than other types of musical settings in the Lullian tradition, which used music in a generally supportive function that reinforced the poetic structure without obstructing its meaning. A greater tension existed between the oracles' short, ambiguous texts and their musical delivery because, as much as the harmonic halo was integral to the envoicing of oracles and sanctified their message, it also had the capability to obscure their meaning.

The relatively late development of harmonic accompaniments was undoubtedly a consequence of the primacy conferred on the literary element in the Lullian esthetic. The protracted gestation of French-language music theater was in part due to the corruptive influence music was perceived to exercise over poetry, and particularly the potential for the musical setting to obscure or otherwise distort the text. Comprehensibility of the text and avoidance of confusion from the musical accompaniment were paramount concerns for Pierre Corneille. When working on *Andromède*, in 1650, he was adamant to confine the musical interludes to episodes, so as to

> have nothing sung that be essential to the understanding of the work, because usually words that are sung are poorly understood by the audience,

46. See Schneider 1988.
47. On this point, see Wood 1981.

Example 9. Lully, *Amadis* (1684), Act III, scene 3. Reproduced from Lully 1684, 145-6. ["Ah! you betray me, miserable woman! Ah! you will betray your oaths. I return from whence I came; the daylight harms me."]

> ... they would create much confusion in the body of the work if they were intended to inform them of something important.[48]

While Corneille felt the need to avoid mixing music and text, he did admit the concurrence of music and spectacular effects, such as the miraculous appearance of divinities. Musical *concerts* served the practical function of disguising the noise of the stage machinery that transported the gods and, like the harmonic accompaniments of oracles, also amplified the supernatural quality of the apparition. In these contexts, Corneille acknowledged (in the *Examen* of *Andromède*) that music served to

> to please the ears of the spectators while their eyes are engaged in watching the descent or ascent of a machine, or are focused on something, such as the fight between Perseus and the monster, that would prevent their paying attention to what the actors might be saying.[49]

Likewise, the *dei ex machina* who descended to the stage of the Académie Royale de Musique were routinely accompanied by instrumental music that heralded their identity – flutes and violins sounded the imminent arrival of Venus or her son, trumpets heralded the arrival of more bellicose gods, and so on. Yet, a half century after *Andromède*, when the apparatus of divine revelation was invoked but now without its accompanying *machine* in the form of oracular voices heard from off stage, the harmonic *concert* had been divorced from theatrical spectacle and, in its place, united with words to represent divine presence. Operatic oracles often resorted to the concise ambiguity that La Fontaine felt compelled to resist, and were not glossed. In place of a gloss, the sheer voluptuousness of the harmonic accompaniments enshrined the decrees with *vérité*. But at the same time, like the glosses of false oracles, the musical component could provide a smoke screen of *verisimilitude* to words that in fact contained no *vérité*, divine or otherwise... or did they divulge a more indirect, ironic truth?

48. Corneille 1963, 466: "faire rien chanter qui fût nécessaire à l'intelligence de la pièce, parce que communément les paroles qui se chantent étant mal entendues des auditeurs, ... elles auraient fait une grande obscurité dans le corps de l'ouvrage, si elles avaient eu à les instruire de quelque chose qui fût important."
49. Corneille 1963, 536: "satisfaire les oreilles des spectateurs, tandis que leurs yeux sont arrêtés à voir descendre ou remonter une machine, ou s'attachent à quelque chose qui les empêche de prêter attention à ce que pourraient dire les acteurs, comme fait le combat de Persée contre le monstre."

Conclusion: "Inventé avec assez d'artifice pour porter les esprits dans un sens contraire à sa vraie intelligence"

Although his treatment of the oracles in *Thétis* and *Énée et Lavinie* demonstrate Fontenelle's scepticism, the small opening they provide for speculation on the nature of oracles is hardly commensurate with the rationalism he expressed in the *Histoire des oracles*. Did Fontenelle see value in retaining oracles at the Opéra beyond obsequious respect for convention? Their presence may have deeper implications than might at first appear, but obsequiousness may still have been the motivating factor. By retaining oracles in the face of better reasoning, Fontenelle took the opportunity to expose their falsity. We can only speculate on what discussions Fontenelle may have engaged in with his artistic collaborators at the Opéra, but if the team agreed that all oracles were shams, then their attempts to stage them tested both opera's power to construct truth and the power of the truth governing the Opéra. After all, behind every oracle was the King's divinely ordained authority which empowered the machinery of theater and state.

Whether it is possible to reconcile the beliefs of Fontenelle the sceptical philosopher with Fontenelle the librettist is difficult to say with any degree of certainty. Fontenelle's own beliefs cannot be read so easily and may not have remained consistent throughout his life. His curiosity for the supernatural was for instance piqued in 1713, when Philippe d'Orléans appointed him to investigate a young woman's prophecy that the Duke would be crowned king. Not only was Fontenelle unable to fault the woman's clairvoyance, he even declared a new-found belief in the occult. Whether the epiphany was genuine and forced Fontenelle to re-evaluate the opinions expressed in his *Histoire des oracles*, or served, as some have argued,[50] as a ruse to assuage antagonism from Jesuit adversaries who had accused him of atheism, Fontenelle left nothing to illuminate his own opinion either way. Although he was considered the ultimate authority on oracles into the eighteenth century, his anti-clericism provoked controversy.[51] Fontenelle, who had been admitted to the Académie française in 1691, followed warnings from literary colleagues that any response could result in imprisonment, and so kept silent. Despite this episode

50. See Fader 2000, 128-9.
51. In 1707, the *Histoire des oracles* was condemned by the Jesuit Jean-François Baltus as heretical, see Baltus 1707.

– or perhaps even because of the reputation it won him as a radical – the *Histoire* continued to exercise considerable influence, particularly in progressive intellectual circles. When Jaucourt compiled the article for the *Encyclopédie* (in 1765), he considered it unnecessary to go further than to La Fontaine's treatise for an authoritative account attuned to the *philosophe*'s ideology.[52]

While the dramatic strategies such as those developed by Fontenelle in his last two libretti could call the credibility and ultimately the authority of oracles into question, oracular proclamations continued to rule at the Opéra and were not openly lampooned until 1705, in the *opéra-ballet La Vénitienne* by Fontenelle's intellectual successor, Houdar de La Motte (music by Michel de La Barre). The first false oracle in a *tragédie en musique* was staged a year later, in La Motte and Marin Marais' *Alcyone*. In Act II, scene 3 of the latter opera, Céix seeks the advice of the magicians Phorbas and Ismène who, unbeknownst to him, are plotting to take the throne of Trachis. To delude Céix, they conjure up a *spectacle infernal* during which Phorbas enters a self-induced prophetic frenzy. Instead of dissolving into the stillness of divine harmony during Phorbas' prophetic utterance, the accompaniment remains charged with frenetic activity, exposing the oracle as a sham.

These works by La Motte heralded neither the demise of the gods nor the silencing of oracles at the Opéra. In addition to earlier operas including *Bellérophon*, *Amadis*, and *Thétis et Pélée* that, along with their attendant divinities and oracles, enjoyed enduring success well into the eighteenth century, oracles continued, in the words of Charles Batteux, to "announce themselves to mortals through works, a language, and vocal inflection that surpass the laws of ordinary credibility,"[53] exercising authoritative presence in newly composed operas up to the Revolution.

52. Diderot & d'Alembert 1751-72, XI, 591: "[Les recherches] de M. de Fontenelle, sans être originales, sont si judicieusement écrites, que je les ai choisies pour en donner le précis dans ce mémoire." ("Fontenelle's studies, although not original, are so judiciously written that I have chosen them to serve as the précis of this article.")

53. Batteux 1746, 212: "s'annoncer aux Mortels par des opérations, par un langage, par une inflexion de voix, qui surpassent les loix du vraisemblable ordinaire."

ADDRESSING THE DIVINE

The 'numinous' accompagnato in opera seria[*]

Bruno Forment

More than any other art, music has the deep-seated ability to evoke the aura of mystery required for theatrical representations of the mythical. When, for instance, Ferruccio Busoni wondered at what particular moments music was truly "indispensable" on the stage, his conclusion read: "During dances, marches, songs, and – at the appearance of the supernatural in the action."[1] Of course, music had already supported unearthly causes long before Busoni even considered writing his *Entwurf einer neuen Ästhetik der Tonkunst* (1916). No later than 1589, Giovanni de' Bardi deployed trombones to convey the gloom of Pluto's subterranean habitat, the 'region of the Demons,' in his five-part madrigal "Miseri habitator del cieco Averno."[2] When opera embarked upon its long history, divine characters were dressed in instrumental garbs indicating their status and identity with increasing precision and idiosyncrasy. In a letter to Alessandro Striggio, Claudio Monteverdi associated Tritons and sea gods with trombones and cornets, "rather than cithers, harpsichords, and harps," and cupids, little zephyrs, and sirens with trebles and winds.[3] In addition, multi-parametric 'conventions' began to crystallize around particular dramatic moments that invoked the divine in either direct or indirect fashion. A conspicuous example is the invocation aria, whose chthonic vocabulary (i.e., featuring such words as

* The author wishes to thank Laurel Zeiss and Carolyn Gianturco for their help, and Jelbrich and Aloïs Forment for their patience.

1. Busoni 1965, 40. In the original (Busoni 1973, 20): "Bei der Frage über die Zukunft der Oper ist es nötig, über diese andere Klarheit zu gewinnen: "An welchen Momenten ist die Musik auf der Bühne unerläßlich?" Die präzise Antwort gibt diese Auskunft: "Bei Tänzen, bei Märschen, bei Liedern und – beim Eintreten des Übernatürlichen in die Handlung." Es ergibt sich demnach eine kommende Möglichkeit in der Idee des übernatürlichen Stoffes."
2. The piece concluded the fourth *intermedio* to *La Pellegrina*, the theatrical extravaganza that was staged in Florence for the wedding of Ferdinando de' Medici and Christine de Lorraine.
3. The letter, dated 9 December 1616, was occasioned by Scipione Agnelli's libretto *Le nozze di Tetide*, which Monteverdi declined to set; it is here cited from Weiss 2002, 25. On the representational use of sonorities in the seventeenth century, see Bianconi 1987, 173 and Kimbell 1991, 28-30.

"harpies," "Erebus," or "Tartarus"), *sdrucciolo* verses (with the accent on the penultimate syllable), and saraband rhythms emphasized the addressee's Otherness.[4] All the more arresting are the magical transformations and divine descents, which called for intermediary music to cover up the rumble of the wooden machinery. In Handel's *Amadigi* (London, 1715), for example, a "loud boisterous Simphony" is heard when an

> Enchanted Porch splits asunder and falls ... the Scene darkens, and it thunders and lightens, but clears up again at the appearing of Oriana, who comes surrounded with enchanted Knights and Ladies; and the Scene changes into most beautiful Rows of Pillars.[5]

The present essay deals with a supernatural trope that emerged from seventeenth-century musical rhetoric and grew into a genuine convention of eighteenth-century Italian opera: the 'numinous' accompagnato. This particular brand of *recitativo accompagnato* or *stromentato*, which consists of a layer of strings superimposed onto a recitative, allowed composers to literally *under-score* those particular moments during which characters invoked the divine.[6]

4. Examples include Medea's "Dell'antro magico" in Cavalli's *Giasone* (1649; Act I, scene 14), Berengario's "Numi Tartarei" in Sartorio's *Adelaide* (1672; Act I, scene 11), and Eleonora's "Le crude Eumenidi" in Carlo Francesco Pollarolo's *Ottone* (Venice, 1694; Act III, scene 3). Arguably the most hilarious instance of this convention is Publicola's "Arpie dell'Erebo" in Legrenzi's *Totila* (1677; Act I, scene 11): it has a servant, Desbo, heave sighs ("Piano... Ahimè... Non più...") in between each of Publicola's phrases. Discussions of the invocation include Glixon 1985, 53-4 and Rosand 1991, 343, both of which, however, overlook the saraband rhythm so relevant in light of seventeenth-century connotations of that dance with the infernal and vulgar (see Gstrein 1997, 20-6, especially 26, where Marino's *Adone* is cited).
5. La Motte 1715, 12-3 (Act I, scene 6): "La Loggia incantata si spezza, e cade al' suono di strepitosa sinfonia; si oscura la Scena, con tuoni, e Lampi, e si rischiara all'apparire d'Oriana, la quale Comparisce circondata da Cavalieri, e Dame incantate; e si cangia la scena in un bellissimo colonnato." Unimpressed by Handel's musical response, a French overture in F Major, Charles Burney (1789, IV, 252) held that it was perhaps "good enough for the opening of any serious opera," but lacked the "picturesque or imitative" demanded by the libretto – "perhaps," Burney added, "the orchestras of these early times were not so powerful or able to execute new and dramatic ideas, as at present." Nonetheless, as one of the anonymous referees of this book noted out, the dotted rhythm can be connoted with the entry of a divinity.
6. General discussions of the accompagnato include Zeller 1911; Monelle 1978, see in particular 262-3, where Semira's invocation in Hasse's *Artaserse* (1730) is examined; Strohm 1998, especially 235, where it is observed that "[i]n der Opera seria des 18. Jh. war das recitativo accompagnato besonders für emotionsgeladene Monologe beliebt, aber auch für spannungsreiche Dialoge, feierliche Ansprachen und Gebete," and where mention is made of the "'numinosen' Streicherbegleitung in ausgehaltenen Akkorden"; Zeiss 1999, 220-38, where the *accompagnato* is connected with "altered states and the supernatural"; Gianturco 2001; Monson, Westrup & Budden 2001.

"Un nume io sento"

Let us immediately clarify the practice through an excerpt from *Andromaca* (1728), a *pasticcio* for the Florentine Teatro della Pergola.[7] In one of the opera's pivotal confrontations, Act II, scene 11, Andromache (Andromaca) rushes into a temple to prevent her son Astyanax (Astianatte) from being sacrificed by the Greek aggressor Pyrrhus (Pirro). The thrilling intervention reverses the relationship between the protagonists: while Hector's widow transforms from an unrelenting heroine, who dares Pyrrhus "to slay her only Son in the face of the Gods,"[8] into a subservient mother, who bows before her male dominator, Pyrrhus lays down his image of scorned lover to become the potential executioner of his future stepson. In true *opera seria* style, the catastrophe leads naturally towards a *lieto fine* lacking the least sign of divine interference,[9] but in the course of matters (see Example 10), Pyrrhus all of a sudden transcends the realm of humanity, exemplified by simple recitative, in order to summon the "guardian gods of Greece" to accept the innocent victim. Four-part, arpeggiated strings in awkward, quasi-modal constellations back each of his utterances, which Andromache seeks to disrupt in vain.[10] When heard within the normative context of simple recitative and eighteenth-century tonal syntax, the brief flashes of string sound accompanying Pyrrhus' eerie vocal line punctuate the flow of human drama with evocations of the mythical. To be sure, the "guardian gods" remain physically absent, yet we can sense their disembodied presence in the two-dimensional sonic space.

Seventy years after the *Andromaca pasticcio*, in autumn 1798, the recently built La Fenice in Venice presented two of Simeone Antonio Sografi's tragic libretti, *Gli Orazi e i Curiazi* and *La morte di Semiramide*, in settings by Marco Portogallo and Sebastiano Nasolini, respectively.[11] Intriguingly, the main ingredient of Pyrrhus' numinous

7. Contextual details in Weaver & Weaver 1978, 253-4. The libretto (Salvi 1728) is based in part on the revision of Antonio Salvi's *Astianatte* (Florence, 1701) for the Teatro Bartolomeo, Naples, where it was set by Leonardo Vinci. As Reinhard Strohm (1976, II, 267) pointed out, the Florentine *Andromaca* contains insertions by Francesco Gasparini, Domenico Sarro, Nicola Porpora, and Vinci himself.
8. Salvi 1728, 50: "Vedrò, s'hai tanto cuore, / Che basti ad eseguir l'empio consiglio / Di trucidarmi, o crudo, / Anche su gli occhi miei / Anche in faccia alli Dei, l'unico Figlio."
9. On the disappearance of the *deus ex machina* in Italian opera, see Forment 2010.
10. See, for instance, bar 28 (Pirro and upper string parts), where it is unclear whether f sharp or natural is asked for.
11. Portogallo's opera was previously given at Ferrara while Nasolini's, which derives from Pietro Giovannini's *La vendetta di Nino ossia la morte di Semiramide* (Venice, 1786), was originally produced in

Example 10. Leonardo Vinci (attr.), *Andromaca* (1728), Act II, scene 11 (scene 14 in the score; recitative, bars 24-38). After Brussels, Koninklijk Conservatorium-Conservatoire Royal, no. 2365, fols. 180-3. ["*Andromache* (Ah, my heart is freezing.) – *Pyrrhus* Ye guardian gods of Greece, to whose divinity I immolate this victim... – *Andromache* (If I resist any longer, my heart will be unrelenting.) – *Pyrrhus* Accept this burnt offering, the blood of which... – *Andromache* (Save the boy and die.) – *Pyrrhus* ... ensures the holy bond of friendship and peace between Greece and Epirus to be eternal and enduring. – *Andromache* Hold, Pyrrhus..."]

accompagnato, the thick 'halo' of strings, surfaces in both works, in each case serving an identical purpose: namely, provide a mysterious atmosphere to an invocation of the powers that lie beyond human existence and reason. In Act I, scene 7 of Portogallo's *Gli Orazi e i Curiazi*, the Roman warrior Marcus Horatius (Marco Orazio) implores the gods for assistance in his upcoming battle against the enemy. A quartet of strings accompanies his *preghiera* with intricate chordal progressions in dramatic *forte-piano* dynamics,[12] eventually (in bar 22) shifting to a heroic obbligato when Horatius alludes to his earthly aspirations (Example 11). Similarly, in Act II, scene 11 of Nasolini's *La morte di Semiramide*, the Assyrian Queen Semiramis loses her way through a dark labyrinth and prays the gods to help her find the urn of her husband Ninus.[13] Sustained strings, enhanced with tremolos and dynamic shadings (*fp*), set the right tone for the 'gothic' situation, while also underscoring the ineffable nature of Semiramis' addressee (Example 12).

Ecclesiastical origins?

When did characters begin to address the gods in this particular type of accompanied recitative? Did the eighteenth century here, too, perpetuate an "infrequent usage"[14] of the seventeenth, artifacts of which could be found in the scores of Monteverdi, Cavalli, Cesti, Steffani, or Stradella?[15] Unfortunately, the answer to that question must remain hypothetical in light of three conditioning elements. First, the preserved corpus of seventeenth-century operatic scores, being tantalizingly incomplete, proves simply inadequate to outline even the origins and development of accompanied recitative in general. Second, there are no clear-cut definitions for such essentially ambiguous terms as *recitativo arioso* and *recitativo stromentato*, as a result of which

1792 at the Teatro Argentina in Rome. On Sografi's innovative *tragedie per musica*, see McClymonds 1989.

12. After making a false start in d minor (bar 14), the harmony hints deceptively at F major via its dominant seventh (bars 15-6), B-flat Major through the third inversion of its dominant seventh (bar 17), D Major (bars 18-9), and c minor via a diminished seventh in inversion (bars 20-1).
13. The original stage setting is described in Sografi 1798b, 44 as a "Sotterraneo con quantità di Colonne, che sostengono le volte a guisa di Labirinto, tra le quali vi sono le urne, che rinchiudono le ceneri degli estinti re di Babilonia, e fra queste quella di Nino nel mezzo."
14. Monson, Westrup & Budden 2001, 2.
15. Carse 1964, 44 offers that "[t]he idea of a voice singing to a soft, sustained, harmonic background of string-tone has long been a commonplace, but was a novelty in the early days of Monody."

Example 11. Marco Portogallo, *Gli Orazi e i Curiazi* (1798), Act I, scene 7 (recitative, bars 14-27). Edited from Portogallo 2003, 152-3. ["Gods, if ever suppliant... and respectful I have worshipped you for the glory of Rome, I prostrate myself before you in this horrific moment for both you and myself. Please see to it, merciful Gods, that I, too, on this beautiful day can shed my blood in the battlefield for the fatherland."]

Example 12. Sebastiano Nasolini, *La morte di Semiramide* (1792), Act II, scene 11 (recitative, bars 47-53). After Naples, Conservatorio 'San Pietro a Majella,' 29.3.24, fol. 193r. ["Gods, assist me, I again move my trembling and hesitant feet... No longer do I know where my steps direct me."]

it is difficult to ascertain whether a passage is conceived in one or the other form (or both).[16] To make matters worse, musical notation prior to 1700 often does not indicate the precise instruments playing along with each fragment, an exception to the rule being of course the printed score of Monteverdi's *Orfeo* (Mantua, 1607). That opera's third act, interestingly, specifies a soft accompaniment ("tocchi pian piano") of three violas da braccio supported by a bass viol when Orpheus (Orfeo) invokes Charon (Example 13). However, whether "Sol tu nobile Dio" can indeed be seen as an embryonic form of our numinous accompagnato remains open to debate.[17]

16. Robinson 1972, 77 makes a valid point when noting that, "[t]he further we go before c. 1720, the more confusing the situation becomes so far as arioso is concerned. In the mid-seventeenth century style and function of aria and recitative were far from rigidly divided, and many musical sections came into a very ambivalent classification zone. Late seventeenth-century Italian opera still contained free lyrical sections in addition to the arias in closed forms. Some of these free sections were similar in style and, more important, possessed similar weight and substance to the aria proper. Others were short, perhaps minute insertions which appeared to fulfil the function of varying the recitative."
17. On this passage, see Ossi 2003, 161. A similar instance, Cavalli's setting of "vaghissimo oggetto dell'alma innamorata" in *La virtù degli strali d'amore* (Venice, 1642; Act III, scene 4), is discussed and characterized as a *recitativo stromentato* in Worsthorne 1968, 67-70.

Example 13. Claudio Monteverdi, *Orfeo* (1607), Act III (Orfeo "Sol tu nobile Dio," bars 1-6). Edited from Monteverdi 1615, 65. ["You alone, noble God, can give me aid. Do not fear, gods, that on a golden lyre..."]

What is undeniable, on the other hand, is the fact that operatic practice did not monopolize the practice on enriching divinity-related passages of recitative with 'haloes' of string sound: in religious genres (e.g., the oratorio, *sacra rappresentazione*, or *historia*), too, divine or holy speeches and characters were given more musical prominence through hymn-like vocal lines, organ-like accompaniments, and learned harmonies – the best-known example being arguably the Vox Christi in Bach's *St Matthew Passion* (Leipzig, 1727). In his *Opinioni de' cantori antichi, e moderni* (1723), furthermore, Pierfrancesco Tosi singled out an "Ecclesiastical" type of recitative that was "sung as becomes the Sanctity of the place, which does not admit those wanton graces of a lighter style" – it was to be performed with "some *messe di voce*, many Appoggiaturas, and a sustained nobility throughout."[18] The German theorist Johann Adam Hiller confirmed Tosi's observations in his *Anweisung zum musikalisch-richtigen Gesange* (1774), arguing that

> More gravely and solemnly one must talk to God than to people: the recitative of the church, especially when being most closely related to this Supreme Being itself, demands the utmost expression, dignity, and a slower tempo.[19]

That Hiller deemed orchestral accompaniments effective for the purpose can be inferred from another passage of his tract, where he hailed the accompagnato as entailing

> much more – or at least a higher degree of – affect, and a far more sublime declamation than ordinary or unaccompanied recitative, which is of little effect in the church, especially when it is sung without reason, emphasis, or dignity.[20]

To pursue the secular-ecclesiastical strand, let us briefly consider works by two composers who deployed homophonic string accompaniments in both their oratorios and operas for numinous effects: Carlo Francesco Pollarolo (c. 1653-1723)[21] and George Frideric Handel (1685-1759). In the B section of "Un'onda che fugge," an aria in Pollarolo's oratorio *La Rosinda* (Vienna, 1685; anonymous libretto),[22] a hermit (Eremito) warns the young virgin Rosinda not to fall into the traps of love and vanity (Example 14). Pollarolo distinguished the graveness of the sermon from the remainder of the set piece by resorting to an arioso in 4/4 (versus a minuet in 3/4), unstable minor-mode harmony (versus A major), a syllabic (versus melismatic) setting, and string accompaniment in long note values (versus quarter notes and eighths). In

18. Cited from Tosi 1742, 66. In the original (Tosi 1723, 41): "Il Recitativo è di tre sorte, e in tre maniere diverse il Maestro lo deve insegnare allo Scolaro. Il primo essendo Ecclesiastico è di ragione, che si canti adattato alla Santità del luogo, che non ammette scherzi vaghi di stile indecente, ma richiede qualche messa di voce, molte Appoggiature, e una continua nobiltà sostenuta."
19. Hiller 1774, 203: "Ernstlicher und feyerlicher als mit Menschen, muß man mit Gott reden: das Recitativ der Kirche, besonders wenn es die nächste Beziehung auf dieses allerhöchste Wesen selbst hat, erfodert daher den meisten Nachdruck, die meiste Würde, und eine langsamere Bewegung."
20. Hiller 1774, 200-1: "Ueberhaupt sollte diese Art von [begleiteten] Recitativen in der Kirche fleißiger gebraucht werden ... Es gehört viel mehr Affect, oder wenigstens ein höherer Grad desselben, und eine weit erhabnere Declamation dazu, als zu dem gemeinen oder unbegleiteten Recitative, welches in der Kirche von sehr geringer Wirkung ist, zumal wenn es ohne Verstand, ohne Nachdruck und Würde gesungen wird."
21. On Pollarolo's pivotal position in operatic history, see Termini 1970 and 1979.
22. In Termini 1970, 388-9 and 453-4, the libretto is falsely attributed to Giovanni Faustini, with whose (secular) *Rosinda* (Venice, 1651) Pollarolo's oratorio has no connection.

another of his oratorios for the Viennese Court, *Jefte* (1692), on a libretto by Girolamo Frigimelica Roberti, Pollarolo highlighted Jephthah's solemn vow to sacrifice the first person he will meet upon his victorious return from the Ammonites – his own daughter, as we know – in near-identical fashion (Example 15). Handel may have based his *Jephtha* (London, 1752; Thomas Morell) on a different libretto, still the corresponding passage in his score retains the basic feature of Pollarolo's: sustained chords performed by four-part strings.[23]

Example 14. Carlo Francesco Pollarolo, *La Rosinda* (1685), part one (Eremito "Un'onda che fugge," B section). Source: Vienna, Österreichische Nationalbibliothek, Mus.Hs.18103, fols. 36v-37r. ["Mortal being, it is you I am addressing. Time will dissolve those machinated ideas into little dust."]

23. See Handel 1886, 58-9: "If, Lord, sustain'd by thy almighty pow'r, Ammon I drive, and his insulting bands, from these our long uncultivated lands, and safe return a glorious conqueror; – what, or whoever shall first salute mine eyes, shall be for ever thine, or fall a sacrifice." (Part I, scene 4 – bars 16-27).

Jefte
Si- gnor, se in ma-no mi - a d'Am-mon la sor-te mi di - a e del po-po-lo tuo di - let - to
Strings

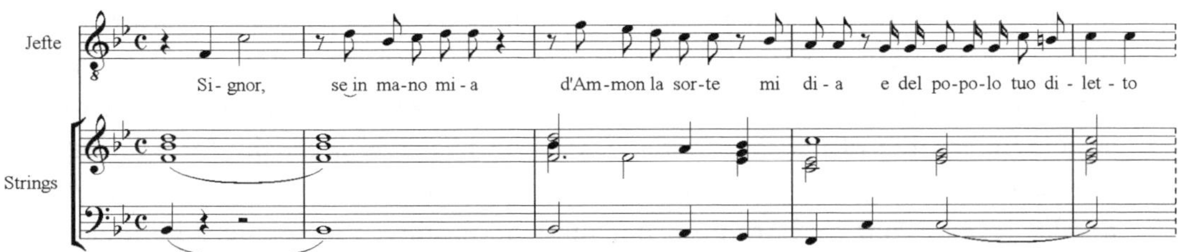

Example 15. Pollarolo, *Jefte* (1692), Act I, scene 1 (recitative). Emended from Termini 1970, 454-5. ["Lord, if you hand over the fate of Ammon and the well-being of your people..."]

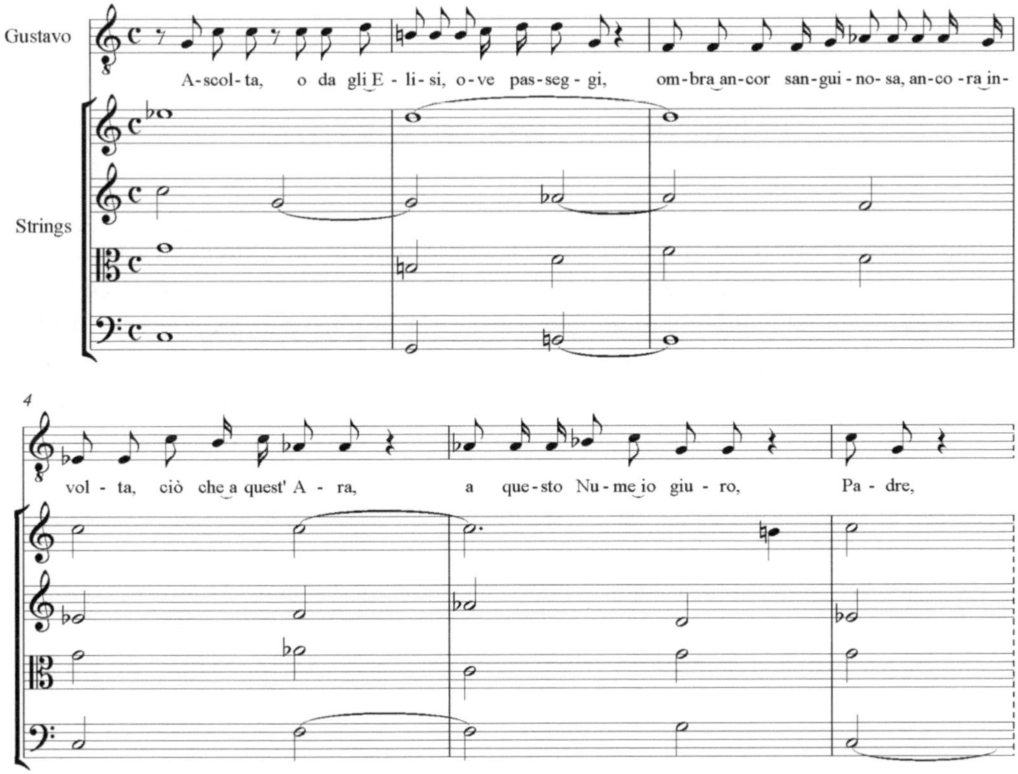
Gustavo
A-scol- ta, o da gli E - li- si, o-ve pas-seg - gi, om-bra an-cor san-gui - no- sa, an-co -ra in-
Strings
4
vol - ta, ciò che a quest' A - ra, a que-sto Nu - me io giu - ro, Pa - dre,

Example 16. Pollarolo, *Il Faramondo* (1698), Act I, scene 7 (recitative, bars 1-6). After Pollarolo 1987, 43. ["Hear, from the Elysian fields where you are strolling, ghost, still bloody and unrevenged, what I on this Altar, to this God I swear, Father ..."]

To return to the *dramma per musica*, a numinous accompagnato is heard in Pollarolo's original setting of Apostolo Zeno's *Faramondo* (Venice, 1698) when Gustavus (Gustavo), King of the Cimbrians and Bohemians, solemnly swears to avenge the murder of his son, Svenus (Sveno).[24] The surviving score for a revival of *Faramondo* (Bologna, 1710) reveals the aforementioned combination of a minor tonality (c) with four-part string accompaniment (Example 16). Handel's setting of the same libretto (London, 1738), while diverging greatly from Zeno's *princeps*, once more corresponds to Pollarolo's in assigning strings to Gustavus' vow.[25] In sum, in five scores produced in two different genres in a period spanning the years 1685 to 1752, two authoritative composers responded with virtually the same idiom to an identical dramatic 'cue' – more striking proof of a convention at work is hard to find.

Paganism and censorship

Supposing that operatic and ecclesiastical applications of the numinous accompagnato did have multiple points in common, it may come as a surprise that, in an age obsessed with religious and moral betterment, the heathen pantheon was invoked with the same musical solemnity as the God of Christianity.[26] Even so, the Italian Inquisition was constantly on the alert for manifestations of heresy, thoroughly reviewing each book or libretto prior to approval, in which case an *imprimatur* was added mentioning the censors' names. Detailed instructions, furthermore, were issued to help poets decide what was illicit or not. One such guidebook, Pietro Francesco Bottazzoni's *Lettere discorsive intorno ad alcuni poetici abusi pregiudizievoli al decoro della religion cattolica come alla buona morale cristiana* ('Discursive letters on a number of poetic abuses disadvantageous to the decorum of both the Catholic religion and good Christian morality,' 1733), strictly forbade the invocation of the "true God" in profane poems and, vice versa, of the "false deities" in sacred texts.[27] As can be

24. Zeno 1698, 18: "Recinto d'alti Cipresse dedicato alla Vendetta, tutto illuminato da notte, con apparato, ed ara nel mezzo." The correct date (27 December 1698) for the premiere of Pollarolo's setting, at the Teatro San Giovanni Grisostomo, is given in Selfridge-Field 2007, 234.
25. See Handel 1884, 6-7: "Ascolta dagli Elisi, ombra di Sveno, ancor inulta ..." (Act I, scene 1 – bars 8-20).
26. See in particular Forment 2010, 199, where Arthur Bedford's stabs at the London stage are cited.
27. Bottazzoni 1733, 105: "Siccome nelle Poesie profane non è lecito l'invocare il vero Dio ec., così nelle Poesie sacre non è lecito l'invocare Numi falsi."

gauged from censorial interventions in a number of libretti, the proscription must have achieved currency long before Bottazzoni's *Lettere* appeared. In, for example, the anonymous libretto to Vivaldi's *Ercole su'l Termodonte* (Rome, 1723), words such as "Heaven" ("Cielo"), "Gods" ("Dei" or "Numi") appear in full, and a chorus of Amazons is allowed to address Diana as the "Chaste Sister of the God of Delos" (i.e., Apollo), all of which made sense within a pagan mythological context: Hercules' conquest of the Amazons. The Almighty's name, by contrast, as in the neutral exclamation "Oh God" ("O Dio"), could not be argued for and was amusingly abbreviated to "O D." (see Illustration 3). Of course, few Italian librettists hesitated to write the Lord's name in full, yet many of them informed their readers – and revisers – in a disclaimer (*protesta*) that potentially blasphemous expressions were to be understood as either jests of poetry[28] or as factual representations of the uncivilized, heathen culture in which their narratives unfolded.[29] While such imprints became more formulaic and superfluous towards the middle of the eighteenth century, when the spirit

28. Early examples include Strozzi 1639, 8 ("Le Favole finalmente sono Favole, le divinità de' Gentili tutte sciocchezze, onde ci si può scherzar sopra allegramente; ma l'allegorie, che nascono da loro, non sono senza profitto. Cosi le voci Fortuna, Fato, Destino, Sorte, e simiglianti sono leggierezze Poetiche, e non sentenze Teologali."); Tirabosco 1642, 96 ("Le parole di Paradiso, Beato, e simili si devono intendere conforme l'uso de Poeti Gentili, che non scherzare tra le delitie di Parnaso se non con simili maniere."); Bissari 1648, 5 and 8 ("Non tanto in' altra cosa pretendon le moderne Scene, quanto nelle Deità, che si vagamente fan comparire; Mà, che ne queste siano nuove ne la causa, perche sono da tal'uno introdotte, l'attesta Cicerone [in *De natura deorum*], *cum explicare argumentum non potestis ad Deum confugitis* ... Parerà d'ammirabil inventione il condur le Deità volanti, il passeggiar l'aere, l'empirla di tuoni, e di saette, l'arricchirla d'eccelse Machine: E pur non habbian cosa in questo, che l'antichità con' i suoi particolari nomi non ci dimostri. ... E condonando quel perfetto, che li si toglie, gradite un passatempo di chi compose; e fate, che per esso la vostra gratia non le si tolga. E che le consuete voci de' Poeti, Fato, Destino, e simili, non pregiudichino al dovuto di buon Christiano."); and Passarelli 1655, 8 ("Le parole Deità, Fato, Destino, e simili le dettesto come Christiano, ne voglio che tu le ammetta da me usate se non in Poetica superficie: io vivo Cattolico, ama ancor tu il prossimo, e vivi lieto.")
29. E.g., Piovene 1714, [5]: "Le voci, Fato, Numi, Dio, e simili, saranno intese da Voi [the 'Cortesi Lettori'] con la dovuta relazione alle persone introdotte; anzi io vengo ad incontrar con piacere l'occasione di mettervi dinanzi agli occhi le azioni de' Numi adorati già da' Pagani, sperando, che ciò possa dar maggiormente a conoscere la cecità del Gentilesimo, ed aumentare la gloria della nostra Cattolica Fede."

14 A T T O
Ip. (Un Uomo in mia difeſa ?)
Teſ. (Ahi che bel volto !)
Ip. (Devi Ippolita dunque
La vita a un tuo nemico ?)
Teſ. (E pur m'hà tolto
Ogni vigor quel ciglio, e vinto Io ſono)
Ip. (E come poſſo, oh D.
Odiare il Donatore, e amare il dono ?)
Teſ. (Ah nò, che non poſs'Io
Toglier la vita à chi pur reſi il giorno.)
Ip. Straniero ; e qual mia ſorte,
Qual tua ſveutura ti guidò quì intorno,
Dove è pena la morte
A ciaſcun del tuo ſeſſo ? ancor non ſai,
Che qui regnan l'Amazoni ?
Teſ. Pur troppo
Bella nemica il tuo rigor provai.
Ip. Come ?
Teſ. Un ſguardo appena
Verſo di me volgeſti,
Che mi apriſti nel ſen piaga mortale.
Ip. Se a te dunque funeſti
Sono i miei ſguardi, or che ſarià il mio ſtrale!
Teſ. Nò nò, troppo gradite
Sono al cor le ferite,
Ch'eſcon dagl'occhi tuoi.
Ip. Dimmi chi ſei ;
Teſ. Del Regnante d'Atene
Figlio, Teſeo ſon Io.
Ip. A queſte infauſte Arene
Chi ti conduſſe mai ?
Teſ. Nobil deſio
D'o-

48 A T T O
Col vendicarti ah ! ch' Io t'uccido, e ſpargo
Il tuo co'l ſangue altrui:
Ah che tè pur vorrà ſvenare il fiero,
Il crudo Greco, e vorrà forſe, ahi viſta !
Ch' Io ti vegga ſvenar sù gl'occhi miei :
Oh figlia ! Oh figlia! ahi perche quì non ſei?
Io ti ſento, Io ti veggio,
Chè mi chiedi pietà, mà ſento ancora
Le voci degli Dei ;
Oh Dei troppo temuti, e troppo avverſi!
Figlia, Dei, che far deggio ? (Numi
Son crudele, ò ſpergiura... Ah ſempre a'
Serbiſi fè ; Miniſtre,
Sù bendate quei lumi ; à lui ſi cinga
La fronte di Cipreſſo, à mè d'Iſopo.
Bendano Teſeo, gli pongono in teſta la Corona di Cipreſſo, e quella d'Iſopo alla Regina.
„ Teſeo, ſoffrilo in pace, omai fà d'uopo
„ Piegare all'Ara le ginocchia, e'l collo
„ Alla ſacra Bipenne.
Teſ. „ Oh crudo amore !
„ Ove mi hai tù condotto !
Ant. „ Or tù d'Apollo
„ Caſta Germana,
„ Al cui freddo ſplendore
„ Delle belle auree Stelle il raggio langue ;
„ Gradiſci l'olocauſto, il di cui ſangue,
„ Che or ſparge il zelo mio, più che il mio ſdegno,
„ Pace renda al mio core, & al mio Regno.
Coro „ Caſta Sorella
„ Del Dio di Delo..
SCE-

Illustration 3. Pages 14 and 48 from the libretto to Vivaldi's *Ercole su'l Termodonte* (Rome, 1723) revealing censorial discrepancies. Brussels, Koninklijk Conservatorium-Conservatoire Royal.

of Enlightenment relaxed religious tensions considerably,[30] religious discipline was maintained by even the most progressive minds.[31]

30. See, for instance, Villeneuve 1756, footnote on 85-6: "un Italien de beaucoup d'esprit semble pousser le scrupule un peu loin sur cette matiere [of knowing "les limites du pouvoir enchanteur qu'on attribue aux Divinités fabuleuses"]; il parle le langage de son pays, où une Tragédie ne peut passer à l'impression si l'Auteur ne prélude par protester que ces paroles, *Destin, Idoles, Adorer, Jupiter, & autres Divinités du Paganisme*, sont des termes purement Poëtiques, contraires à la sainte Morale, qu'il les déteste dans le cœur, comme soumis au Saint Siége. C'est une espece d'excuse de ce qu'il n'ose mettre dans la bouche du pieux Enée les sentiments d'un Catholique Romain."
31. Planelli 1772, 249-50 demanded that the impresario "Procurerà in esso [libretto], che i personaggi non parlino troppo della Divinità, nè (ove sieno pagani) secondo la grossolana Religione del volgo

Censorship was not alone in disciplining the gods' presence on the operatic stage, however. The Church found an ally in dramatic criticism, and more particularly in Aristotle's demand that divinities and irrational elements be confined to prologues and appendages outside the actual drama.[32] The precept found operatic applications from the mid-seventeenth century onwards, resulting in both the dramatic and visual relegation of the mythical to the asylum of linguistic discourse – put bluntly, the gods could be spoken of, but not speak for themselves. Intriguingly, the gods' very elimination provided conditions congenial for the introduction of the numinous accompagnato. Nothing can better illustrate this idea than a comparison between three libretti adapted from Vergil's *Aeneid*: *Enea in Italia* (Venice, 1675), *Enea negli Elisi, ovvero Il tempio dell'Eternità* (Vienna, 1731), and *Didone abbandonata* (Naples, 1724).

The voice of Destiny

Giacomo Francesco Bussani culled his libretto *Enea in Italia* from *Aeneid*, books VII to XII, which relate Aeneas' (Enea's) battle with the Latin warrior Turnus (Turno) over the hand of Lavinia. The musico-dramatic scope of Bussani's plot was by no means restricted to the human dimension, though, for already in the opening scene, Bussani staged and sonified the divine forces underlying Aeneas' deeds. In a nocturnal tableau, Fate (il Fato) and Venus (Venere) discuss the warrior's mission and reveal

de' gentili, la quale trasferiva a' suoi Dei le più umilianti debolezze degli uomini: ma che dieno a conoscere ne' loro ragionamenti qual idea aver si debba dell'Essere Supremo. Il qual linguaggio non sarà punto inverisimile in bocca loro: ben si sapendo, che dalla Teologia del volgo pagano era tutt'altra quella delle colte persone; le quali rigettando la moltiplicità degli Dei, e le ingiuriose favole, che si spacciavano di essi, un solo Dio, e perfettissimo ammetteano." Similarly, Gamerra 1789, 53 contended that "Una religione qual'è la nostra sì grande, sì santa, sì augusta, che consola il povero, che ritiene l'infelice sull'orlo del precipizio aperto dalla disperazione; che fa brillar di gioja l'indigenza nel seno della miseria; che sparge lo spavento sul felice oppressore; che fa tremare i tiranni vittoriosi e impuniti, e che apre la strada al rimorso nel cor dei Monarchi, una tal religione, io dico, sarà rispettata dagli Autori."

32. *Poetics*, 54a31: "The *deus ex machina* should be employed only for events external to the drama – for antecedent or subsequent events, which lie beyond the range of human knowledge, and which require to be reported or foretold; for to the gods we ascribe the power of seeing all things. Within the action there must be nothing irrational. If the irrational cannot be excluded, it should be outside the scope of the tragedy." A fuller account of the impact of Aristotelian poetics on the demise of the *deus ex machina* is to be found in Forment 2009 and 2010a.

the future city of Rome.[33] Venus sings two arias ("Ombre cieche" and "Dimmi: Enea trionferà?"), and the scene concludes with a duet ("Sinche il Sol dai Globi erranti"). The phenomenological space in this scene is therefore 'continuous' in that deities and mortals are conjured up simultaneously, with genuine arias being allotted to both of them, yet the earthly is distanced from the heavenly since both realms are mapped onto different vertical coordinates – the deities above (*ex machina*), Aeneas and his men below (stagefloor). Typical for Baroque illusionism, moreover, the joints between theatrical reality and play, auditorium and stage, are blurred to the extent that Carlo Pallavicino, the composer of *Enea in Italia*, incorporated melodic material from the overture in Venus' opening aria (Examples 17a and b).

Example 17a. Carlo Pallavicino *Enea in Italia* (Venice, 1675), overture (bars 13-4 and 23-4). Source: Venice, Biblioteca Nazionale Marciana, Cod. It. IV 412 (= 9936), fols. 1r-1v.

Example 17b. Pallavicino *Enea in Italia*, Act I, scene 1 (aria, bars 1-2 and 25-7). Same source, fols 2r-2v.

33. Bussani 1685, 1: "Reggia del Fato in Cielo Stellato. In Terra spiaggia Latina ingombrata da Padiglioni con l'Essercito addormentato di Enea. In Mare Armata Navale illuminata da Faci, e da Fanali." All of a sudden, a backdrop is lifted to show Rome in the distance ("*Quì da nubi si svela Roma in lontananza*") while Fate exclaims to Venus: "Mira colà, come trà fasce eterne / D'auree zone rotanti / Bambin vagisce il formidabil Soglio: / Vedi nascente il Tebro, e il Campidoglio," after which Aeneas awakens.

Like Bussani, Pietro Metastasio did not shrink from staging the mythical, yet he wisely reserved it for such 'secondary' or 'occasional' entertainments as his *feste* and *azioni teatrali*. Thus, at the rise of the curtain in *Enea negli Elisi*, which was originally set by Johann Joseph Fux, the audience witnessed Aeneas (Enea) together with the sibyl Deiphobe (Deifobe) in a dark wood crossed by two roads, the one leading to the underworld, the other to the Elysian fields. An elm tree in the middle of both roads conjures up the seat of the dreams, the monstrous forms produced by sleep.[34] Ensuingly, night becomes day and the wood transforms into a celestial temple with transparent columns and portraits of ancient heroes and heroines. Eternity (Eternità) is seated in its middle, flanked by Virtue (Virtù), Glory (Gloria), and Time (il Tempo), the shadows of Linos (Lino, i.e. Hercules' lyre teacher), Orpheus (Orfeo), and choirs.[35] A handful of recitatives and arias later, clouds descend to reveal the habitat of Venus (Venere), a supernatural utopia populated by doves, roses, the Graces (Grazie), cupids, and stars.[36] Aeneas has a happy encounter in this locale with his dead father Anchises (Anchise), who imparts providential knowledge about the past and future, up to the "remote century to which the invincible Charles [VI] will give his name"[37] – needless to add, Metastasio's *festa* was staged for the birthday of a royal, the Emperor's spouse, Elisabeth Christina. But what matters here is that all the supernatural material Bussani assigned to the prologue of his *Enea in Italia* shows up in a courtly revel by the *poeta cesareo*.

34. Metastasio 1965, II, 174: "Nell'aprir della scena comparirà una piccola ed oscura selvetta divisa in due strade; delle quali una, più caliginosa e funesta, conduce a Dite, e l'altra, più luminosa ed allegra, agli Elisi. Nel mezzo di esse l'olmo foltissimo rammentato da Virgilio come sede de' Sogni. Si vedranno fra i rami del medesimo varie forme mostruose rappresentanti le immagini corrotte del Sonno."
35. Metastasio 1965, II, 178: "nel terminar della preghiera appena depone Enea il ramo fatale, che si cangia in un istante la notte in giorno, la funesta in allegra armonia, e l'orrore dell'angusta selva nell'amenità de' vastissimi Elisi. Si vede in essi il tempio dell'Eternità, sostenuto da colonne trasparenti, fra le quali saranno ordinatamente disposte le immagini delle eroine e degli eroi dall'antichità più celebrati. Sederà nel mezzo l'Eternità: a' lati di lei la Virtù e la Gloria: più basso il Tempo; e nelle due estremità, l'uno a fronte dell'altra, l'ombre di Lino e d'Orfeo coronate d'edera e di lauro, con la cetra accanto, e con numeroso accompagnamento de' loro seguaci, che formano i Cori."
36. Metastasio 1965, II, 184: "ad un cenno dell'Eternità si vede occupata la parte superiore del tempio da un gruppo di nuvole, che dilatandosi a poco a poco scoprono alla vista degli spettatori l'aspetto del cielo di Venere. Da un lato vedrassi la conca marina, che serve di carro alla deità suddetta, con le colombe accoppiate con freni di rose alla medesima: dall'altro le tre Grazie; e per tutto Amorini che scherzano. Sarà adorno il cielo di varie stelle; nella più grande e più luminosa delle quali comparirà adombrata l'immagine di Augusta [i.e., Empress Elisabeth Christina]".
37. Metastasio 1965, II, 195: "il remoto / Secolo ... a cui l'invitto Carlo / Nome darà."

In *opera seria*, on the other hand, "the gods no longer speak, and we are never told whether they hear."[38] As a rule, the irrational was kept from the stage in the century between Pollarolo's *Faramondo* and Portogallo's *Gli Orazi e i Curiazi*, surfacing in mere words and music rather than scenic actions. And yet, *opera seria* heroes, too, can be driven by exterior forces which, in constituting more than human passions, demand to be voiced accordingly. In the opening lines of Metastasio's *Didone abbandonata*, Aeneas (Enea) thus motivates his decision to leave Dido (Didone) – and Carthage – in a statement to Dido's sister, Selene, and confidant, Osmidas (Osmida):

> No, princess, friend, believe *not fear or hatred*
> Unmoors the Phrygian fleet and drives me hence:
> ... *destiny* commands
> Once more to expose my life on Neptune's waves.
> Such is the will of *the gods*! Ah me unhappy!
> The crime of *Fate* must thus appear my own.[39]

Aeneas' pagan "destiny," "gods," and "Fate," for whose verbal presence Metastasio duly apologized in a *protesta*,[40] do of course not intervene in the drama; one will search in vain for an aria sung by Fate or Venus, or a revelation of Rome painted on a backcloth. Nonetheless, the divine pops up orchestrally when Aeneas summons up the vision of Anchises, for which Metastasio felt no need to have the old man's *ombra* appear on stage. Rather, he assembled a *hypotyposis*, a vivid description, from two episodes of the *Aeneid* – Mercury's appearance, through which Jupiter orders Aeneas to leave Carthage (Book IV, lines 222-78), and Aeneas' dream of Anchises (V, lines 721-40) – in order to make clear what supernatural powers caused Aeneas to abandon Dido.[41] Domenico Sarro, the first composer to try his hand at *Didone*, underscored the relevant description with an array of orchestral gestures (Example 18): from brisk chordal accents (bars 29-33 and 36-7), over stormy sixteenths and thirty-seconds (bars 34 and 49-50), to numinous haloes in sostenuto (bars 38-42). Harmonically, the preponderance of diminished sevenths and bold modulations verges on the whimsical, suggesting once more that such passages should be heard and understood as belonging to a realm different from that associated with simple recitative.

38. Strohm 2002, 62-3.
39. Translation emended from Hoole 1800, II, 232. In the original: "No, principessa, amico, / *Sdegno non è, non è timor* che move / Le frigie vele e mi trasporta altrove. ... Ma ch'io di nuovo esponga / All'arbitrio dell'onde i giorni miei / Mi prescrive il *destin*, voglion *gli dei*; / E son sì sventurato / Che sembra colpa mia quella del *fato*." (emphases mine)
40. Metastasio 2002-4, CD-ROM (*princeps*): "Tutte l'espressioni di sensi e di parole che non convengono co' dogmi cattolici o sono scritte per proprietà del carattere rappresentato o sono puri adornamenti poetici."
41. The latter is actually unrelated to the Carthaginian episode!

29
Enea
"Fi - glio" (ei di - ce e l'a - scol - to) "in - gra - to fi - glio, ques - to è d'I - ta - lia il re - gno
Strings

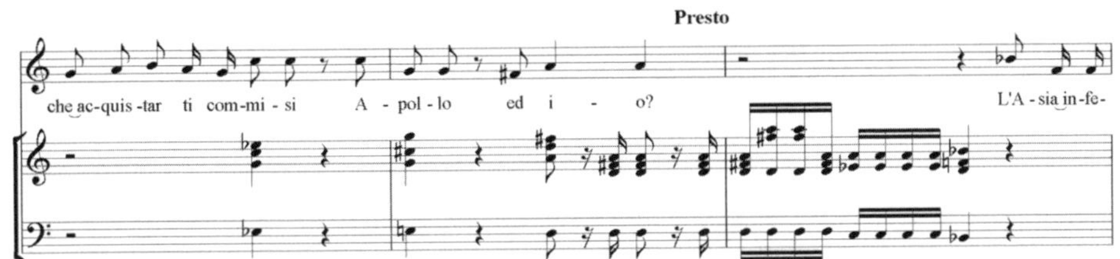
Presto
che ac - quis - tar ti com - mi - si A - pol - lo ed i - o? L'A - sia in - fe -

35
li - ce a - spet - ta che in un al - tro ter - re - no, o - pra del tuo va - lor, Tro - ia ri - na - sca; tu il pro - met - tes - ti;
f
dolce

40
io nel mo - men - to e - stre - mo del vi - ver mi - o la tua pro - mes - sa in - te - si, al - lor che ti pie - ga - sti a ba - ciar que - sta

45
de - stra e mel giu - ra - sti. E tu frà tan - to in - gra - to al - la pa - tria, a te stes - so, al ge - ni - to - re
f

Example 18. Domenico Sarro, *Didone abbandonata* (Naples, 1724), Act I, scene 1 (recitative, bars 29-53). After the autograph in Naples, Conservatorio 'San Pietro a Majella,' Rari 1.6.6, fols. 15-8. [*Aeneas.* "O son! (he cries, I hear his well-known voice) ungrateful son! Are these the Italian realms, whose conquest oft to thee have Phœbus [Apollo] and myself enjoin'd? Ill-fated Asia from thy valour hopes in other climes renew'd another Troy. This didst thou promise, this, in life's last moments I heard thee swear, when kneeling, on this hand thy filial kiss confirm'd the solemn compact. And now, ungrateful to thyself, thy country, thy father, here thou dwell'st in sloth and love – Rise, cut the cords that hold thy tardy vessels, and loose thy spreading sails." – Such warning given he darts an angry glance and disappears.][42]

Paradoxically, then, the louder the cry for an opera devoid of miracles and deities, the more 'indispensable' orchestral phantasmagorias became in the score. While the deities hid their persona behind the wings, the conveyed their disembodied presence through prayers and dreams with compelling accompaniments. In this respect, the numinous accompagnato did not solely enhance the expressive scope of opera. Rather than serving as a pleasant diversion from ordinary recitative, it provided a much-needed substitute for a visual deficit, which explains why the trope persisted as long as opera remained bereft of mythical bodies. The numinous accompagnato thus merits to be reckoned with, either superficially, as a conventional folly of the *teatro alla moda*, or with deeper hermeneutic urgency, as the musico-dramatic testimony of an epoch that craved for rationalism but could not help but override the logocentric borders of classicist drama.

42. Translation cited from Hoole 1800, II, 232.

IPHIGENIA'S CURIOUS MÉNAGE À TROIS IN MYTH, DRAMA, AND OPERA*

Reinhard Strohm

The desire to assimilate or equate opera and myth seems unstoppable today. We feel that opera and myth have much in common, not only when operas take their plots from classical mythology – such as Orpheus, Ulysses, Iphigenia, or Hypermnestra – but also when the 'metaphysical' potential of the genre itself is being invoked. This happens regularly in discussions of 'the meaning' or 'the essence' of opera. The observation that opera may *utilize as well as resemble myth* seems also to reflect the non-verbal dimensions of its communication.[1] On the other hand, the mythical associations of opera are somewhat suspect since they have often, in varied forms, been used to glamorize the genre to enhance its public appeal. If opera is both 'myth' – in the sense of an 'ancient tale about humans and gods' – and an artistic product, it can be allowed to speak of the supernatural and yet be a subsidized commercial enterprise: a synthesis that other art forms have failed to reach.

This essay is based on the assumption that opera, as a dramatic text and performance, does not have a single transhistorical meaning, but that its identity constitutes and reconstitutes itself historically. In this regard, it should be distinguished from myth and its transhistorical implications. Structuralist analyses, such as those introduced by Claude Lévi-Strauss or Roland Barthes, have different functions, depending on whether they concern the nature of underlying stories (*fabulæ*), or that of dramatic texts or performances.[2] I also believe that the historical fluctuations of the *fabulæ* in dramatic texts are quite unlike those in the theoretical and historical literature, notwithstanding mutual influences.[3] Very similar fluctuations to those of

* I am most grateful to James Morwood for his helpful criticism and comments on an earlier version of this essay.

1. Mythical inclinations are ascribed to eighteenth-century opera in Feldman 2007; in this case, a figurative, critical meaning of the term 'myth' ('false tale') is half-implied. By contrast, Tomlinson 1999 does not use the term 'myth,' as his discussion privileges the non-verbal aspect of opera.
2. A structuralist case study of operas on the Iphigenia myth is Forment 2007a, 122-70.
3. An influential anthropological-philosophical investigation that does not address literary works, is Blumenberg 1985.

opera, however, exist in spoken drama, which has its own mythical ambitions and an even longer-lasting association with mythical subjects. In the seventeenth and eighteenth centuries, the uses of myth in opera and drama almost seem like a single discourse: an insoluble entanglement of given 'sentences' with new textual and performative initiatives. The various appearances of a particular myth in operas and dramas sometimes accentuate the difference between the genres, but may equally bring them closer together, or act as conduits for external influences (cultural ideologies, for example). The relative invariance of the *fabula*, when put to theatrical uses, tends to allow for a multiplicity of interacting textual solutions, a shared discourse. We shall consider such a shared discourse – a curious *ménage à trois* – by surveying a selection of operas and spoken plays based on the Iphigenia myth. First of all, however, we should enquire how myth, history, and poetry as sources of dramatic *fabulæ* can actually be distinguished, and what selection from each source the various theatrical repertoires have made.

On the classicist stage of the Renaissance, spectators had been accustomed to hear spoken tragedies (with occasional choruses or songs), spoken comedies, sung or spoken *intermedii*, and pastoral fables. The new genre of opera, despite the claim that it revived the performance practice of Greek mythical *drama*, was conceived as an all-sung *favola pastorale*, and the rule that it be sung confirmed the separation of the genre from the Aristotelian genres of tragedy and comedy. Opera did not utilize mythical drama, but for its secular subjects selected pastoral fables from epic poetry, both classical and modern. Heroic-tragic myths were shunned: before the mid-seventeenth century, only Orpheus and Ariadne were allowed to sing on stage, not Achilles, Orestes, or Andromache. It is surprising to realize at hindsight how carefully the genre in its first half century of existence avoided actual Greek tragedies as models, while during the same period several national traditions of spoken drama were thriving on this very heritage. This distinction within the literary tradition seems to reflect the contrast between the 'pastoral' and the 'heroic' spheres, the latter of which was at first deemed unfeasible for the musical theater.[4]

A striking development, therefore, was the diversification of subjects in mid-seventeenth-century Italian opera. Giovan Francesco Busenello and Claudio Monteverdi's *L'incoronazione di Poppea* (Venice, 1643) inaugurated *historical* drama on the operatic stage. From around 1660, the first operas derived from actual Greek *tragedies* appeared in Venice, Munich, and Paris.[5] Thus opera began to occupy two domains at once, which had hitherto been reserved to the spoken (or only incidentally sung) theater.

How real, however, was the genre distinction between 'myth,' 'history,' and 'poetry'? In fact, the authors of operas based on ancient drama or on ancient history seem to have made only a gradual difference between myth and *poetry*. Giacomo Badoaro and Monteverdi's *Il ritorno d'Ulisse in patria* (Venice, 1640), for example, is based ultimately on Homer, but the story is rebuilt from the bottom up with non-classical episodes, characters, and stage-sets. This mythological opera cast in modern literary forms might well be compared to the several operas based on Fénelon's *Les aventures de Télémaque* (1699), a *roman* interpolated into a Homeric plot lacuna, which in its literary form and moral ideology is entirely a product of its own time.[6] While, in such works, the *ancienneté* of the mythical models could be fragile, the changes to a *fabula* could be robust. Dido and Aeneas were allowed to get married in Ortensio Mauro and Agostino Steffani's *I trionfi del fato* (Hannover, 1695) – making it seem immaterial whether these protagonists were actually called Dido and Aeneas, or bore the names of some pseudo-historical princes from Mediterranean romance. Production modalities – added ballets, intermezzi, stagecraft, and so forth – could blur any remaining distinction between transmitted and invented materials.

Although the story of Nero and Poppæa was the first historical subject ever used in opera, this distinction fades, too, when we appreciate that Busenello made much use of the Pseudo-Senecan *Octavia*, the only surviving Roman tragedy on a historical rather than mythical subject.[7] Aristotle himself in the *Poetics* had called all traditional dramatic plots 'mythoi' (*fabulæ*, tales), regardless of whether they were myths or just venerable history. And, why should early modern audiences have made such distinctions when

4. Brown 2006 attempts to bypass such distinctions, proposing a synthesis of the Orpheus, Orlando, and Orestes myths in opera and drama, with a climax in Gluck and Goethe.
5. On the appearance of ancient tragedies on the opera stage, see Strohm 2010b.
6. See Forment 2007b.
7. 7 See Manuwald 2005; Manuwald 2008.

not even erudite poets did so?[8] Finally, the boundaries between myth, history, and literature appear negligible from the moment it is appreciated that the ancient poets had been using myth as a vehicle for their own worldviews all the time.

Whatever the merits of a theoretical distinction between these sources of the *fabula*, the repertoire selections made by opera and drama in their various stages of development do not unambiguously map onto such a distinction. It is true that historical subjects were shunned in French opera until the mid-eighteenth century.[9] Subjects based on ancient tragedies were accepted in European opera – as said – only from the mid-seventeenth century onwards. But why, for example, did the opera career of heroic Iphigenia begin only in 1699 – an entire century later than Eurydice's?[10] Tragic Electra was denied the opera stage until 1708, when the taste for tragic opera was growing in Italy: Girolamo Frigimelica Roberti in his *tragedia per musica* entitled *Mitridate Eupatore* (music by Alessandro Scarlatti) faithfully transferred the *Electra* plot to the pseudo-historical kingdom of Cilicia. King Oedipus arrived on the musical stage as late as 1729.[11] Such exclusions suggest that theatrical practice was governed not only by a theoretical awareness of genres, but by cultural ideologies, social rituals, national preferences, and literary topics.[12]

A survey of the early modern Iphigenia plays from the beginning to the late eighteenth century would require more than one book.[13] I shall concentrate here on selected Iphigenia plays of the century between Jean Rotrou (1640) and Johann Elias

8. Pietro Metastasio's manuscript *Annotazioni di soggetti* is a miscellaneous list of mythical, literary, and historical subjects as possible sources for future libretti, among them the mythical ones of Aegisthus, Electra, Helen, Helen in Egypt, Hercules Trachinius [i.e., Sophocles' *Women of Trachis*], Iphigenia in Tauris, Paris, Polydorus, Polyxena, Pylades, Talestris, Telemachus, and Theonoe and Leucippe. See Metastasio 1965, II, 1279-85.
9. Rushton 1976.
10. On the special case of Duke Anton Ulrich's *Iphigenia* (1661), see below.
11. See Strohm 2010b.
12. The strictly performative characteristics of the genres, such as arias or spoken dialogue, were quite neutral to the question of myth. Besides, the distinction between spoken drama and opera according to such criteria also fluctuated, as will be seen.
13. A valuable attempt is Gliksohn 1985. Much more limited in repertoire and approach is Heitner 1964.

Schlegel (1737).[14] The two Iphigenia stories were equally popular in this period; the Tauris plays show a somewhat greater variety in characters, story-line and dramaturgical solutions. The Aulis dramas after 1674 all reflect the influence of Jean Racine's *Iphigénie*. This work galvanized later dramatists, whose prefaces regularly refer to it, whether because of Racine's general reputation or of his particular approach to Euripides. In fact, it must be ascribed to this influence that around 1700 a spate of Iphigenia plays – on both myths – suddenly appeared in several countries simultaneously, having some of its most faithful repercussions in Arcadian opera. This is already an example of the *ménage à trois*, as opera and drama undergo a common influence almost against the grain of their performative genre identities.

Jean Rotrou's *Iphigénie* (1640, published 1641) may well be the earliest modern version of the Aulis myth in dramatic form, as distinct from the Renaissance revivals and translations (for example by Lodovico Dolce, 1551). Rotrou's tale of kingship, love, sacrilege, and redeeming innocence sets a pattern that would still serve opera and drama for two centuries. The driving force of the work, according to Robert J. Nelson, are its moral intentions: "Whatever the intention of the generals at the outset, it has been purified by the *consistently* good intention of Iphigénie."[15] Modernity found here an open space in the classical texts that could be filled with personal 'motivations' because the ancient dramas were read as determined by fate and religion, whereas the modern approach was based on subjectivity.

The German *Singe-Spiel*, *Iphigenia ein königliches Fräulein* (Wolfenbüttel, 1661) by Duke Anton Ulrich of Braunschweig-Lüneburg has been classified as an 'opera,' and thus as the first opera on the subject altogether.[16] This is slightly misleading, because this author's *Singe-Spiele* were spoken plays with incidental music, as the stage directions referring to musical interludes and songs make clear – although the term 'Singspiel' was later used synonymously with 'opera,' this equation does not apply here as yet. We may nevertheless regard this play as somehow operatic: it contains lyrical solos (some of which are performed by extra singers from outside the list of characters), choruses, elaborate stagecraft, and machines; the extended comical subplot with a stammering servant is a virtual import from Venetian opera; eroticism and jealousy disguise the tragic constellation of the play; a romantic relationship between

14. *L'Ifigenìa* by Niccolò Jommelli (Rome, 1751) and later Iphigenia operas are discussed in Forment 2007a, 122-70 and Forment 2010b.
15. Nelson 1969, 111-8: 117.
16. Anton Ulrich 1982-5, I-2, 260-324. The music is lost. See Brockpähler 1964, 88-9. On the plays by Anton Ulrich, see Smart 1989, 158-72.

Iphigenia and Pylades is introduced and doubled by that of Hermione and Orestes. The *dea ex machina* is comically doubled, furthermore: the servant Thersites appears first as a fake Diana; he orders the sacrifice of Pylades to please his master, the wicked Aegisthus, who loves Iphigenia and wishes to eliminate his rival. Then Diana appears in person to correct this scandalous fiction and let Iphigenia fly to her in the sky.

An early clash between opera and drama over their respective loyalties (or disloyalties) to classical myth – which must be considered here although it is not directly concerned with Iphigenia – could have been the renowned *Querelle d'Alceste* of 1674-5. This was a debate on the respective merits of Philippe Quinault's *tragédie en musique, Alceste, ou Le triomphe d'Alcide* (Paris, 1674; music by Jean-Baptiste Lully) and the Euripidean *Alcestis*.[17] Quinault's friend Charles Perrault, a leader of the group of the *Modernes* in French classicist circles, welcomed the opera and accused Euripides of certain faults which, he contended, were corrected in Quinault's libretto version of the story.[18] The disagreement of the opposing group of the *Anciens* was first articulated by Jean Racine, who in the preface (1675) to his tragedy *Iphigénie* (first performed Versailles, 18 August 1674) went out of his way to defend Euripides against the criticism of Perrault and, by implication, against the changes to the *Alceste* story introduced by Quinault.[19] Other contributions to this debate followed on the heels. Is this now a case where the identities of opera and spoken drama could be deduced from their divergent attitudes towards a common mythological source?

It is striking that none of the contributors to this literary quarrel ever mentioned what every commentator would emphasize today: the genre difference between opera and spoken drama. Quinault's libretto was read as a literary text just like Euripides' original tragedy; the musical setting was never considered. The contested differences between the two dramas involved such things as a moral impropriety imputed to Euripides' Admetus, who asks his parents to die for him, and dramaturgical questions, for example whether Admetus and Alcestis were a young or old couple, or whether Admetus should suffer from an illness or be injured in a duel. A distinguishing feature in Quinault's plot is that Hercules (Alcide) is himself in love with Alcestis, whom he rescues from Hades, although in the end he gives her up for Admetus: the language is transparent enough to recognize in this magnanimous Hercules – a departure from Euripides *not* criticized by Racine – an allegory of Louis

17. See Quinault 1994.
18. See Quinault 1994, 79-102.
19. Racine's preface is in Quinault 1994, 103-10. The entire story is also reassumed in Fumaroli 2001, 163-78.

XIV. A study of Lully's score might demonstrate how certain key phrases that are musically enhanced well beyond their spoken impact, for example the words of the triumphant chorus "Alcide est vainqueur du trépas" in Act V, were intended as an unmistakable homage to the King. In matters political and moral, opera and drama shared a common ideology.

Racine was sometimes closer to the 'operatic' approach than he may have wished to admit, especially in his preference for the expression of tender feelings.[20] Pierre Perrault (brother of Charles) criticized Racine only for not acknowledging that in his poetry he had himself surpassed the ancients.[21] But there were more austere critics. Fénelon criticized the language of modern tragedies, including those of Racine, for their 'pompous' and 'flowery' phraseology, which he regarded as a deviation from the ideals of esthetic simplicity and social decorum that he had espoused and saw in the ancients.[22] Pierre de Villiers, on the other hand, disliked the introduction of romantic love (*amours*) into the dramas, which made the myths appear modern and sentimental.[23] The entire culture, however, was interested in 'la mythologie galante': the majority of Pierre Corneille's tragedies, and all those of Racine, introduced *galanterie* where the ancient models did not have it. In Rotrou's *Iphigénie* of 1640, and even more in Racine's of 1674, the character of Achilles was perceived as the intrusion of love and passion into Euripides' moral and political plot. In Racine's drafted first act of an *Iphigénie en Tauride* (c. 1676), romantic love is introduced through an additional character, the son of Thoas, whose love for Iphigenia is opposed by his father. French and Italian critics of the time saw the topic of romantic love as the one that distinguished modern sensibilities most clearly from classical drama. Although that view of classical drama was a huge simplification – Sophocles' *Antigone* and *Women of Trachis* are obvious counterexamples – early modern plays were sometimes deliberately left without love interest, and by no means only spoken dramas: Frigimelica Roberti's *Mitridate Eupatore* (see above), among other examples, conforms to the classical plays by only having a faithfully married couple.

For contemporaries, the most significant issues arising from the dramatization of myths were two: the precept of verisimilitude, *vraisemblance*, or *verosomiglianza* (to

20. Boileau's criticism of Quinault (see Fumaroli 2001, 155: "Les héros chez Quinault parlent bien autrement, / et jusqu'à 'Je vous hais' tout s'y dit tendrement") is of course applicable to Racine as well.
21. Quinault 1994, 133-4.
22. Fénelon 1970.
23. Gliksohn 1985, 100-4 and 118. On heroism and the *amours* in drama, see also Porée 2000, 40-5 and the editor's commentary on xxxiv-vi.

which the dramaturgical options of happy or tragic endings could be subordinated), and the issue of cruelty and sacrifice, central to most classical tragedies. In his preface to *Iphigénie*, Racine addresses both issues. He rejects the supernatural interference and miraculous substitution of the sacrificial animal, which in the (altered) Euripidean version and in Ovid's *Metamorphoses* leads to the protagonist's rescue, calling this solution "too absurd and unbelievable for our age"; at the same time, he objects to the human sacrifice on ethical grounds:

> What a spectacle if I had stained the scene through the horrible murder of the utterly virtuous, amiable person that Iphigenia had to be represented as being! And what a spectacle, also, to solve my tragedy through the assistance of a deity and a machine, and through a metamorphosis that could have readily found some credence in Euripides's time but would be too absurd and unbelievable among us.[24]

Racine's solution to these two shortcomings of his model, although ostensibly following Aristotelian precepts, is a rationalization based on modern morality and theories of passion. Eriphyle, the substitute victim, is a character driven by jealousy; the coincidence that she is present at the intended sacrifice is made credible by her excessive passion and jealous persecution of her rival Iphigenia. Eriphyle commits suicide at the altar as a self-punishment: an action not familiar from classical tragedy.[25] Iphigenia, in turn, deserves to be rescued because of her virtue.

Throughout the 'enlightened' century, Iphigenia plays remained fixated on the dialectic between Racinian, 'credible' dramaturgies, and the option of miraculous divine interferences and rescues, which the ancients had already introduced in many dramas to restrain cruelty. In any case, human sacrifice had to be avoided or averted.[26] But just how could a *lieto fine* be achieved under the conditions of modern rationality? The question posed by the mythical plots, for which solutions were sought, was in fact identified as a conflict between cruelty on the one hand, and verisimilitude on the other: verisimilitude was what society ordained or found acceptable.[27] The Iphigenia

24. Racine 1999, I, 698: "Quelle apparence que j'eusse souillé la scène par le meurtre horrible d'une personne aussi vertueuse et aussi aimable qu'il fallait représenter Iphigénie? Et quelle apparence encore de dénouer ma tragédie par le secours d'une déesse et d'une machine, et par une métamorphose, qui pouvait bien trouver quelque créance du temps d'Euripide, mais qui serait trop absurde et trop incroyable parmi nous?"
25. The suicide of Sophocles' *Ajax* is differently motivated. Metastasio used a guilt-ridden suicide only in *Issipile* (1732).
26. Further on this matter, see Hughes 2007; Strohm 2010a.
27. See Gliksohn 1985, 86-8.

plays by Euripides became test pieces of this preoccupation, not least because this dramatic pair was transmitted with happy endings since antiquity. In addition, it enabled a meaningful variation to the problem, Iphigenia herself being the potential victim of the sacrifice in the first play, the potential perpetrator in the second. Some authors wrote or set a pair of Iphigenia dramas to exploit this potential.

Verisimilitude was seen differently in the various camps, however: supernatural elements, magic, and miracle (*le merveilleux*) enjoyed a special licence in French opera until the revolutionary period, almost qualifying for a 'secondary' kind of verisimilitude, believed to be more suitable for the musical theater.[28] From about 1690 onwards, the Arcadian poets of the *dramma per musica* sought to rationalize the mythical substance and to find credible 'solutions' in the French *spoken* dramas which could be transferred to opera.[29] This rationalization was not the same as a replacement of myth by history, because in the same era historical plots were often narrated, in both genres, with the help of supernatural and magic appearances.

The first genuine Iphigenia opera seems to have been *Die wunderbahr-errettete Iphigenia* by Christian Heinrich Postel, set to music by Reinhard Keiser for Hamburg (1699).[30] This opera on the Aulis story includes sung dialogue, arias, ensembles, and a chorus; the lyrical texts are sometimes sentences, sometimes direct expressions of passion. Postel replaces Eriphyle with a character simultaneously at home in the Achilles myth and in Venetian opera: Achilles' abandoned fiancée Deidamia, princess of Scyros, arrives in Aulis – disguised in male clothes – to challenge him over his infidelity. Achilles is interested in marrying Iphigenia out of ambition, but she loves Anaximenes, the disguised Scythian King Thoas. Such multiplication of the *amours* (including their denial) had already served in Anton Ulrich's play as a mechanism to lend credibility to actions. But while the passions could enhance verisimilitude, they

28. See Weiss 1984.
29. See Weiss 1982; Strohm 1997, 121-200.
30. Postel 1699. Repeat performances took place in Hamburg 1705 and 1710. A revised version was newly set by Carl Heinrich Graun for Braunschweig (1728) and repeated in Braunschweig and Hamburg (1731); see Marx & Schröder 1995, 418-9 and 248. I have used the text version in Flemming, 255-308.

could make supposedly heroic characters more ambiguous. Iphigenia's character change in Euripides was a much-debated issue (following Aristotle's comments in *Poetics*, 1454a32-3). Racine's heroine, who is ready to die for Achilles' glory out of love, is more unified; Postel re-introduces an Euripidean ambiguity in her motivations. In the final scenes, Achilles' armed protest against the sacrifice leads to his belated recognition of Deidamia, who offers herself as the victim out of desperation. Averting the sacrifice, Diana appears with thunderbolts, produces the white hind, and sanctions the two correct marriages. Postel's most original invention, highlighted in the editor's preface, is the figure of Thoas and his bond with Iphigenia: an attempt to connect the two stories without supernatural means, but also a dramaturgical challenge to whoever would wish to write a Tauris drama as a follow-up to Postel's libretto.[31]

An early operatic adaptation of Racine's drama that rejected miracle was Pietro Riva's *Ifigenia* (Venice, 1707; music by Agostino Bonaventura Coletti).[32] According to the preface, the author adopted a "tempered solution, without the miracle alleged by the [ancient] Authors."[33] Yet the opera abounds in extra episodes, spectacle, and subplots; the characters are Agamemnon, Iphigenia, Eriphyle, Deidamia, Achilles, Patroclus, Ajax, Choruses of Mycenean Virgins, Captains and Soldiers, and Royal Guards, and a High Priest – but no Diana. The individual characters of the *personaggi* are delineated in the libretto; for example, Iphigenia is called "magnanimous and constant," Eriphyle "ferocious and resolute," Achilles "fiery, impetuous and passionate."[34] This idea of a fixed characterization was taken up in 1719 by Pasqualigo (see below).

Apostolo Zeno reproduced Racine much more faithfully in his *Ifigenia in Aulide* (Vienna, 1718; music by Antonio Caldara). His libretto was often set and made the subject popular all over Europe. Zeno follows Racine's 'third opinion' of the outcome of the Aulis story: the wicked rival Eriphyle (here called Elisena) has to carry the burden of the tragic curse. Although Zeno enlarges upon Racine's assertion that this solution is prefigured in ancient authors, there is actually no ancient testimony for the sacrificial death of the 'other Iphigenia.' Yet Racine's play deeply influenced the opera tradition by its stark moral differentiation between the two female leads.[35]

31. Brief references to Postel's "most famous libretto" are found in Haufe 1994, 63-4 and 81.
32. The libretto, whose author, Pietro Riva, had died some years before, was revised by Aurelio Aureli.
33. Cited from Selfridge-Field 2007, 273: "soluzione moderata, e ridotta dal miracolo allegato dagli Auttori".
34. Selfridge-Field 2007, 273.
35. An 'other woman' who is sacrificed for the benefit of the *prima donna* also appears in, for example, *Idoménée*, a *tragédie en musique* by Danchet and Campra (1712), and *Idomeneo* by Varesco and Mozart

Also significantly, Zeno's final peripety is only communicated by a messenger's report, as in Racine but in no other adaptation known to me.

In 1700, the Huguenot emigrant Abel Boyer translated Racine's *Iphigénie* for the London theater of Drury Lane.[36] In the preface Boyer polemizes against John Dennis and his *Iphigenia*, previously performed at the rival theater of Little Lincoln's Inn Fields (see below), which distracted audiences from his own show.[37] Act IV begins with an inserted song, "Morpheus thou gentle god of soft repose, / Th'unruly Tumults of my mind compose" (see Example 19), which illustrates the lonely suffering of the jealous Eriphyle; this was "composed by Mr [Daniel] Purcell" and "sung by Mrs Erwin" – a professional singer not on the list of characters, as was the practice in German and English plays.[38] Act V ends spectacularly with a sacrificial chorus and symphony, thunder and lightning, "subterranean groans and howlings," and an eclipse of the sun; while the clashing of swords is heard behind the scene, Achilles and Patroclus storm in to threaten Calchas, followed by Eriphyle's suicide on stage (!) and Diana's apparition in a machine. Whereas Postel's German opera had changed the plot and its characters in such a way as any poet of the spoken theater could have done, Boyer's Racine translation introduced elements of an even more melodramatic (and more English) conception of theater.

A very different response to Racine emerges in a context where academic interest in Euripides crossed with college performances of French tragedies: *Ifigenia*, a *dramma per musica*, performed in Carnival 1705 at the Teatro Obizzi, Padua.[39] The dedication is signed by one Bortolo Tardivelo (perhaps an anagram), who says he has written the poem years ago but now revised it for the stage. The frontispiece (Illustration 4) shows the abduction of Iphigenia in the clouds over the burning altar, surrounded by temple maidens resembling vestal virgins. Names are changed and many other *personaggi* are introduced, completing a love-jealousy quartet of characters. The libretto also offers pastoral scenes (royal hunt), magnificent stage-sets,

(1781). Danchet's Electra has fewer negative traits than Varesco's.

36. Boyer 1700. The drama was plagiarized in a version by Charles Johnson, *The victim* (Drury Lane, 1714), which held the stage for several decades afterwards. See also Hall & Macintosh 2005, 32-5.

37. "This tragedy came out upon the Neck of another of the same Name, which being the product of a Giant-Wit, and a Giant-Critick, like Horace's Mountain in Labour, had miserably balk'd the World's Expectation; and most People having been tir'd at Lincolns-Inn-Fields, did not care to venture their patience at Drury-lane, upon a false Supposition that the two Iphigenia's were much alike: Whereas they differ no less than a young, airy Virgin, from a stale, antiquated Maid." (Boyer 1700, [5])

38. The song is erroneously assigned to the *Iphigenia* of John Dennis (1699) in the reference works.

39. Tardivelo 1705.

Example 19. Daniel Purcell, "Morpheus thou gentle god of soft repose" (1700) from *A collection of the choicest songs & dialogues composd by the most eminent masters of the age* (c. 1720). Oxford, Bodleian Library, Harding Mus. E 118 (111).

Example 19. (continued).

spectacle (sea storm and earthquake in Act I), heroic and amorous motifs (Iphigenia has two suitors, one of whom is pursued by his jilted lover in male disguise).

The influence of Zeno's *Ifigenia in Aulide* has already been stressed; many of the operas of the period c. 1720-50 listed in reference works as independent productions are in fact versions of Zeno's *dramma per musica*.[40] This is not the case with the libretto *Ifigenia in Aulide* by Paolo Rolli, performed with music by Nicola Porpora in London's Haymarket Theatre in May, 1735.[41] Rolli seems to understand his version as an alternative to Zeno's and returns in important aspects to Euripides, leaving aside Racine – there is no Eriphyle, and the peripety comes through the *dea ex machina*. The Haymarket audience will have known of Handel's *Oreste* (1734), the Taurian opera performed at the rival Covent Garden Theatre just five months before (see below): music and, in particular, singers had become debated issues in London at the time. Since Carlo Broschi *detto* Farinelli sang Achilles in Porpora's opera and Francesca Cuzzoni, Iphigenia, it is no surprise that Rolli conveyed the myth partly through the musical numbers – just as modern commentators would expect from *any* opera. The poetic and musical characterization of Calchas, Agamemnon and, in particular, Clytemnestra and Achilles links up with the Racinian tradition: innermost feelings and conflicts appear which Euripides had not made explicit; action vibrates in the lyrical numbers, for example in Agamemnon's angry arias and his duet with Calchas in Act II. Family tensions are expressed and compressed in a remarkable *terzetto* for Agamemnon, Clytemnestra, and Iphigenia in Act III. The stagecraft was important, too, with seven sets, choruses of soldiers and priests, and the *machina*. A stage direction in Act III makes Agamemnon cover his head in his cloak, in direct reference to the famous ancient painting and to the Euripidean version itself. This opera attempted, perhaps for the first time, to translate into music and image a vision of an ancient drama that was still basically Racinian, while at the same time deploying new operatic gestures invoking the classical tradition of the myth.

40. Not all of them are as easily recognizable as is Geminiano Giacomelli's *Achille in Aulide* (Rome, 1739). An opera by Antonio Bioni performed in Breslau in 1732 under the unspecific title *La verità conosciuta* is in fact Zeno's version with the protagonist renamed Ernelosia.

41. Rolli 1993.

Illustration 4. Frontispiece (*contropiatto*) of Bortolo Tardivelo's *Ifigenia* (Padua, 1705). Milan, Biblioteca Nazionale Braidense, Racc.dramm.2434.

François-Joseph Lagrange-Chancel's *tragédie Oreste et Pilade, ou Iphigénie en Tauride* (1697) was this author's second drama and surely intended as the Taurian counterpoint to Racine's *Iphigénie*. Although several Euripidean motifs are preserved (for example that of Iphigenia's letter to Orestes), the action is about as far removed from Euripides as Quinault's *Alceste* had been from its model. A Sarmatian princess, Thomyris, has been betrothed to Thoas, for which he has obtained the realm from her father; as he begins to favor Iphigenia, Thomyris becomes an ally of the Greeks out of jealousy.[42] Thoas' attempt to send Thomyris surreptitiously away by ship leads to the escape of the Greeks and his own death.[43] There are unmistakably 'operatic' elements in the solos for Iphigenia and Orestes, displaying furious passions. Wedding and sacrifice are a typical concern of the dialogues.

The Taurian Iphigenia appeared quite early in England, although most of the early sources are lost. The 'musical tragedy' *Circe* by Charles Davenant (London, 1677) is a version of Euripides' play, with the added figure of Circe as evil queen.[44] For a revival (in 1685?), Henry Purcell composed incidental music, which accentuates the magical and ceremonial aspect.[45] This work was of course known to John Dennis, whose *Iphigenia* was first performed in London in 1699.[46] In the preface, Dennis mentions Lagrange and other models, also reporting the (now discarded) notion that the Roman playwright Marcus Pacuvius (220-130 BC) had written an *Iphigenia*: the play cited by Cicero and others, *Dulorestes*, nevertheless had utilized the Euripidean scene where Orestes and Pylades both offer to die for each other. This important friendship motif, and the 'wonderful moment' of recognition of the siblings (both absent from the Aulis myth), are Dennis' main reasons for the strong impression he claims to have made on the audience. In the play he goes as far as transforming Thoas himself into a female character, an unnamed 'Scythian Queen,' who represents Barbarian attitudes (in a slightly chauvinistic manner) and contrib-

42. The constellation of this triangle is reminiscent of both Racine's *Andromaque* (1669) – with Hermione, Pyrrhus, and Andromache – and Jacques Pradon's *Tamerlan* (1676) – with Irène, Tamerlane, and Astérie.
43. The death of Thoas seems to be derived from a passage in Hyginus (*Fabulæ*, no. CCLXI): see Heitner 1964.
44. See the evaluation in Hall & Macintosh 2005, 36-41.
45. See Various 1997: "The first play based on a Greek model was Charles Davenant's unusual musical tragedy *Circe*, produced in 1677 at Dorset Gardens in London. It takes the plot of Euripides' *Iphigenia in Tauris*, adds the witch Circe in the role of King Thoas' wife, and centres much of the spectacle, emotion, and rhetoric upon her. It is a remarkable fusion of operatic sung sequences with long spoken scenes, and benefitted from excellent musical scores by both Bannister and later, for a 1685 revival, by Purcell."
46. Dennis 1700. A detailed discussion is found in Hall & Macintosh 2005, 42-53.

utes to exoticism and eroticism. The play introduces an erotic passion of Orestes for Iphigenia from which he recovers when recognizing her to be his sister. Struck by the self-sacrificing attitudes of all three Greeks, the Queen agrees to a reconciliation and marries Orestes; they all leave with the Diana statue. These events in Act V are also adorned with a magnificent choral-ceremonial scene.

The plot of *Iphigénie en Tauride*, a *tragédie en musique* by Joseph-François Duché de Vancy, with music by Henri Desmarets and André Campra (Paris, 1704),[47] focuses on erotic conflicts and the character of Thoas. The dominant figure is at first Electra, who has accompanied her brother to Tauris, where Thoas wants to force her into marriage, while she is accompanied by her lover Pylades. All five acts, however, problematize Thoas' self-doubting cruelty and his fluctuating attempts to bargain with both women over love and sacrifice. Iphigenia is rarely heard at first, but later takes the initiative, as in Euripides; instead of the goddess Athena a popular uprising and final battle bring about the escape and the death of Thoas. The operatic garnish is one of the richest ever, offering choruses of soldiers, maidens and sea-gods, sacrifical ceremonies directed by a *Grand sacrificateur*, large symphonies, military marches and dances, an apparition of the ocean-god, and other numinous soliloquies. But the action between the main characters is guided by verisimilitude, exactly as in many historical dramas of the period, for example by Thomas Corneille.

With his *Ifigenia in Tauris* (Rome, 1709),[48] Pier Jacopo Martello rivaled Racine in mediating Euripides to a large crowd of imitators, although his influence was more restricted to Italy. The work, written in Italian alexandrines (so-called *versi martelliani*), is of a decidedly classicist inspiration, in sharp contrast to earlier playwrights who had introduced *amours* to enhance verisimilitude (or vice-versa). In his preface, Martello quotes Ovid's version of the story (*Ex Ponto*, III, 2, 45-96) and dialogizes with Euripides about a solution without *dea ex machina*, while also discussing the mode of recognition as the main problem of verisimilitude. Euripidean episodes and motifs neglected by other authors are restored, for example the shepherd's report. Iphigenia's dream, however, is not only narrated but directly experienced in the first few lines of the drama. The nub of the passionate action is Iphigenia's god-fearing character and emerging infatuation with Pylades, which she finally resists when understanding that he is betrothed to Electra: her 'virginal' heroism almost functions as a legitimation for her flight from the barbarian duties in Tauris. The

47. Desmarets & Campra 1711.
48. Martello 1981, II, 423-84.

friendship motif is emphasized. Thematic parallels with the Italian oratorio tradition – which often shows the constancy and self-sacrifice of saints and the conversion of sinners – suggest that Martello's intended audiences were academic and ecclesiastic colleges of central-northern Italy. Accordingly, the three main pious characters appear proto-Christian in contrast to the barbaric-pagan Thoas, whom Orestes and Pylades let live once they have defeated him before Act V even begins.

In Carnival 1713, Carlo Sigismondo Capeci produced both an *Ifigenia in Aulide* and an *Ifigenia in Tauri* for the private theater of the Polish ex-Queen Maria Casimira in Rome (at Palazzo Zuccari).[49] The two operas, both set by Domenico Scarlatti, formed a pair, reflecting much classical precedent for successive and paired stories (e.g., Ariadne, Oedipus, Orestes, etcetera). In Italian opera, paired works, usually designed for a single Carnival season and theater, conveyed a feeling of ceremonial balance and also carried extra moral significance.[50] For example, Maria Casimira's operas of 1711 by the same authors (*Tolomeo et Alessandro* and *Orlando*) were unified by a common theme of magnanimity. In the prefaces of the two *Ifigenia* librettos, Capeci emphasizes their interdependence, which he also strengthens by introducing Pylades as a lover of Iphigenia already in Aulis. He mentions Euripides as the only source for the Aulis drama; in the Tauris drama he also acknowledges Martello – while stressing his deviations from both models in order to adapt the action "to the Characters and taste of modern libretti."[51] In fact, there are extra love and family interests: the recognition of Pylades as abducted son of Thoas, the love of Thoas' daughter Doriphyle for Orestes. These, and Iphigenia's heroism in offering herself as the Greek victim on the altar, all lead to reconciliation and a double wedding. By contrast, the Aulis libretto retains a *machina* that carries Iphigenia away. In line with the Arcadian reform, the narrative is diluted into many short dialogue scenes between two or three characters, without any of the ensemble scenes or large ceremonial tableaux that the English and French versions were cultivating. Apart from the exit arias, Capeci's tributes to musical performativity are minimal, and even the several scene changes – an Italian convention – usually move only a few architectural pieces or trees around the stage.

The Arcadian Benedetto Pasqualigo made himself known as the author of a *tragedia da cantarsi*, *Ifigenia in Tauride*, given at the Venetian Teatro San Giovanni

49. Capeci 1713a and 1713b.
50. See Strohm 2006.
51. Capeci 1713b, 3-4: "è convenuto allontanarmi in qualche parte da loro [Euripides and Martello] nel fine dell'Opera, per adattarlo ai Personaggi, & al gusto de' moderni Drammi."

Grisostomo in Carnival 1719. The music was by Giuseppe Maria Orlandini. In the 1725 Carnival, the same theater repeated the opera, but now with music by Leonardo Vinci, for whom all aria texts were changed, probably by the poet himself. This somehow indifferent attitude towards aria poetry contrasted with a peculiar approach to the plot: the libretto gives fixed characterizations of the *personaggi* – as had been done in 1707 (see above) – and contradicts all previous versions by making Thoas an "obliging, kind, and not entirely Barbarian" character.[52] Iphigenia is "superstitious and passionate," Pylades predictably a "friend of heroic virtue," Orestes also predictably "variable of mood and agitated by the maternal furies." Two extra characters, Thoas' virginal daughter Theonoe ("hospitable and amorous") and her "contemptible lover," the Scythian prince Almireno, form a subsidiary pair.[53] The poet imitates Martello in his classicist allure of quoting Ovid's account in the preface, boasts a double peripety and "recognition by dialogue and signs," and stresses the difficulties of reconciling poetry and myth, and of adapting them both to the stage and the Carnival conventions.[54] Is Pasqualigo's portrait of Thoas a first glimmer of Goethe's? A fuller investigation is needed.[55]

Within the tradition of the Tauris myth, and within the genre of the *dramma per musica*, solutions and characterizations have now begun to oscillate from one extreme to the other. While Pasqualigo made Thoas a friend, another young poet, Gianguelberto Barlocci, discovered in him the stock character of a bloodthirsty tyrant. Barlocci's *Oreste* was performed with music by Benedetto Micheli at the Teatro Capranica in Rome in Carnival 1723. A revised version under the same title was given by George Frederic Handel at London's Covent Garden in December 1734; the composer assembled the music in a *pasticcio* manner from his other operas.[56] This necessitated changes of many aria texts, but hardly affected the plot and scenes. The inspiration for Barlocci's version seems to be Duché de Vancy (1704),

52. Pasqualigo 1719, [8] ('Persone, che cantano'): "D'animo condiscente, amatorio, e meno che Barbaro."
53. Pasqualigo 1719, [8]: "Superstiziosa, e passionata"; "Amico d'Eroica virtù"; "Vario di spirito, & agitato dalle Furie materne"; "Ospitale, & amorosa"; "Amante spregevole di Teonoe".
54. Pasqualigo 1719, 4-5 ('Agli uditori'), at 5: "io per la prima volta, ho osato di maneggiarlo ... in gratia del canto, su le Venete Scene, con invenzione di doppia Peripezia, e riconoscimento per discorso, e per segni, e con qualche disperata difficoltà avvenutami nel framischiare la Dignità della Mitologia, la puntualità della Poetica, e l'Eccellenza dell'Esemplare, con la delicatezza dell'armonia, con le ripugnanze del Teatro, dell'uso, e del Carnovale senza una mostruosa deformità."
55. For the possibility of a humane characterization of Thoas already in Euripides, see Morwood 2002. I am hoping to discuss this and yet other Iphigenia dramas, together with their music, in a different publication.
56. Handel 1991. See Jacobshagen & Mücke 2009, II, 417-21.

with a loving couple added to the brother-sister pair. However, this time it is Orestes who brings his wife, Hermione, with him to Tauris. As a result, the sadistic tyrant can threaten a total of four opponents with death, first individually in varying hostage situations, then all of them together. Iphigenia is ordered to kill Orestes herself on the altar – but Hermione intervenes offering herself in his stead; Iphigenia finds support in her secret lover Phyloctetes, a servant of Thoas who ultimately assembles the rebellious people to overthrow and kill the tyrant. The theatrical ingredients are similar to Capeci's in their restraint. The arias, by contrast, harbor considerable passion, Orestes being particularly vociferous about his rapidly changing emotions. When he and Hermione are both captured, we witness a heart-wrenching contest between the spouses about who is going to die for the other. In conclusion, it seems that the dialogue between Arcadian authors such as Martello, Capeci, Pasqualigo, and Barlocci was only ostensibly about adapting Euripides to the modern stage; it was more essentially about psychology, moral stature, and human relationships.

In the versions after Martello, the issue of recognition was gradually superseded by that of the final reversal, and both these aspects of verisimilitude were eclipsed, in turn, by themes of morality and relationships. This was in fact the general direction European dramaturgy took in those decades: Italian opera participated in it without any interference of the supposed performative needs of the genre. Morality and divine justice are the main themes of our last example, the German *Trauerspiel*, *Orest und Pylades* (originally entitled *Die Geschwister in Taurien*) by Johann Elias Schlegel (1737).[57] Nevertheless, a different spirit seems to breathe in this drama. The poet wrote it aged eighteen and revised it five years later (1742); it is written in elegant alexandrines and suitable as a closet drama, although performances did take place. Schlegel (a friend of Gottsched and later of Holberg) seems not to have read Italian opera libretti, nor even Martello, but he certainly knew the French dramatists, including Lagrange. He aspired to interpreting the great themes of the classics, above all the morality of the gods and of religion: his play opens a chasm between Thoas, on the one hand, and the gods, who abandon cruel sacrifices, on the other. This subject is skillfully moulded through the dialogue, involving several priests and occasionally recalling the critical stance towards formalized religion in Voltaire's *Œdipe* (1718). The ambivalent status of Iphigenia between those worlds is well expressed in these dialogues; she is neither a heroine nor an *innamorata*. Schlegel also realizes the Euripidean concern with purification and with the liberation of Orestes from his

57. Schlegel 1963, 86-123. See also Heitner 1964, 295-7.

furies. The concluding scenes show Thoas, already defeated and mortally wounded, still insisting on revenge and being offered the sacrifice by one after another of the Greeks, until the High Priest can read the divine verdict from a holy book, which justifies Orestes and condemns Thoas.

It seems difficult to classify these ten operas and nine dramas according to their respective approach to the Euripidean version of the myth, or to group them by any other criterion. To start with, we cannot distinguish between a Euripidean and a modern line, insofar as of the three dramas and two operas that adhere most closely to the Greek models – Racine, Zeno, Martello, Rolli, and Schlegel – all but one (Rolli) also remove the *dea ex machina*. There is no distinction either between tragic and happy endings (supposedly a generic difference between Baroque opera and spoken tragedy), because all the nineteen plays have happy endings, as have the two ancient models. Thoas is killed in three dramas and in one opera. Racine and Zeno introduce the tragic death of Eriphyle as if to pay a price for verisimilitude. Of these two most closely related works in the whole group, one is, notably, a French spoken play, the other an Italian opera. Most of the plays elaborate on love and jealousy motivations; only Martello thematicizes a denial of erotic love in Iphigenia, and Schlegel follows the classical model in not having a love element at all. Divine intervention or miracle is avoided in five Italian operas, and the group as a whole is almost evenly split over this issue:

> *Miracle:* Rotrou, Anton Ulrich, Davenant, Postel, Boyer, Duché de Vancy, Tardivelo, Capeci (*Aulide*) , Rolli (four dramas, five operas);
>
> *No miracle:* Racine, Lagrange, Dennis, Riva, Martello, Capeci (*Tauri*) , Zeno, Pasqualigo, Barlocci, Schlegel (five dramas, five operas)

The greatest distance from Euripides' plot is found in the English Tauris drama by Dennis, whereas the Italian Tauris drama by Martello follows the classical text in the closest detail – despite removing the *dea ex machina*. The greatest contrast in the use of spectacle, music, and action exists between the word-centered Racine/Zeno on the one hand, and the spectacle-centered Duché de Vancy on the other, corresponding to a perceived contrast between *tragédie* and *tragédie en musique*. Yet the English plays are more spectacular than most of the Italian operas, despite the fact that one of them presents itself as a translation of Racine's tragedy. Lagrange and Postel cumulate verisimilitude and love interests, but whereas the French author manages without divine apparition, the German indulges in it. The balance between spectacle, *amours*, divine intervention, and verisimilitude is about the same in the two earlier German plays, although Anton Ulrich's work is a play with incidental music, Postel's a fully sung opera. Schlegel stands apart and is closest to Euripides in character treatment; he problematizes divine justice – but he does circumvent the *dea ex machina*.

It is apparent that the social contexts of the performances – the distinctions that can easily be drawn between courtly, academic, and public theater productions – have little relevance for the contents of the works themselves, nor for their respective contributions to the myth. The resources of a courtly *tragédie en musique* were undeniably more spectacular than those of an Italian academic drama such as Martello's; but then, Capeci's *Tauride* libretto for an Italian palace performance imitated Martello's drama in avoiding any spectacle, and Zeno's excessively austere *dramma per musica* was written for the theatrically and musically most resourceful court of the period. A grouping along national or regional lines may be marginally more effective, given some explicit similarities within the Italian tradition, or the relative coherence between the early German and the English plays. The Italian opera performed in England, Rolli's *Ifigenia in Aulide*, may have inherited an English preference for the spectacular. Other evidence nevertheless suggests a general permeability of national traditions, at least allowing for the reception of the French models by all the other nations. In conclusion, we almost physically observe how one poet read and imitated the other, regardless of genre, language or social context, regardless even of whether the play was to be sung or recited. Opera and drama based on classical myth were cultivated by a supranational educated community with little respect for genre divisions: Iphigenia's two lovers obviously enjoyed the dialogue with one another, which partly even disguised their own generic identities.

SPECTATORSHIP AND INVOLVEMENT IN GLUCK'S *IPHIGÉNIE EN TAURIDE*

Bram van Oostveldt

for Gerard Mortier and Valéry De Smedt

COMPASSION

> 3. Je souffrirai donc avec l'autre, mais sans *appuyer*, sans me perdre. Cette conduite, à la fois très affective et très surveillée, très amoureuse et très policée, on peut lui donner un nom: c'est la *délicatesse*: elle est comme la forme 'saine' (civilisée, artistique) de la compassion.
>
> Roland Barthes, *Fragments d'un discours amoureux* (1977)[1]

In an intriguing scene in *Dangerous liaisons* (1988), Stephen Frears' superb film version of Christopher Hampton's homonymous play, Gluck's *Iphigénie en Tauride* is performed at the Paris Opéra. From her box, the wicked Marquise de Merteuil (played by Glenn Close) surveys the public with her binoculars. Her gaze falls upon Chevalier Danceny (Keanu Reeves), who is moved to tears by Iphigenia's famous aria "Ô malheureuse Iphigénie" (Act II, scene 6). Merteuil mocks Danceny's emotional response to her friends by calling him one of those rare eccentrics who attend the opera to listen to the music. The scene subtly interprets the construction of a new and ideal type of spectator in French operatic culture during the last decades of the Ancien Régime. For unlike the Marquise de Merteuil, who goes to the opera to see and be seen, Danceny forgets his surroundings, being totally absorbed by the action on stage.

It is not surprising that Frears' movie touches upon this changing mode of spectatorship and involvement precisely in the context of Christoph Willibald von Gluck and Nicolas François Guillard's *Iphigénie en Tauride*. In his penultimate opera, which premiered at the Académie Royale de Musique on 18 May 1779, Gluck brought French

1. Barthes 1996, III, 514: "COMPASSION. 3. So I shall suffer with the other, but without *pressure*, without losing myself. Such behavior, at once very affective and very controlled, very amorous and very civilized, can be given a name: *delicacy*: in a sense it is the 'healthy' (civilized, artistic) form of compassion." (Translation emended from Barthes 1990, 58.)

operatic reform to its full conclusion. Epitomizing Gluck's ideal of a unified musical drama characterized by "noble simplicity" and subordinating music to poetry "in order to strengthen the expression of the sentiments,"[2] *Iphigénie en Tauride* not only offers a successful answer to the 'abuses' of the past; above all it embodies the ultimate goal of operatic reform as theorized and practiced in the second half of the eighteenth century: to produce a spectator like Chevalier Danceny, whose position vis-à-vis the pain of others is transformed from detachment into emotional involvement.

In this essay, I want to examine how this historical shift in spectatorship can be retraced in *Iphigénie en Tauride*, and how it fits into a wider network of contemporary French discourses on spectatorship. To do so, I will first of all focus on the popularity of the Iphigenia in Tauris myth in reform opera, paying particular attention to the ways in which the story itself answered to new views on spectatorship. Secondly, I will contextualize those views within a contemporary body of theories on drama, theater, and visual arts in order to argue that their concern with the beholder was not merely esthetic, but involved ethics as well.

Shipwreck with spectator

In what follows, the moral dimensions of spectatorship will be explored using *Shipwreck with spectator: paradigm of a metaphor for existence* (*Schiffbruch mit Zuschauer*, 1979), an elegant essay by the German philosopher Hans Blumenberg.[3] In it, Blumenberg investigates the use and development of the seafaring metaphor as a rhetorical figure to describe human existence, its limits, and anxieties from Antiquity to modern times. Until the conquest of the air by the Montgolfières, Blumenberg writes, humans sought to grasp the movement of their existence through the metaphor of the perilous sea voyage. Although the repertory of this metaphor is very rich, its content is somehow disturbing in that it exposes the limits and extremes of human existence. For that particular reason, the metaphor is often used as a warning not to challenge the limits of human condition, since such testing inevitably results into shipwreck. As a cautionary sign for human *hubris*, however, the figure of the

2. Preface to the printed score of *Alceste* (1769) as translated in Newman 1967, 238-9.
3. Blumenberg 1997.

shipwreck is only useful with someone witnessing it. In that case, the spectator in question becomes the locus determining and historicizing the moral dimensions of man's natural boundaries.

In Antiquity, Blumenberg notes, witnessing a shipwreck constituted a profoundly philosophical and epistemological experience. According to Lucretius' *De rerum naturum* (first century BC), for instance, watching a ship perish has nothing to do with taking pleasure in the sufferings of others; rather, it reveals the essential relationship between philosophers and reality. The firm ground of the shore in this case establishes an epistemological basis that gives the spectator the enjoyment of knowing the world and his own position within it.[4]

The beholder's delight in watching shipwrecks acquired new interpretations in the Renaissance. For instance, in the essay *De la solitude* (1588), Montaigne did not justify the pleasure of such spectatorship on account of the right to enjoy one's self-awareness from a distanced position, but rather on the basis of man's successful self-preservation: "By virtue of his capacity for distance," Blumenberg writes, "Montaigne's man stands unendangered on the solid ground of the shore. He survives through one of his most useless qualities: the ability to be a spectator."[5] For Montaigne, in other words, spectatorship becomes a locus of comfort, a pleasure in setting one's own life at stake with as little risk as possible.

On the other hand, Early Modernity also disputed the distanced position of the spectator. In the age of great sea explorers, the oceans had become the true 'global media' in the exchange of capital and goods.[6] Shipwreck having thus become "the price that must be paid in order to avoid that complete calming of the sea that would make all worldly commerce impossible,"[7] the distanced and uninvolved spectator became untenable within the dynamics of early capitalism and imperialism. Instead, spectatorship grew into a state of burning curiosity that demanded full involvement with the drama of human life. No longer was it a question of whether or not to embark on a dangerous sea voyage, or to stay in the safety of the harbor to ensure happiness; in the end, as Blaise Pascal contended in his famous wager, there was no choice but to embark – "Cela n'est pas volontaire, vous êtes embarqué!"[8]

4. Blumenberg 1997, 10-4 and 26-8.
5. Blumenberg 1997, 17.
6. See Sloterdijk 2004, 47-54.
7. Blumenberg 1997, 29.
8. Pascal 2004, 249 (fragment 397): "That is not voluntary, you are embarked."

Iphigenia, operatic reform, and Enlightenment

The 'life-as-sea voyage' metaphor, with its implications of shipwreck and spectatorship, offers an exemplary instrument for understanding the story of Iphigenia and its fame as dramatic subject matter in the Enlightenment. Having been sacrificed in Aulis by her father in order to incite the winds necessary to bring the Greek fleet to Troy, and obliged in Tauris to sacrifice the shipwrecked Greeks (including her own brother Orestes), there is no question of Iphigenia finding consolation in her distanced position on the firm ground of the shore. In both episodes, her spectatorship requires total involvement, which explains why the myth was so favored by attempts to reform opera into an all-round, deeply affecting drama.[9] Its appeal to the enlightened beholder is here to be found in what Francis Lamport has aptly called "cosmic optimism."[10] Indeed, in Enlightenment versions of the story, the ultimate benevolence of divine powers regarding man's fate is increasingly replaced by human agency, which in turn depends on active involvement.

In the eighteenth century, the Iphigenia theme was largely dominated by Racine's tragedy *Iphigénie* (1674). Even when, in 1730, Pierre Brumoy's *Le théâtre des Grecs* was first published, the acquaintance with and beauty of Euripides' *Iphigenia in Aulis* continued to be represented more by Racine's version of the play than by Euripides' tragedy itself.[11] This had mainly to do with Racine's radical adaptation of the ancient story to the strictly rationalist and classicist rules of decorum (*bienséance*) and verisimilitude (*vraisemblance*), which precluded violence and excesses of the marvelous (*merveilleux*).[12] In his famous preface to *Iphigénie*, Racine indeed argued against killing a character as beautiful and virtuous as Iphigenia, while also dismissing the Euripidean intervention of the *deus ex machina*. A supernatural dénouement might have been plausible for the ancients, he asserted, yet it seemed absurd to a 'civilized' seventeenth-century audience, including himself.[13] As a solution, he introduced the character of Eriphyle, who as a mirror image replaces Iphigenia on the altar of human sacrifice.

9. Cummings 1995. See also Gliksohn 1985.
10. Lamport 2004, 41.
11. See Brumoy 1730, I, 103, where he admits that "il m'a parû qu'on ne pouvait mieux sentir les beautés d'Euripide qu'en les rapprochant de celles de Racine." (cited from Cummings 1995, 220)
12. See Oostveldt & Bussels 2012, Garlington 1963, and Reinhard Strohm's chapter in this volume.
13. Racine 1999, 36.

According to Roland Barthes (in *Sur Racine*, 1963), Racine's version of Iphigenia can be seen as an attempt to secularize the tragedy by defining every character in strictly psychological and social terms.[14] Although this process of secularization excludes the divine and mythical completely, which results in the rational triumph of man, Racine's tragedy became problematic for the eighteenth century despite, or even because of, its reputation. First, it rendered every sequel, as envisaged by Euripides' *Iphigenia in Tauris*, impossible, or made it at least implausible. In his own scenario for an *Iphigénie en Tauride* published by his son Louis in 1747, Racine tellingly had pirates kidnap Iphigenia on the shores of Aulis and take her to Tauris – given the presence in Aulis of the entire Greek army, this solution, Lamport ironically remarks, is surely no more *vraisemblable* than a divine miracle.[15]

But Racine's denial of a sequel was not the sole problem faced by eighteenth-century adapters of the Iphigenia theme. To be sure, the clarity and strictness of his tragedy set a promising example to Italian librettists following the ideals of the Arcadian Academy, such as Apostolo Zeno, whose *Ifigenia in Aulide* (Vienna, 1718) enjoyed great popularity. And when, in the second half of the eighteenth century, the arts showed a marked tendency towards neoclassicism, the Iphigenia in Aulis even became a point of reference.[16] Boasting such ancestors as Euripides and Racine, moreover, the play proved very suitable for reforming opera. Thus, in his *Saggio sopra l'opera in musica* (1755), Francesco Algarotti included a scenario for an opera based on Racine's version of the play.[17] And in *Entretiens sur le fils naturel* (1757), Denis Diderot upheld Racine's *Iphigénie* as a perfect libretto that portrayed emotions in their widest nuances, thus deeply affecting the listener.[18] Within this context, it should be no surprise that Gluck and Du Roullet's *Iphigénie en Aulide* (1774), too, was based on Racine's model. But in spite of its popularity, it was not the first Iphigenia that became central to neoclassical opera reform. In her essay on the sources of Gluck's Iphigenia operas, Julie E. Cummings explained why: first, the Aulis plot was too complex to comply with the 'noble simplicity' of neoclassical esthetics; secondly, the character of Agamemnon – as a *pater familias* – proved too morally ambiguous for

14. Barthes 1996, I, 1058-63.
15. Lamport 2004, 44.
16. Cummings 1995, 220-1.
17. Cummings 1995, 221.
18. Diderot 1996, IV, 1186-7: "Je ne connais ni dans Quinault, ni dans aucun poète, des vers plus lyriques, ni de situation plus propre à l'imitation musicale. L'état de Clytemnestre doit arracher de ses entrailles le cri de la nature; et le musicien le portera à mes oreilles dans toutes ses nuances."

bourgeois ethics; finally, Racine's authority was so overwhelming that no playwright or librettist seemed able to surpass his version.[19]

Instead of Aulis, Tauris furnished the ideal subject for operatic reform. Although virtually wiped out by Racine, the myth gained notoriety through François-Joseph de Langrage-Chancel's *Oreste et Pylade* (1697), which remained in print until 1758. This tragedy probably inspired Guimond de La Touche in his *Iphigénie en Tauride* (1757), which twenty-two years later furnished the basis for Gluck and Guillard's *Iphigénie en Tauride*.[20] A narrative explanation for this development can be found in Euripides' version, which constitutes one of the simplest Greek tragedies, featuring only four characters and a plot that is symmetrically constructed around the impending sacrifice of Orestes and Pylades on the one hand, and the recognition of brother and sister on the other.

Morally speaking, Iphigenia's resistance of the cruel tyrant Thoas not only supports the bourgeois ethic of neoclassicism, it also dramatizes the enlightened overthrow of barbarity in favour of a more humane society.[21] This process of emancipation requires human agency, for only when Iphigenia herself has the courage to step out of the darkness into the light of Reason will she be able to throw off her obedience to Thoas and Diana. From this perspective, *Iphigénie en Tauride* can be regarded as a drama of human autonomy, in keeping with the priest Hierarchis' statement in Johann Elias Schlegel's *Orest und Pylades* (1737) – "no Greek will be sacrificed by us any more. You yourselves are worthy of sacrifices and gods on earth"[22] – or with Goethe's *Iphigenie auf Tauris* (1779), which has the relationship between Iphigenia and Thoas evolve according to a more 'governmental' regime of power that highlights the equality of men and their independence from the gods.[23] In this light also we can regard the different eighteenth-century versions of Iphigenia in Tauris as the moral and even political outcome of what Kant advanced as the true nature and the historical significance of Enlightenment.[24]

19. Cummings 1995, 221-2. The morally ambiguous character of Agamemnon as a father who kills his virtuous daughter out of *raison d'état* can be compared to the father-daughter relationships in eighteenth-century bourgeois drama, see Szondi 1973 and Heeg 2000.
20. Lamport 2004, 44-8.
21. Cummings, 223. An interesting perspective on the relationship between divine clemency and human autonomy can be found in Ivan Nagl's study on Mozart's operas, Nagl 1985.
22. Quoted from Lamport 2004, 46-7: "kein Grieche mehr von uns soll geopfert werden / Ihr selbst seyd Opfer werth, und Götter auf der Erden."
23. On the notion of 'governmentality,' see Foucault's essay *La gouvernementalité* (Foucault 1994, III, 635-57).
24. See his epochal answer to the question *Was ist Aufklärung?* as quoted in Cassirer 1962, 163: "Enlightenment is man's exodus from his self-incurred tutelage. Tutelage is the inability to use

To step out of the barbaric darkness is of course no small thing to do. As a fundamental restructuring of society, it shakes that society to the core. It is no coincidence that this societal reform, the logical outcome of which Kant perceived to be the French Revolution,[25] was often described by contemporaries in terms of sublime, natural disasters, such as eruptions, earthquakes, and... storms.[26]

It is indeed as if a gigantic storm can be heard from the very beginning of Gluck's *Iphigénie en Tauride*. Until then, no opera had ever opened in more threatening and convincing a fashion. Striving for a completeness and compactness of drama that could rival that of the Ancients, Gluck no longer separated the overture from the operatic action. "The piece starts," a contemporary critic noted, "with the first strike of the bow and has no Symphony one names properly Overture."[27] As early as in the famous preface to *Alceste* (1769), Gluck himself had argued that the function of the operatic sinfonia was to alert the spectator to the nature of the action to be expected.[28] The overture to *Iphigénie en Tauride* goes even further, presenting a genuine scene that no longer prepares the spectator for the forthcoming action, but itself propels all the action to come.

As Julie Cummings stated, Gluck took the storm idea from Gian Francesco de Majo's *Ifigenia in Tauride* (Mannheim, 1764) whose overture, too, constitutes an autonomous scene. The piece starts with an Allegro con brio, during which Orestes and Pylades' ship is wrecked on the coasts of Tauris. In the ensuing Cantabile, the survivors reach the shore; during the Allegro bellicoso they are captured by the Scythian soldiers, at which moment Iphigenia enters.[29] Gluck reversed the order of the action. His overture begins with a minuet, 'le calme,' which soon turns into a rapidly approaching tempest. At the height of the turmoil, Iphigenia and her priestesses enter, beg for mercy, and summon heaven to end the storm.

one's understanding without the guidance of another person. This tutelage is self-incurred if its cause lies not in any weakness of the understanding without the guidance of another person but in indecision and lack of the courage to use the mind without the guidance of another. 'Dare to know' (*sapere aude*)! Have the courage to use your own understanding; this is the motto of the Enlightenment." On the moral and political dimensions of Kant's question, see also Foucault's essay *Qu'est-ce que les Lumières?* in Foucault 1994, V, 562-78.

25. Safranski 2007, 30-2.
26. See Starobinski 2006, 229-36; Ankersmit 2005, 317-68.
27. Anonymous quoted in Cummings 1995, 227: "La Pièce commence avec le premier coup d'archet, et n'a pas de Symphonie qu'on appelle proprement Ouverture."
28. Newman 1967, 239: "I have thought that the overture should prepare the spectators for the character of the coming action, and give them an indication of its subject."
29. Cummings 1995, 227-8. See the edited score in de Majo 1996, 3-22.

Iphigenia as spectator

From its very outset, *Iphigénie en Tauride* confronts us with interesting insights into the role of the shipwreck metaphor. First, the storm itself precipitates the shipwreck of Orestes and Pylades, and their ensuing search for security on the coasts of Tauris. Secondly, it represents the internal torment of Iphigenia, who is introduced as a witness precisely when the tempest is at its peak. Granted, it is mentioned nowhere in Guillard's libretto that the temple of Diana would be close to the sea.[30] Still, a near-contemporary, the Prince de Ligne, did locate it on the shores of the Black Sea in his *Lettre de Parthenizza* (1787), not on archeological grounds, but rather in response to collective cultural memory.[31] Clearly visible from the seaside, the temple in this location functions as a warning that Tauris is not a safe harbor for seafaring strangers.[32]

But even without geographical 'proof,' Iphigenia is highlighted as a spectator who witnesses the tempest through her inner eye and considers the frightening threat of a sinking ship. Since her spectatorship is in no way detached from the disaster in which she has to take part in her obligation to sacrifice survivors of shipwrecks, there is no question that her position on firm ground constitutes a locus of knowledge, as it did for Lucretius, or a locus of comforting modesty, as was the case for Montaigne. To some extent, we could say that Iphigenia's spectatorship is more closely related to Pascal's interpretation of the seafaring metaphor, in that it affects everyone and allows no escape. The emphasis in Gluck's opera on Iphigenia as a profoundly affected spectator is to be noted particularly when the storm has abated somewhat and Iphigenia cries out: "Le calme reparoit; mais au fonds [sic] de mon cœur, / Hélas! l'orage dure encore."[33] The inner storm that her words allude to will end only when her life – or sea voyage – has ended, a wish she expresses in her most

30. Guillard 1779, 1: "Le Théâtre représente dans le fonds [sic], l'entrée du Temple de DIANE; sur le devant le bois sacré qui le précéde [sic] & l'entoure."
31. Ligne 1902, 23: "'T is on the silvery shores of the Euxine ... at the foot of a rock on which still stands a column, sad relic of the Temple of Diana so famous for the sacrifice of Iphigenia, to the left of the rock whence Thoas hurled strangers ... that I write these words."
32. One should also remark here that the antique name of the Black Sea, *Pontos Euxeinos*, which literally means 'hospitable sea,' was in fact a euphemism for *Pontos Axeinos* or 'inhospitable sea,' mentioned in Strabo's *Geography* (c. 17 AD), Book VII, Chapter 3, section 6.
33. Guillard 1779, 3: "Calm reappears; but deep in my heart, alas! The storm still rages."

beautiful aria to Diana: "O toi, qui prolongeas mes jours, / Reprends un bien que je déteste, / Diane! je t'implore, arrêtes-en le cours."[34]

For the Enlightenment, however, the solution of Christian resignation was of course not an option. As noted earlier, fate could in the enlightened view be overcome only through a public act of human autonomy, as in Goethe's rendering of the Iphigenia story. This transformative act can be traced in *Iphigénie en Tauride*. In its first scenes, Iphigenia still confides in the mercy of the mute gods, most notably Diana; yet gradually she grows aware of the fact that the only way to alter the situation in Tauris is offered not by devout worship, but rather by human agency. At her own risk, she chooses the second path when liberating Pylades and sending him off to Greece with a letter for her sister Electra to call for help. This very act of resistance will change the course of the opera. For only in the aftermath of Thoas' execution, when his guards are fleeing the Greeks, does Diana descend from heaven to stop what has already been accomplished. This delayed appearance of the goddess acknowledges that the divine order can be executed solely through human agency. The intervention of the Greeks alone enables Diana to blame the Scythians, who for much too long have savagely dishonored her laws and altars. And when man is capable of doing what gods cannot achieve, the latter have no choice but to forgive man's sins, which in turn lifts the curse of the Tantalides.[35] In this respect, Guimond de La Touche's tragedy, which served as the basis for Guillard's libretto and also inspired Goethe, was "probably intended as an enlightened, Voltairean critique of religious bigotry and obscurantism."[36]

Iphigenia's spectatorship thus demands to be rethought in the light of the idea that the gods behave as detached, scarcely interested, or even powerless onlookers of the *theatrum vitæ humanæ*. Although as a spectator she is clearly involved or 'embarked,' to use Pascal's term, Iphigenia is not willing to let her 'ship of life' drift on stormy seas, but for the time being she does everything to protect it from shipwreck. To explain thus the relationship between shipwreck and spectator in *Iphigénie en Tauride* we do better to move from Pascal to Voltaire. For Voltaire the relationship between shipwreck and spectator is not one of distance, as it happened to be for

34. Guillard 1779, 5: "O you who prolonged my days, take back a good I detest! Diana! I implore thee, halt their [my days'] course!"

35. King Tantalus was the son of Zeus, the father of Pelops, and the ancestor of Atreus, Agamemnon, Orestes, Iphigenia, and Electra. For his challenging of the Gods, not merely was he himself punished, but his descendants were doomed as well. See Calasso 1993, 149-64.

36. See Lamport 2004, 47.

Lucretius and Montaigne, but one of close involvement as well. This type of involvement clearly differs from Pascal's in that it does not emerge from human fate, but is born out of curiosity.[37] According to Blumenberg, this curiosity in Voltaire's discussion of the metaphor is not merely a sensationalist feeling, but reflects the profoundly passionate state of man. Curiosity is a natural feeling of man that goes along with sensitivity and brings with it the drive to interfere. In Voltaire's view, passions constitute the energy that sets the human world in motion. In his oriental novel *Zadig ou La Destinée* (1748), for instance, he described passions as the "wind that fills the sail of a ship, which, although it sometimes capsizes the ship, is also responsible for its moving at all. ... This life is in fact kept going only by means of things that can also be fatal to us: *Tout est dangereux ici-bas, et tout est nécessaire.*"[38]

Involvement born out of curiosity is not merely the natural state of man; it also provides the key to happiness. In her *Discours sur le bonheur* (published 1779), Voltaire's friend the Marquise du Châtelet held lingering in the harbor and calculating one's chances to be responsible for one not achieving happiness in life. To the doubtful, she said: "Let us hinder them to lose their precious and short time that we have for feeling and thinking and let them prepare their vessels during this time so they can procure the pleasures they will taste during their voyage."[39] Rather than offering an alternative to shipwreck, the harbor can thus only be conceived of as the place of foregone pleasures.[40]

Now that curiosity lies at the basis of Iphigenia's spectatorship, this excitement of mind and body has nothing to do with the pleasure in merely *observing* the sufferings of others. Her view incites involvement, and, once involved, only human agency can bring salvation. Dreams of better worlds will never become reality when they are dreamt on the soft pillows of safety and security. For the Enlightenment, a better and happier world is built by sailors who, despite all difficulties, try to control their ship and show us the audacity through which to conquer the hazardous sea voyage of life.

37. Voltaire 1762, 134-135.
38. Blumenberg 1997, 34. See also Blumenberg 1993, 403-36.
39. Châtelet 1961, 3-4: "Empêchons-les de perdre une partie du temps précieux et court que nous avons à sentir et à penser, & de passer à calfater leur vaisseau le temps qu'ils doivent employer à se procurer les plaisirs qu'ils peuvent goûter dans leur navigation." Châtelet's thoughts on happiness are also dealt with in Mauzi 1994, 460-72.
40. Blumenberg 1997, 35.

The spectator

When life is a sea voyage in which everyone is involved, according to the old *theatrum mundi* topos, theater must be one as well. And what about the spectator in the theater? What is his or her relationship to the shipwrecks witnessed on stage? On this matter, Blumenberg refers to Abbé Ferdinando Galiani,[41] who in a letter to Madame d'Épinay (31 August 1771) agreed with Voltaire that curiosity is inherent in human nature, but at the same time endowed the concept with fewer capabilities than Voltaire did. According to Galiani, it is only because the spectator is standing on firm ground that he is fascinated by the shipwreck: "Curiosity is a passion, or, if you like, a sensation ... The least danger dispels our every curiosity, and we don't occupy ourselves any longer with ourselves and our individuality."[42] The theater, consequently, offers the perfect locus to illustrate the human condition. For only when witnessed from the safe theatre seat is the drama of human shipwreck bearable:

> Here lies the origin of a spectacle. Begin by assuring safe places to the spectators and then expose to their eyes a great risk. Everybody comes to see it and is occupied by it. This brings us to another true idea: the more the spectator is safe, the more the risk he sees is dangerous, the more he is interested in the performance, and this is the key to the entire secret of tragic, comic, and epic art, and so on.[43]

This move from seashore to theater is explained by Blumenberg in terms of a restriction of spectatorship to its purely esthetic dimension. Even so, when seen against the theatrical reforms of the second half of the eighteenth century, Galiani's interpretation of spectatorship is still firmly embedded within an ethics of spectatorship.

Theater reform, as most vividly debated in France, was fundamentally constructed round the problem of spectatorship. In order to enhance the spectator's involvement in the theatrical representation, a series of strategies were developed which, as Michael Fried argued, emerged from the *tableau* esthetic which, oddly enough, was

41. Blumenberg 1997, 39. See also Blumenberg 1993, 406-7.
42. Galiani 1881, 434: "Curiosité est une passion, ou si vous voulez une sensation ... La moindre péril nous ôte toute curiosité, et nous ne nous occupons plus que de nous mêmes et de notre individu."
43. Galiani 1881, 434: "Voilà, l'origine de tous les spectacles. Commencez par assurer de places sûres aux spectateurs, ensuite exposez à leurs yeux un grand risque à voir. Tout le monde court et s'occupe. Cela conduit à une autre idée vraie, c'est que plus le spectateur est sûr, plus le risque qu'il voit est grand, plus il s'intéresse au spectacle, et ceci est la clef de tout le secret de l'art tragique, comique, épique, etc."

built on the exclusion of the spectator.[44] With respect to the paintings by Chardin and Greuze exhibited in the bi-annual *Salons* from the mid 1750s onwards,[45] Diderot and other French art critics were fascinated by the ways in which they depicted characters "in a state or condition of rapt attention, of being completely occupied or engrossed or ... absorbed in what he or she is doing, hearing, thinking, feeling."[46] Their state of absorption gave the illusion that the characters depicted were not aware of being the object of observation. The artist thus neutralized, or even negated, the beholder's presence, which established the fiction that no one was standing in front of the canvas, or that the spectator was altogether excluded from the representation.[47] But precisely because this fiction was established, the beholder's attention could be caught so that his exclusion was transformed into total involvement, resulting in an experience of representation as reality and an emotional attachment to the scene represented.

In order to make the theater approach the naturalness of Chardin and Greuze's paintings – *ut pictura theatrum* – Diderot advocated the introduction of theatrical tableaus. In *De la poésie dramatique* (1758), he advised actors to perform behind an imaginary fourth wall separating the stage from the auditorium.[48] In line with Chardin and Greuze, furthermore, he demanded that the performers on stage create the illusion of not being observed. This plea for naturalness would be supported by a more corporeal style of acting which strove to complement the verbal performance.[49] By producing a maximal visual and auditory impact, Diderot contended, the spectator would be inclined to experience what he saw as real, and this would eventually attach him or her emotionally to the action on stage.

Interestingly, Diderot explained the efficacy of pantomime on the spectator's sensorial experience by using an extract from Act II, scenes 3 and 4 of Guimond de La Touche's *Iphigénie en Tauride*, in which Orestes is haunted by the Eumenids. Instead of merely crying out his despair, Diderot advised that Orestes have his lament accompanied by a variety of physical convulsive movements, as if he were

44. Fried 1988.
45. See among others in particular Diderot's *Salons* of 1759, 1761, and 1767.
46. Fried 1988, 10.
47. The idea of the tableau as excluding the spectator was first expressed by Barthes in his essay *Diderot – Brecht – Eisenstein* (Barthes 1994, II, 1592): "Le tableau (pictural, théâtral, littéraire) est un découpage pur, aux bords nets, irréversible, incorruptible, qui refoule dans le néant tout son entour, innommé, et promeut à l'essence, à la lumière, à la vue, tout ce qui qu'il fait entrer dans son champ." See also Frantz 1998.
48. Diderot 1996, IV, 1310: "Soit donc que vous composiez, soit que vous jouiez, ne pensez non plus au spectateur que s'il n'existait pas. Imaginez sur le bord du théâtre un grand mur qui vous sépare du parterre; jouez comme si la toile ne se levait pas."
49. See Oostveldt 2005, 236-309.

totally absorbed in his psychosis. Only by such action, he stated, would effect of the scene be one of naturalness, attaching the viewer to the representation.[50]

Although these strategies of absorption seemed to exclude the spectator altogether from theatrical representation, this did not at all mean that the latter became the detached, uninvolved onlooker to the sufferings of others. On the contrary, the effect of naturalness served to increase the plausibility or *vraisemblance* of the theatrical representation, which in turn compelled the spectator to identify himself with the emotions performed on the stage. This appeal for emotional attachment was emphasized by contemporary ideas on the transmission of emotions. From his *Pensées sur l'interprétation de la nature* (1751), through *Le rêve de d'Alembert* (1769), to his *Éléments de physiologie* (1780), Diderot himself developed and refined a psychophysical theory that described the working of emotions in terms of highly contagious energy. His arousal theory not only found its way to theoretical notions on acting, as expounded in the writings of Pierre Rémond de Saint-Albine, Antoine-François Riccoboni, and Diderot himself,[51] but also influenced the debate on the effect of music on the passions.[52]

Whether related to painting or theatrical staging, late-eighteenth-century French theater reform developed a number of strategies that advanced the theatrical representation as an autonomous, closed field aiming at the total exclusion of the spectator. Paradoxically, though, these strategies of exclusion were univocally intended to enhance the spectator's involvement in the drama of human shipwreck. As Diderot argued in his *De la poésie dramatique*, full engagement with the theatrical characters made man want to escape the wicked whose company he kept, and made him reconcile himself with the true nature of the human race. Because of this involvement, furthermore, the good and the bad shed their tears together and made them less inclined to do evil in society:

> The auditorium of the theater is the only place where the tears of the virtuous man and of the wicked are fused. There, the wicked man is irritated by the injustices he would have committed; he is compassionate for the sorrows he would have caused and is criticizing a man of his own character. But the impression is received, it stays with us, in spite of us; and the wicked man leaves his box less disposed to do evil then if he was lectured by harsh and strict orator.[53]

50. Diderot 1996, IV, 1338-9.
51. See Oostveldt 2005, 276-309, and Roach 1985, 116-59.
52. See Kivy 1988, 97-178.
53. Diderot 1996, IV, 1282-3: "Le parterre de la comédie est le seul endroit où les larmes de l'homme vertueux et du méchant soient confondues. Là, le méchant s'irrite contre des injustices qu'il aurait

In sum, the distanced spectator Galiani spoke of did not merely estheticize the shipwreck-and-spectator metaphor, as Blumenberg suggested; contextualized within contemporary French theory regarding spectatorship, this distanced position surprisingly enough increased the interest or involvement of the spectator.

Conclusion: The Moral Tears of the Impartial Spectator

The popularity of the Iphigenia in Tauris theme in eighteenth-century opera and drama can be explained by its optimistic stance towards human progress. In Enlightenment versions of the story, the ultimate benevolence of divine powers regarding man's fate was substituted by human agency. Yet, the transgression of barbaric darkness in favour of Reason and autonomy required utter involvement. An uninvolved Iphigenia, in this respect, was not permitted within the enlightened realm of fiction. To free herself from tyranny, religious bigotry, and obscurantism, and to ensure happiness in life, Iphigenia could not leave her ship adrift on stormy seas, but had to control it with audacity and risk.

Should it appear that the mortal dangers of life as sea voyage were experienced solely as an esthetic pleasure, late eighteenth-century theater reform also employed specific strategies to attach the spectator to the theatrical performance. As a result, the auditorium was ideally the place where a righteous man like Chevalier Danceny shed his tears in the company of others. And even though this artistic compassion was 'civilized' and 'delicate,' not to say sentimental, he transcended the purely esthetic pleasure of observing the pain of others. In its renewed claim as legitimate heir of ancient tragedy, the late-eighteenth-century (musical) theater inscribed itself within a bourgeois enlightened ideology that ensured its operation as a public school of morals. At best, it established a community of spectators whose capacity for compassion helped constitute the identity of the rightful and respectable Citizen. In our

commises; compatit à des maux qu'il aurait occasionnés, et s'indigne contre un homme de son propre caractère. Mais l'impression est reçue; elle demeure en nous, malgré nous; et le méchant sort de sa loge moins disposé à faire le mal que si'il eût été gourmandé par un orateur sévère et dur."

postmodern society of consumers, by contrast, this idea of theater as instrument for humanist *Bildung* is often considered the charming, but unprofitable and hopelessly outdated, legacy of modernity. Maybe we should think again!

BIBLIOGRAPHY

ALGAROTTI, Francesco (1763). *Saggio sopra l'opera in musica* [rev. ed.; orig. publ. 1755]. Livorno: Coltellini.

ALLEN Walter jr. (1940). The epyllion: a chapter in the history of literary criticism. *Transactions of the American Philological Association*, 71, 1-26.

ANDERSON, David (1988). *Before the knight's tale: imitation of classical epic in Boccaccio's* Teseida. Philadelphia, PA: University of Pennsylvania Press.

ANDREINI, Francesco; Tessari, Roberto (Ed.) (1987). *Le bravure del capitano Spavento*. Pisa: Giardini.

ANDREINI, Giovanni Battista (2004). *La Centaura*. Genoa: Il Nuovo Melangolo.

ANKERSMIT, Frank R. (2005). *Sublime historical experience*. Stanford, CA: Stanford University Press.

ANONYMOUS; Fabbri, Paolo; Pompilio, Angelo (Eds.) (1983). *Il Corago, o vero Alcune osservazioni per metter bene in scena le composizioni drammatiche* [written c. 1628-37]. Florence: Olschki.

ANTON ULRICH of Braunschweig-Lüneburg; Spahr, Blake Lee (Ed.) (1982-5). *Bühnendichtungen*. Stuttgart: Hiersemann.

APOLLODORUS; Frazer, James G. (Ed. and Trans.) (1921). *The library*. Cambridge, MA; London: Harvard University Press.

APULEIUS, Lucius; Adlington, William (Trans.) (1566). *The story of Cupid and Psyche* [orig. publ. 1639]. Online: http://ancienthistory.about.com/library/bl/bl_cupid-andpsyche.htm (Accessed 28 December 2009).

APULEIUS, Lucius (s.d.). Apulei Psyche et Cupido. In *Metamorphoseon*, IV. Online: www.thelatinlibrary.com/apuleius/apuleius.cupid.shtml (Accessed 28 December 2009).

ARISTOPHANES; Dover, Kenneth James (Ed.) (1993). *Frogs*. Oxford: Clarendon.

ARISTOPHANES; Henderson, Jeffrey (Ed. and Trans.) (2002). *Frogs, Assemblywomen, Wealth*. Cambridge, MA; London: Harvard University Press.

ARISTOTLE; Lucas, D. W. (Ed.) (1972). *Poetics*. Oxford: Clarendon.

ARISTOTLE; Janko, Richard (Ed.) (1987). *Poetics with the Tractatus Coislinianus; a hypothetical reconstruction of Poetics II; The fragments of On the poets*. Indianapolis, IN; Cambridge: Hackett.

ASPDEN, Suzanne (2001). Ariadne's clew: politics, allegory and opera in London (1734). *Musical quarterly*, 85(4), 735-70.

AUBIGNAC, François Hédelin d' (1715). *La pratique du théatre* [orig. publ. 1657]. Amsterdam: Bernard.

AUBIGNAC, François Hédelin d'; Baby, Hélène (Ed.) (2001). *Pratique du théâtre* [orig. publ. 1657]. Paris: Champion.

BADOARO, Giacomo (1644). *L'Ulisse errante. Opera musicale*. Venice: Pinelli.

BALTUS, Jean-François (1707). *Réponse à l'histoire des* oracles. Paris: s.l.

BANIER, Antoine (1715). *Explication historique des fables, où l'on découvre leur origine et leur conformité avec l'histoire ancienne* [2nd ed.; orig. publ. 1711]. Amsterdam: Le Breton.

BARTHES, Roland; Howard, Richard (Trans.) (1990). *A lover's discourse: fragments* [orig. publ. as *Fragments d'un discours amoureux*, 1977]. Harmondsworth: Penguin.

BARTHES, Roland; Marty, Eric (Ed.) (1996). *Œuvres complètes*. Paris: Seuil.

BARTOLINI, Nicolò Enea (1643). *La Venere gelosa* [genre unspecified]. Padua: Frambotto.

BATTEUX, Charles (1746). *Les beaux-arts réduits à un même principe*. Paris: Durand.

BIANCONI, Lorenzo; Bryant, David (Trans.) (1987). *Music in the seventeenth century* [orig. publ. as *Il Seicento*, 1982]. Cambridge: Cambridge University Press.

BIRKERICK, Anne (1998). *Reading undercover: audience and authority in Jean de La Fontaine*. Lewisburg, PA: Bucknell University Press.

BISSARI, Pietro Paulo [ps. Rincorto, Academico Olimpico] (1648). *La Torilda. Dramma*. Venice: Valvasense.

BLONDEL, David (1649). *Des Sibylles célèbres tant par l'antiquité payenne que par les S. Pères*. Paris: Perier.

BLUMENBERG, Hans; Wallace, Robert M. (Trans.) (1985). *Work on myth* [orig. publ. as *Arbeit am Mythos*, 1979]. Cambridge: Cambridge University Press.

BLUMENBERG, Hans; Wallace, Robert M. (Trans.) (1993). *The legitimacy of the modern age* [orig. publ. as *Die Legitimität der Neuzeit*, 1966]. Cambridge, MA; London: MIT Press.

BLUMENBERG, Hans; Rendall, Stephen (Trans.) (1997). *Shipwreck with spectator: paradigm of a metaphor for existence* [orig. publ. as *Schiffbruch mit Zuschauer*, 1979]. Cambridge, MA: MIT Press.

BOSSUET, Jacques-Bénigne (1681). *Discours sur l'histoire universelle* [written 1679]. Paris: Marbre-Cramoisy.

BOTTAZZONI, Pietro Francesco (1733). *Lettere discorsive intorno ad alcuni poetici abusi pregiudizievoli al decoro della religion cattolica come alla buona morale cristiana opera postuma*. Naples: Moscheni.

BOUCHARD, Marcel (1947). *L'histoire des oracles de Fontenelle*. Paris: SFELT.

BOUCHET, Laurent (1645). *Les oracles des sybilles* [sic] *et leurs profonds respects envers Jésus-Christ naissant en Bethléem*. Paris: Jolybois.

BOYER, Abel (1700). *Achilles, or, Iphigenia in Aulis. A tragedy as it is acted at the Theatre Royal in Drury-lane*. London: Bennet.

BOYLE, Anthony James (1997). *Tragic Seneca: an essay in theatrical tradition.* London; New York, NY: Routledge.

BRACCIOLINI, Francesco (1628). *Lo scherno degli Dei.* Rome: Ferroni.

BROCKPÄHLER, Renate (1964). *Handbuch zur Geschichte der Barockoper in Deutschland.* Emsdetten: Lechte.

BROWN, Jane K. (2006). Orest, Orlando, Orpheus oder: der Held von Goethes *Iphigenie.* In Udo Bermbach & Hans Rudolf Vaget (Eds.), *Getauft auf Musik: Festschrift für Dieter Borchmeyer* (pp. 55-65). Würzburg: Königshausen & Neumann.

BRUMOY, Pierre (1730). *Le théâtre des Grecs.* Paris: Rollin; Coignard.

BURGESS, Geoffrey (1998). *Ritual in the tragédie en musique from Lully's* Cadmus et Hermione *(1673) to Rameau's* Zoroastre *(1749).* Ph.D. dissertation, Cornell University.

BURKERT, Walter (1979). *Structure and history in Greek mythology and ritual.* Berkeley and Los Angeles, CA; London: University of California Press.

BURNEY, Charles (1789). *A general history of music from the earliest ages to the present period.* London: Payne et al.

BURROWS, Donald (1994). *Handel.* Oxford: Oxford University Press.

BUSENELLO, Giovan Francesco (1656). Gli amori di Apollo e Dafne. In *Delle hore ociose* (s.n.). Venice: Giuliani.

BUSONI, Ferruccio (1973). *Entwurf einer neuen Ästhetik der Tonkunst* [orig. publ. 1916]. Hamburg: Wagner.

BUSONI, Ferruccio; Ley, Rosamond (Trans.) (1965). *The essence of music and other papers.* New York, NY: Dover.

BUSSANI, Giacomo Francesco (1685). *Enea in Italia. Drama per musica.* Venice: Nicolini.

CABANI, Maria Cristina (2002). La *Franceide* di Giambattista Lalli. In Various, *I capricci di Proteo: percorsi e linguaggi del barocco. Atti del convegno di Lecce, 23-26 ottobre 2000* (pp. 693-716). Rome: Salerno.

CALASSO, Robert; Parks, Tim (Trans.) (1993). *The marriage of Cadmus and Harmony* [orig. publ. as *Le nozze di Cadmo e Armonia*, 1988]. New York, NY: Vintage.

CALZABIGI, Ranieri de' (1994). *Dissertazione su le poesie drammatiche del Signore Abate Pietro Metastasio* [orig. publ. in 1755]. In Anna Laura Bellina (Ed.), *Scritti teatrali e letterari*, I (pp. 22-146). Rome: Salerno.

CAPECI, Carlo Sigismondo (1713a). *Ifigenia in Aulide. Dramma per musica.* Rome: de' Rossi.

CAPECI, Carlo Sigismondo (1713b). *Ifigenia in Tauri. Dramma per musica.* Rome: de' Rossi.

CARSE, Adam (1964). *The history of orchestration* [orig. publ. 1925]. New York, NY: Dover.

CASSIRER, Ernst; Kölln, Fritz & Pettegrove, James (Transl.) (1962). *The philosophy of the Enlightenment* [orig. publ. as *Die Philosophie der Aufklärung*, 1932]. Boston, MA: Beacon.

CATULLUS; Kroll, Wilhelm (Ed.) (1989). *C. Valerius Catullus*. Stuttgart: Teubner.

CHÂTELET, Émilie du; Mauzi, Robert (Ed.) (1961). *Discours sur le bonheur*. Paris: Les Belles Lettres.

CHAVANNES, Claire (2004). *Aurelio Aureli et l'opéra vénitien du XVIIe siècle*. MA thesis, Université de Paris III – Sorbonne-Nouvelle.

CHIARELLI, Alessandra; POMPILIO, Angelo (2004). *"Or vaghi or fieri": cenni di poetica nei libretti veneziani (circa 1640-1740)*. Bologna: CLUEB.

CLAUSTRE, André de; Anonymous (Trans.) (1793). *Dizionario mitologico ovvero delle favole. Ricavate dalla poetica istoria per istruzione della gioventù* [orig. publ. as *Dictionnaire de mythologie*, 1745]. Rome: Mercante.

COLLASSE, Pascal (1690). *Énée et Lavinie*. Full score, Paris: Ballard.

COLLASSE, Pascal (1716). *Thétis et Pelée* [2nd ed.; premiered 1689]. Short score, Paris: Ballard.

CORNEILLE, Pierre; Stegmann, André (Ed.) (1963). *Œuvres complètes*. Paris: Seuil.

CORRADI, Giulio Cesare (1675). *La divisione del mondo. Dramma per musica*. Venice: Nicolini.

CRUMP, Mary M. (1931). *The epyllion from Theocritus to Ovid*. Oxford: Blackwell.

CUMMINGS, Julie E. (1995). Gluck's Iphigenia operas: sources and strategies. In Thomas Bauman & Marita Petzoldt McClymonds (Eds.), *Opera and the Enlightenment* (pp. 217-40). Cambridge: Cambridge University Press.

GAGLIANO, Marco da (1608). *La Dafne*. Florence: Marescotti.

DALE, Antoine van (1683). *De oraculis ethnicorum dissertationes duæ: quarum prior de ipsorum duratione ac defectu, posterior de eorundem auctoribus. Accedit et schediasma de consecrationibus ethnicis*. Amsterdam: Boom.

DALLA VALLE, Daniela (1982). Les dieux cachés (ou le conceptisme des dieux): les oracles dans le genre pastoral au XVIIe siècle. In Louise Godard de Donville (Ed.), *La mythologie au XVII siècle* (pp. 145-52). Marseille: CMR.

DEAN, Winton (2006). *Handel's operas, 1726-1741*. Woodbridge, Suffolk: Boydell.

DEAN, Winton; KNAPP, J. Merrill (1995). *Handel's operas, 1704-1726* [Rev. ed.; orig. publ. 1987]. Oxford: Clarendon.

DE MAJO, Gian Francesco de; Corneilson, Paul (Ed.) (1996). *Ifigenia in Tauride. Dramma per musica*. Full score, Madison, WI: A-R Editions.

DENNIS, John (1700). *Iphigenia. A tragedy acted at the theatre of Little Lincoln's Inn-Fields*. London: Parker.

DESMARETS, Henri & CAMPRA, André (1711). *Iphigénie en Tauride. Tragédie mise en musique*. Paris: Ballard.

DI CEGLIE, Roberto (1997). Il *Dialogo sopra la poesia dramatica* di Ottaviano Castelli. *Studi secenteschi*, *38*, 319-55.

DIDEROT, Denis; Versini, Laurent (Ed.) (1996). *Œuvres*. Paris: Laffont.

DIDEROT, Denis; D'ALEMBERT, Jean le Rond (Eds.) (1751-72). *Encyclopédie ou dictionnaire raisonné des sciences des arts et des métiers*. Paris: Briasson et al.

DONALDSON, Ethelbert Talbot (1985). *The swan at the well: Shakespeare reading Chaucer*. New Haven, CT; London: Yale University Press.

DRYDEN, John (1713). *Fables, ancient and modern*. London: Tonson.

ELIADE, Mircea (1991). Toward a definition of myth. In Y. Bonnefoy et al. (Eds.), *Mythologies*, I (pp. 3-5). Chicago, IL; London: University of Chicago Press.

ERRICO, Scipione (1634). *I liti di Pindo*. Messina: Bianco.

ERRICO, Scipione; Ricci, Gino (Ed.) (2004). *Le guerre di Parnaso*. Lecce: Argo.

EURIPIDES (1703). *Tragœdiæ Medea et Phœnissæ, Græco-Latinæ*. Cambridge: Cambridge University Press.

EURIPIDES; Jouan, François; Van Looy, Herman (Ed. and Trans.) (1998-2003). *Fragments*. Paris: Les Belles Lettres.

EURIPIDES; Collard, Christopher; Cropp, Martin (Ed. and Trans.) (2008). *Fragments*. Cambridge, MA; London: Harvard University Press.

FABBRI, Paolo (1984). Lessico monteverdiano: intorno al "genere rappresentativo." In F. Passadore (Ed.), *La musica nel veneto dal XVI al XVIII secolo* (pp. 89–97). Adria: Antiquæ Musicæ Italicæ Studiosi.

FADER, Don (2000). *Musical thought and patronage of the Italian style at the Court of Philippe II, Duc d'Orléans (1674-1723)*. Ph.D. dissertation, Stanford University.

FELDMAN, Martha (2007). *Opera and sovereignty: transforming myths in eighteenth-century Italy*. Chicago, IL; London: University of Chicago Press.

FÉNELON, François de Pons de Salignac de La Motte (1970). Projet d'un traité sur la tragédie. In Ernesta Caldarini (Ed.), *Lettre à l'Académie (avec les versions primitives)* (pp. 89-99). Geneva: Droz.

FIASCHINI, Fabrizio (2006). *L'"Incessabil agitazione": Giovan Battista Andreini tra professione, cultura e religione*. Pisa, Rome: Serra.

FLEMMING, Willi (Ed.) (1933). *Die Oper*. Leipzig: Reclam.

FLETCHER, John; SHAKESPEARE, William; Waith, Eugene M. (Ed.) (1989). *The two noble kinsmen* [orig. publ. 1634]. Oxford: Clarendon.

FLETCHER, John; SHAKESPEARE, William; Potter, Lois (Ed.) (1997). *The two noble kinsmen* [orig. publ. 1634]. Walton-on-Thames, Surrey: Nelson.

FONTENELLE, Bernard Le Bovier de; Maignon, Louis (Ed.) (1908). *Histoire des oracles* [orig. publ. 1687]. Paris: Cornély.

FORD, Andrew (2002). *The origins of criticism: literary culture and poetic theory in classical Greece*. Princeton, NJ; Oxford: Princeton University Press.

FORMENT, Bruno (2007a). *'La terra, il cielo e l'inferno': the representation and reception of Greco-Roman mythology* in opera seria. Ph.D. dissertation, Ghent University.

FORMENT, Bruno (2007b). Dall''effeminato' al 'virtuoso': modelli d'identità di genere nel 'Telemaco' (1718) di Alessandro Scarlatti. *Rivista italiana di musicologia*, 40(1-2), 85-112.

FORMENT, Bruno (2009), Trimming scenic invention: oblique perspective as poetics of discipline. *Music in art: international journal of music iconography*, *34*(1-2), 31-43.

FORMENT, Bruno (2010a). The gods out of the machine... and their comeback. In Peter Brown & Suzana Ograjenšek (Eds.), *Ancient drama in music for the modern stage* (pp. 193-209). Oxford: Oxford University Press.

FORMENT, Bruno (2010b). Jommelli's 'tenacious memory': replications in L'*Ifigenìa* (1751). *Studi musicali*, *38*(2), 361-87.

FOUCAULT, Michel (1994). *Dits et écrits* [orig. publ. 1954-88]. Paris: Gallimard.

FRANTZ, Pierre (1998). *L'esthétique du tableau dans le théâtre du XVIIIe siècle*. Paris: Presses Universitaires de France.

FRIED, Michael (1988). *Absorption and theatricality: painting and beholder in the age of Diderot*. Chicago, IL: Chicago University Press.

FUMAROLI, Marc (1997). *Le poète et le roi: Jean de La Fontaine en son siècle*. Paris: Fallois.

FUMAROLI, Marc (2001). Les abeilles et les araignées. In Anne-Marie Lecoq (Ed.), *La querelle des anciens et des modernes, XVIIe-XVIIIe siècles* (pp. 7-218). Paris: Gallimard.

FURETIÈRE, Antoine (1690). *Dictionnaire universel: contenant generalement tous les mots françois tant vieux que modernes, et les termes de toutes les sciences et des arts*... Amsterdam, The Hague: Leers.

GAISSER, Julia Haig (2007). Threads in the labyrinth: competing views and voices in Catullus 64. In *Catullus* (pp. 217-58). Oxford: Oxford University Press.

GALILEI, Vincenzo (1581). *Dialogo della musica antica e moderna*. Florence: Marescotti.

GALIANI, Ferdinando (1881). *Correspondance avec Madame d'Épinay, Madame Necker, Madame Geoffrin, etc. Diderot, Grimm, de Sartine, d'Holbach, etc.* Paris: Calmann Lévy.

GAMERRA, Giovanni de (1789). Osservazioni sullo spettacolo in generale. In *Novo teatro*, I (pp. 6-56). Pisa: Prosperi.

GANTZ, Timothy (1993). *Early Greek myth: guide to literary and artistic sources*. Baltimore, MD; London: Johns Hopkins University Press.

GARLINGTON, Aubrey S. (1963). 'Le merveilleux' and operatic reform in 18th-century French opera. *Musical quarterly*, 49(4), 484-97.

GAUTRUCHE, Pierre; D'Assigny, Marius (Trans.) (1701). *The poetical history, being a compleat collection of all the stories necessary for the perfect understanding of the Greek and Latine poets ... now Englished* [8th ed.; orig. publ. as *Historia poetica ad faciliorem pœtarum et veterum auctorum intelligentiam*, s.d.]. London: Collins.

GIANTURCO, Carolyn (2001). Accompanied recitative in seventeenth-century Italy: a brief history. In Nicole Ristow et al. (Eds.),"*Critica musica*": *Studien zum 17. und 18. Jahrhundert. Festschrift Hans Joachim Marx zum 65. Geburtstag* (pp. 83-96). Stuttgart, Weimar: Metzler.

GLIKSOHN, Jean-Michel (1985). *Iphigénie de la Grèce antique à l'Europe des lumières*. Paris: Presses Universitaires de France.

GLIXON, Beth Lise, *Recitative in seventeenth-century Venetian opera: its dramatic function and musical language*. Ph.D. dissertation, Rutgers University.

GRAF, Fritz; Marier, Thomas (Trans.) (1993). *Greek mythology: an introduction* [orig. publ. as *Griechische Mythologie*, 1987]. Baltimore, MD: Johns Hopkins University Press.

GRENE, David; LATTIMORE, Richmond (Eds.) (1960). *The complete Greek tragedies*. Chicago, IL: University of Chicago Press.

GRONDA, Giovanna (1990). *La carriera di un librettista: Pietro Pariati da Reggio di Lombardia*. Reggio Emilia: Il Mulino.

GSTREIN, Rainer (1997). *Die Sarabande: Tanzgattung und musikalischer Topos*. Vienna: Studien; Lucca: LIM.

GUILLARD, Nicolas-François (1779). *Iphigénie en Tauride. Tragédie*. Paris: Lormel.

HALL, Edith & MACINTOSH, Fiona (2005). *Greek tragedy and the British theatre 1660-1914*. Oxford: Oxford University Press.

HANDEL, George Frideric; Chrysander, Friedrich (Ed.). (1874). *Teseo. Opera* [premiered 1713]. Full score, Leipzig: Deutsche Händelgesellschaft.

HANDEL, George Frideric; Chrysander, Friedrich (Ed.). (1881). *Arianna in Creta. Opera* [premiered 1734]. Full score, Leipzig: Deutsche Händelgesellschaft.

HANDEL, George Frideric; Chrysander, Friedrich (Ed.). (1884). *Faramondo. Opera* [premiered 1737]. Full score, Leipzig: Deutsche Händelgesellschaft.

HANDEL, George Frideric; Chrysander, Friedrich (Ed.). (1886). *Jephtha. Oratorium* [premiered 1752]. Full score, Leipzig: Deutsche Händelgesellschaft.

HANDEL, George Frideric; Baselt, Bernd (Ed.) (1991). *Oreste. Opera* [premiered 1734]. Full score, Kassel a.o.: Bärenreiter.

HARDIE, Phillip (1997). Virgil and tragedy. In Charles Martindale (Ed.), *The Cambridge companion to Virgil* (pp. 312-26). Cambridge: Cambridge University Press.

HARRIS, Ellen (Ed.) (1989). *The librettos of Handel's operas*. New York, NY; London: Garland.

HAUFE, Eberhard (1994). *Die Behandlung der antiken Mythologie in den Textbüchern der Hamburger Oper 1678-1738*. Frankfurt a.o.: Lang.

HEARTZ, Daniel; BAUMANN, Thomas (1990). *Mozart's operas*. Berkeley and Los Angeles, CA; London: California University Press.

HEEG, Gunther (2000). *Das Phantasma der natürlichen Gestalt: Körper, Sprache und Bild im Theater des 18. Jahrhunderts*. Frankfurt, Basel: Stroemfeld.

HEITNER, Robert R. (1964). The Iphigenia in Tauris theme in drama of the eighteenth century. *Comparative literature*, 16(4), 289-309.

HELLER, Wendy (2005). The beloved's image: Handel's *Admeto* and the statue of Alcestis. *Journal of the American Musicological Society*, 58(3), 559-638.

HILLER, Johann Adam (1774). *Anweisung zum musikalisch-richtigen Gesange*. Leipzig: Junius.

HOXBY, Blair (2005). The doleful airs of Euripides: the origins of opera and the spirit of tragedy reconsidered. *Cambridge opera journal*, 17(3), 253-69.

HUGHES, Derek (2007). *Culture and sacrifice: ritual death in literature and opera*. Cambridge: Cambridge University Press.

IVANOVICH, Cristoforo (1681). Memorie teatrali di Venezia. Appendix to *Minerva al tavolino*. Venice: Pezzana.

JACOBSHAGEN, Arnold & MÜCKE, Panja (2009). *Händels Opern*. Laaber: Laaber.

JANKO, Richard (1992). From catharsis to the Aristotelian mean. In Amélie Oksenberg Rorty (Ed.), *Essays on Aristotle's* Poetics (pp. 341-58). Princeton, NJ: Princeton University Press.

KERMAN, Joseph (1988). *Opera as drama* [rev. ed.; orig. publ. 1956]. Berkeley and Los Angeles, CA: California University Press.

KETTERER, Robert C. (2001). Handel's *Scipione* and the neutralization of politics. *Newsletter of the American Handel Society*, 15(1), 1 and 4-8.

KETTERER, Robert C. (2003). Why early opera is Roman and not Greek. *Cambridge opera journal*, 15(1), 1-14.

KETTERER, Robert C. (2009). *Ancient Rome in early opera*. Urbana and Chicago, IL: University of Illinois Press.

KIMBELL, David R. B. (1963). The libretto of Handel's 'Teseo.' *Music & Letters*, 44(4), 371-9.

KIMBELL, David R. B. (1991). *Italian opera*. Cambridge; New York, NY: Cambridge University Press.

KINTZLER, Catherine (1991). *Poétique de l'opéra français de Corneille à Rousseau*. Paris: Minerve.

KIVY, Peter (1988). *Osmin's rage: philosophical reflections on opera*. Princeton, NJ: Princeton University Press.

LA FONTAINE, Jean de; Marmier, Jean (Ed.) (1965). *Œuvres complètes*. Paris: Seuil.

LA GORCE, Jérôme de (2002). *Jean-Baptiste Lully*. Paris: Fayard.

LA MESNARDIÈRE, Hippolyte-Jules Pilet de (1639). *La poëtique*. Paris: Sommaville.

LA MOTTE, Antoine Houdar de; Haym, Nicolà or Rossi, Giacomo (Trans.) (1715). *Amadis of Gaul. An opera* [*Amadigi*]. London: Tonson.

LAMPORT, Francis (2004). "Und Götter auf der Erden": humanity and divinity in some Enlightenment versions of the Iphigenia story. *Forum for modern language studies* 40(1), 41-55.

LATTARICO, Jean-François (2008). 'Quand les mouches contre-attaquent': à propos de la *Moscheide* de Giambattista Lalli (1624). *Italies*, 12, 59-82.

LAURENTI, Jean-Noël (2002). *Valeurs morales et religieuses sur la scène de l'Académie Royale de Musique (1669-1737)*. Geneva: Droz.

LIGNE, Charles Joseph de; Prescott Wormeley, Katharine (Trans. & Ed.) (1902). *The Prince de Ligne: his memoirs, letters and miscellaneous papers*. Boston, MA: Hardy, Pratt & Company.

LOPE DE VEGA; Garcia Santo-Tomas, Enrique (Ed.) (2006). *Arte nuevo de hacer comedias en este tiempo* [orig. publ. 1609]. Madrid: Catedra.

LOREDANO, Giovan Francesco (1654). *L'Iliade giocosa* [orig. publ. 1653]. Venice: Guerigli.

LULLY, Jean-Baptiste (1684). *Amadis*. Full score, Paris: Ballard.

LULLY, Jean-Baptiste (1697). *Bellérophon* [premiered 1679]. Short score, Paris: Ballard.

LULLY, Jean-Baptiste (1720). *Psyché* [premiered 1678]. Full score, Paris: Ballard.

LULLY, Jean-Baptiste (2008). *Psyché* [Boston Early Music Festival Orchestra and Chorus directed by Paul O'Dette and Stephen Stubbs]. Compact disc, CPO 7773672.

LYNE, R. O. A. M. (Ed.) (1978). *Ciris: a poem attributed to Virgil*. Cambridge: Cambridge University Press.

MAIRET, Jean de (1925). *Chryséide et Arimand* [premiered 1625]. Paris: Presses Universitaires de France.

MANUWALD, Gesine (2005). Nero and Octavia in Baroque opera: their fate in Monteverdi's 'Poppea' and Keiser's *Octavia*. *Ramus: critical studies in Greek and Roman literature*, 34(2), 152-66.

MANUWALD, Gesine (2008). Study on Seneca's fate and the reality significance of Seneca in the *Octavia* and in Monteverdi's opera *L'incoronazione di Poppea*. *Antike und Abendland*, 54, 129-40.

MARTELLO, Pier Jacopo; Noce, Hannibal S. (Ed.) (1981). *Teatro*. Bari: Laterza.

MARX, Hans Joachim & SCHRÖDER, Dorothea (1995). *Die Hamburger Gänsemarkt-Oper: Katalog der Textbücher (1678-1748)*. Laaber: Laaber.

MAUZI, Robert (1994). *L'idée du bonheur dans la littérature et la pensée françaises au XVIIIe siècle*. Paris: Michel.

McCLYMONDS, Marita Petzoldt (1989). The Venetian role in the transformation of Italian opera seria during the 1790s. In Maria Teresa Muraro and David Bryant (Eds.), *I vicini di Mozart* (pp. 221-40). Florence: Olschki.

MENEGATTI, Tiziana (2000). *"Ex ignotos notus": bibliografia delle opere a stampa del principe degli Incogniti, Giovan Francesco Loredano*. Padua: Il Poligrafo.

METASTASIO, Pietro; Hoole, John (Trans.) (1800). *Dramas and other poems of the Abbé Pietro Metastasio*. London: Otridge et al.

METASTASIO, Pietro; Brunelli, Bruno (Ed.) (1965). *Tutte le opere* [2nd ed.; orig. publ. 1947]. Milan: Mondadori.

METASTASIO, Pietro; Selmi, Elisabetta (Ed.) (1998). *Estratto dell'arte poetica di Aristotile* [orig. publ. 1783]. Palermo: Novecento.

METASTASIO, Pietro; Bellina, Anna Laura (Ed.) (2002-4). *Drammi per musica*. Venice: Marsilio.

MILLS, Sophie (1997). *Theseus, tragedy and the Athenian empire*. Oxford: Clarendon.

MOLIÈRE; Wall, Charles H. (Trans.) (s.d.) *Psyché*. Online: http://www.fullbooks.com/Psyche.html (Accessed 30 December 2009).

MOLIÈRE; Jouanny, Robert (Ed.) (1962). *Œuvres complètes*. Paris: Garnier.

MONELLE, Raymond (1978). Recitative and dramaturgy in the dramma per musica. *Music & Letters*, 59(3), 245-67.

MONSON, Dale E.; WESTRUP, Jack; BUDDEN, Julian (2001). Recitative. In Stanley Sadie (Ed.), *The new Grove dictionary of music and musicians*, XXI (pp. 1-6). London: Macmillan.

MONTEVERDI, Claudio (1615). *L'Orfeo. Favola in musica* [premiered 1607]. Full score, Venice: Amadino.

MORINI, Agnès (1994). *Sous le signe de l'inconstance: la vie et l'œuvre de Giovan Francesco Loredano (1606-1661), noble vénitien, fondateur de l'Académie des Incogniti*. Ph.D. dissertation, Université de Paris-IV Sorbonne.

MORWOOD, James (2002). *The plays of Euripides*. Bristol: Bristol Classical.

MURATORI, Lodovico Antonio; Soli Muratori, Gian Francesco (Ed.) (1767-73). *Opere del proposto Lodovico Antonio Muratori gia' bibliotecario del serenissimo signore Duca di Modena*. Arezzo: Bellotti.

NAGL, Ivan (1985). *Autonomie und Gnade: über Mozarts Opern*. Munich, Vienna: Hanser.

NELSON, Robert J. (1969). *Immanence and transcendence: the theater of Jean Rotrou 1609-1650*. Columbus, OH: Ohio State University Press.

NEWMAN, Ernest (1967). *Gluck and the opera: a study in musical history*. London: Gollancz.

NIDERST, Alain (1972). *Fontenelle à la recherche de lui-même*. Paris: Nizet.

NUSSBAUM, Martha (1992). Tragedy and self-sufficiency: Plato and Aristotle on fear and pity. In Amélie Oksenberg Rorty (Ed.), *Essays on Aristotle's* Poetics (pp. 261-90). Princeton, NJ: Princeton University Press.

OOSTVELDT, Bram van (2005). *Tranen om het alledaagse: het verlangen naar natuurlijkheid en de enscenering van burgerlijke identiteit in drama en theater in de Oostenrijkse Nederlanden*. Ph.D. dissertation, Universiteit Gent.

OOSTVELDT, Bram van; BUSSELS, Stijn (2012, forthcoming). 'One never sees monsters without experiencing emotions': le merveilleux and the sublime in theories on French performing arts (1650-1750). In Caroline Van Eck & Jürgen Pieters (Eds.), *Pre-histories of the sublime*. Leiden: Brill.

OSSI, Massimo (2003). *Divining the oracle: Monteverdi's seconda prattica*. Chicago, IL; London: University of Chicago Press.

OTTONELLI, Domenico (1652). *Della christiana moderazione del teatro*. Florence: Bonardi.

PALLAVICINO, Ferrante (1640). *La rete di Vulcano*. Venice: Guerigli.

PARIATI, Pietro; ROLLI, Paolo (1734). *Ariadne in Crete, an opera* [orig. *Teseo in Creta*, 1715]. London: Wood.

PASCAL, Blaise; Le Guern, Michel (Ed.) (2004). *Pensées*. Paris: Gallimard.

PASQUALIGO, Benedetto. (1719). *Ifigenia in Tauride. Tragedia da cantarsi*. Venice: Rossetti.

PASSARELLI, Almerico (1655). *L'Endimione. Drama*. Ferrara: Suzzi.

PIERI, Marzio (2003). Opera and Italian literature. In Lorenzo Bianconi & Giorgio Pestelli (Eds.), *Opera in theory and practice, image and myth* [orig. publ. as *Storia dell'opera italiana: teorie e tecniche, immagini e fantasmi*, 1988] (pp. 221-86). Chicago, IL: Univerity of Chicgao Press.

PIOVENE, Agostino (1714). *Marsia deluso. Favola pastorale*. Venice: Rossetti.

PLANELLI, Antonio (1772). *Dell'opera in musica*. Naples: Campo.

PLUTARCH (1702-11). *Plutarch's lives, translated from the Greek, by several hands*. London: Tonson.

POLLAROLO, Carlo Francesco (1987). *Il Faramondo* [premiered 1699-1710]. Full score, Milan: Ricordi.

PORÉE, Charles; Flamarion, Édith (Ed.) (2000). *De Theatro (1733) avec la traduction en regard du P. Brumoy*. Toulouse: Société de littératures classiques.

PORTOGALLO, Marco (2003). *Gli Orazi e i Curiazi* [premiered 1798]. Full score, San Giuliano Milanese: BMG / Ricordi.

POSTEL, Christian Heinrich (1699). *Die wunderbahr-errettete Iphigenia. In einem Singe-Spiel auff dem Hamburgischen Schau-Platz vorgestellet*. Hamburg: Spieringk.

POWELL, John (2001). Music and the scenic portrayal of gods, men, and monsters in Corneille's *Andromède*. Unpublished paper presented at the symposium *Gods, men, and monsters*, Oxford, New College, 2-4 April 2001. Online: http://www.personal.utulsa.edu/ffijohn-powell/Andromede/HTM_files/Introduction.htm (Accessed 3 January 2010).

POWELL, John (2004). The metamorphosis of *Psyché*. In Carine Barbafieri & Chris Rauseo (Eds.), *Les métamorphoses de* Psyché (pp. 223-50). Valenciennes: Presses Universitaires.

PROPP, Vladimir (1968). *Morphology of the folktale* [2nd ed.; orig. publ. as *Морфология сказки*, 1928]. Austin, TX: University of Texas Press.

QUINAULT, Philippe; Brooks, William et al. (Eds.) (1994). Alceste *suivi de* La querelle d'Alceste: *anciens et modernes avant 1680*. Geneva: Droz.

QUINAULT, Philippe; Norman, Buford (Ed.) (1999). *Livrets d'opéra*. Toulouse: Société de littératures classiques.

QUINAULT, Philippe; HAYM, Nicolà (1715). *Teseo. Dramma tragico*. London: Buckley.

RACINE, Jean (1675). *Iphigénie*. Paris: Barbin.

RACINE, Jean (1962). *Œuvres complètes*. Paris: Seuil.

RACINE, Jean; Forestier, Georges (Ed.) (1999). *Œuvres complètes*. Paris: Gallimard.

RAGLAN, Fitzroy Richard Sommerset, Baron (1956). *The hero* [repr.; orig. publ. 1936]. New York, NY: Vintage.

REBAUDENGO, Maurizio (1995). *Giovan Battista Andreini: tra poetica e drammaturgia*. Turin: Rosenberg & Sellier.

REEVE, M. D. (1972). Euripides, *Medea* 1021-1080. *Classical quarterly*, 22, 51-61.

RIGINOS, Alice Swift (1976). *The anecdotes concerning the life and writings of Plato*. Leiden: Brill.

ROACH, Joseph R. (1985). *The player's passion: studies in the science of acting*. Newark, DE: University of Delaware Press.

ROBINSON, Michael F. (1972). *Naples and Neapolitan opera*. Oxford: Clarendon.

ROLLAND, Romain (1931). *L'histoire de l'opéra en Europe avant Lully et Scarlatti* [rev. ed.; orig. publ. 1895]. Paris: Boccard.

ROLLI, Paulo (1734). *Ariadne in Naxus: an opera*. London: Aris.

ROLLI, Paolo (1993). Ifigenia in Aulide. In Carlo Caruso (Ed.), *Libretti per musica* (pp. 423-51). Milan: Angeli.

ROSAND, Ellen (1991). *Opera in seventeenth-century Venice: the creation of a genre*. Berkeley and Los Angeles, CA; Oxford: University of California Press.

RUSHTON, Julian (1976). Philidor and the tragédie lyrique. *Musical Times*, 117(1603), 734-7.

RUSSELL, Donald A. (2001). *Plutarch* [2nd ed.; orig. publ. 1972]. Bristol: Bristol Classical Press.

SAFRANSKI, Rudiger (2007). *Romantik: eine Deutsche Affäre*. Munich: Hanser.

SALVI, Antonio (1728). *L'Andromaca. Drama per musica* [premiered 1701]. Florence: Verdi.

SBARRA, Francesco (1667). *Le disgrazie d'amore. Dramma giocosomorale*. Vienna: Cosmerovio.

SCHLEGEL, Johann Elias; Schubert, Werner (Ed.) (1963). *Ausgewählte Werke*. Weimar: Arion.

SCHNEIDER, Herbert (1988). Les monologues dans l'opéra de Lully. *XVIIe siècle*, 161, 353-63.

SCHOLES, Robert (1974). *Structuralism in literature: an introduction*. New Haven, CT; London: Yale University Press.

SELFRIDGE-FIELD, Eleanor (2007). *A new chronology of Venetian opera and related genres, 1660-1760*. Stanford, CA: Stanford University Press.

SENECA, Lucius Annæus; Fitch, John G. (Ed. and Trans.) (2002). *Hercules, Trojan women, Phoenician women, Medea, Phaedra*. Cambridge, MA; London: Harvard University Press.

SLOTERDIJK, Peter (2004). *Im Weltinnenraum des Kapitalismus: für eine philosophische Theorie der Globalisierung*. Frankfurt am Main: Suhrkamp.

SMART, Sara (1989). *Doppelte Freude der Musen: court festivities in Brunswick-Wolfenbüttel 1642-1700*. Wiesbaden: Harrassowitz.

SMITH, Ruth (1995). *Handel's oratorios and eighteenth-century thought*. Cambridge: Cambridge University Press.

SOGRAFI, Simeone Antonio (1798a). *Gli Orazi e i Curiazi. Tragedia per musica*. Venice: Valvasense.

SOGRAFI, Simeone Antonio (1798b). *La morte di Semiramide. Dramma per musica* [premiered 1792]. Venice: Valvasense.

SOLERTI, Angelo (1903). *Le origini del melodrama*. Turin: Bocca.

SOMMERSTEIN, Alan H. (2005). Tragedy and myth. In Rebecca W. Bushnell (Ed.), *A companion to tragedy* (pp. 163-80). Malden, MA: Blackwell.

SOPHOCLES; Lloyd-Jones, Hugh (Ed. and Trans.) (1996). *Fragments*. Cambridge, MA; London: Harvard University Press.

SPOOR, Heinrich (1707). *Favissæ, utriusque antiquitatis tam Romanæ quam Græcæ*. Utrecht: Mutendam.

STAROBINSKI, Jean (2006). *L'invention de la liberté 1700-1789: les emblèmes de la raison*. Paris: Gallimard.

STATIUS, Publius Papinius; Dewar, Michael (Ed. and Trans.) (1991). *Thebaid IX*. Oxford: Clarendon.

STERNFELD, Frederick William (1993). *The birth of opera*. Oxford: Clarendon.

STROHM, Reinhard (1976). *Italienische Opernarien des frühen Settecento (1720-1730)*. Cologne: Volk.

STROHM, Reinhard (1997). *Dramma per musica: Italian opera seria of the eighteenth century*. New Haven, CT; London: Yale University Press.

STROHM, Reinhard (1998). Rezitativ. In Ludwig Finscher (Ed.), *Die Musik in Geschichte und Gegenwart*, Sachteil VIII (columns 224-42). Kassel et al.: Bärenreiter.

STROHM, Reinhard (2002). Zenobia: voices and authorship in opera seria. In Szymon Paczkowski & Alina Zorawska-Witkowska (Eds.), *Johann Adolf Hasse in seiner Epoche und in der Gegenwart: Studien zur Stil- und Quellenproblematik* (pp. 53-81). Warsaw: Instytut Muzykologii Uniwersytetu Warszawskiego.

STROHM, Reinhard (2006). Dramatic dualities: opera pairs from Minato to Metastasio. In Melania Bucciarelli, Norbert Dubowy & Reinhard Strohm (Eds.), *Italian opera in Central Europe*, I (pp. 275-95). Berlin: Berliner Wissenschafts-Verlag.

STROHM, Reinhard (2008). Memories of ancient rituals in early opera. Paper delivered at the conference *Ritual dynamics and the science of ritual*, University of Heidelberg, 29 September-2 October 2008.

STROHM, Reinhard (2010). Ancient tragedy in opera, and the operatic debut of *Oedipus the King* (Munich, 1729). In Peter Brown & Suzana Ograjenšek (Eds.), *Ancient drama in music for the modern stage* (pp. 160-76). Oxford: Oxford University Press.

STROZZI, Giulio (1639). *La Delia, o sia la Sera sposa del Sole. Poema drammatico.* Venice: Pinelli.

SZONDI, Peter (1973). *Die Theorie des bürgerlichen Trauerspiels im 18. Jahrhunderts: der Kaufmann, der Hausvater und der Hofmeister.* Frankfurt: Suhrkamp.

TARDIVELO, Bortolo (1705). *Ifigenia. Drama per musica.* Venice: Corona.

TEDESCO, Anna (2003). "All'usanza spagnola": el *arte nuevo* de Lope de Vega y la òpera italiana del siglo XVII. *Criticon*, 87-88-89, 737-852.

TEDESCO, Anna (2006). "Scrivere a gusti del popolo": l'*arte nuevo* di Lope de Vega nell'Italia del Seicento. *Il saggiatore musicale*, *13*(2), 221-45.

TERMINI, Olga Ascher (1970). *Carlo Francesco Pollarolo: his life, time, and music with emphasis on the operas.* Ph.D. dissertation, University of Southern California.

TERMINI, Olga Ascher (1979). Carlo Francesco Pollarolo: follower or leader in Venetian opera? *Studi musicali*, *8*, 223-71.

TIRABOSCO, Marc'Antonio (1642). *L'Alcate. Drama rappresentato in musica.* Venice: Surian.

TOMLINSON, Gary (1999). *Metaphysical song: an essay on opera.* Princeton, NJ: Princeton University Press.

TOSI, Pierfrancesco (1723). *Opinioni de' cantori antichi e moderni o sieno osservazioni sopra il canto figurato.* Bologna: dalla Volpe.

TOSI, Pierfrancesco; Galliard, John Ernest (Trans.) (1742). *Observations on the florid song or, Sentiments on the ancient and modern singer* [orig. publ. as *Opinioni de' cantori antichi e moderni o sieno osservazioni sopra il canto figurato*, 1723]. London: Wilcox.

TRONSARELLI, Ottavio (1626). *La catena d'Adone. Favola boschereccia.* Rome: Corbelletti.

VARIOUS (1703-45). *Recueil général des opéra [sic] représentés par l'Académie Royale de Musique depuis son établissement.* Paris: Ballard.

VARIOUS (1612). *Vocabolario degli Accademici della Crusca.* Venice: Albert. Online: http://vocabolario.signum.sns.it (Accessed 17 March 2011).

VARIOUS (1997). *Archive for the Performance of Greek and Roman drama.* Online: http://www.apgrd.ox.ac.uk/people/imagesdocs/eh1566-1997.htm (Accessed 1 March 2010).

VILLENEUVE, Josse de (1756). *Lettre sur le méchanisme de l'opéra italien.* Paris: Duchesne & Lambert.

VINCI, Leonardo et al. (1728). *L'Andromaca.* Full score, Brussels, Koninklijk Conservatorium-Conservatoire Royal, no. 2365.

VERGIL; Austin, R. G. (Ed.) (1963). *Aeneidos: liber quartus*. Oxford: Clarendon.

VERGIL; Mynors, R. A. B. (Ed.) (1990). *Georgics*. Oxford: Clarendon.

VERGIL; Pease, Arthur Stanley (1935). *Publii Vergilii Maronis Aeneidos liber quartus*. Cambridge, MA: Harvard University Press.

VOLTAIRE (1762). *Dictionnaire philosophique ou introduction à la connoissance de l'homme*, Paris: Durand-Guillyn.

WEAVER, Robert Lamar; WEAVER, Norma Wright (1978). *A chronology of music in the Florentine theater 1590-1750*. Detroit, MI: Information Coordinators.

WEISS, Piero (1982). Teorie drammatiche e "infranciosamento": motivi della "riforma" melodrammatica nel primo settecento. In Lorenzo Bianconi & Giovanni Morelli (Eds.), *Antonio Vivaldi: teatro musicale cultura e società*, II (pp. 273-98). Florence: Olschki

WEISS, Piero (1984). Baroque opera and the two verisimilitudes. In Edmond Strainchamps (Ed.), *Music and civilization: essays in honor of Paul Henry Lang* (pp. 117-26). New York, NY: Norton.

WEISS, Piero (1988). Opera and neoclassical dramatic criticism in the seventeenth century. In *Studies in the history of music. Volume 2: music and drama* (pp. 1-30). New York, NY: Broude.

WEISS, Piero (Ed.) (2002). *Opera: a history in documents*. New York, NY; Oxford: Oxford University Press.

WISEMAN, Thomas P. (2004). *The myths of Rome*. Exeter: University of Exeter Press.

WOOD, Caroline (1981). Orchestra and spectacle in the *tragédie en musique*, 1673-1715: oracle, *sommeil* and *tempête*. *Proceedings of the Royal Musical Association* 108, 25-46.

ZARDINI, Francesca; ZARDINI LANA, Grazia (2007). *Gli Ulissi di Giacomo Badoaro: albori dell'opera a Venezia*. Verona: Fiorini.

ZEISS, Laurel E. (1999). Accompanied recitative in Mozart's operas: "The chef d'œuvre of the composer's art". Ph.D. dissertation, University of North Carolina, Chapel Hill.

ZELLER, J. G. Bernhard (1911). *Das recitativo accompagnato in den Opern J.A. Hasses*. Ph.D. dissertation, Universität Halle-Wittenberg.

ZENO, Apostolo (1699). *Faramondo. Drama per musica*. Venice: Nicolini.

CONTRIBUTORS' BIOGRAPHIES

GEOFFREY BURGESS is a freelance scholar and Adjunct Professor at the Eastman School of Music. An active Baroque oboist, he has performed extensively in Europe, Australia, and the USA with renowned orchestras such as Les Arts Florissants. His doctoral dissertation on ritual in French Baroque opera (Cornell University, 1997) won the Donald J. Grout Award. His book *The oboe* (Yale University Press, 2007; with Bruce Haynes) has become a standard reference work and won the Bessaraboff Prize from the American Musical Instrument Society. An earlier version of his contribution to this volume was presented at the annual meeting of the Society for Seventeenth-Century Music (Rochester, NY, 25 April 2009).

BRUNO FORMENT is Postdoctoral Fellow (FWO) at Ghent University and Lecturer at the Vrije Universiteit Brussel. His essays on operatic poetry, music, and stage design appeared in international journals like *Early music* and the *Journal of seventeenth-century music*, and in the volume *Ancient drama in music for the modern stage* (Oxford University Press, 2010). He is the recipient of grants and awards from the Belgian American Educational Foundation, the Fulbright-Hays Commission, the Goldberg Early Music Foundation, and the Swiss Musicological Society. His chapter derives from a paper delivered at the twelfth International Biennial Conference on Baroque Music (Warsaw, 29 July 2006).

ROBERT C. KETTERER is Professor of Classics at the University of Iowa and former vice president of the American Handel Society. He is the author of *Ancient Rome in early opera* (University of Illinois Press, 2009) and the co-editor of *Crossing the stages: the production, performance and reception of ancient theater* (*Syllecta classica*, X, 1999). Recent publications include articles in the *Händel-Jahrbuch* and the *International journal of the classical tradition*, as well as a chapter in *Ancient drama in music for the modern stage* (2010). He read an earlier draft of his contribution to this book as Howard Serwer Lecturer at the American Handel Festival (Centre College, 28 February 2009).

JEAN-FRANÇOIS LATTARICO is Professor of Italian Literature and Opera history at the Université 'Jean-Monnet' of Saint-Étienne. He recently published a translation of Francesco Pona's novel *La Messalina* (Les Translatives, 2009) and a critical edition of Busenello's unpublished libretto *Il viaggio d'Enea all'inferno* (Palomar, 2010). He is currently preparing monographs on Busenello and the Accademia degli Incogniti. Originally entitled "*Lo scherno degli dei*: mythe et dérision dans le *dramma per musica* du XVIIe siècle," his contribution to this book was presented in the colloquium *The embodied myth in the dramma per musica* (Brussels, 7 December 2006).

Reinhard Strohm is Emeritus Professor of Music at the University of Oxford and Emeritus Fellow of Wadham College. He has published widely on late-medieval music, eighteenth-century opera, and music historiography. His recent books include *Dramma per musica: Italian opera seria of the eighteenth century* (Yale University Press, 1997) and *The operas of Antonio Vivaldi* (Olschki, 2008). He is a corresponding member of the American Musicological Society, a fellow of the British Academy, and the recipient of various awards, among which the Dent medal of the Royal Musical Association and the Glarean-Preis of the Swiss Musicological Society. He read an early version of his chapter at *The embodied myth in the dramma per musica*.

Bram van Oostveldt is Assistant Professor of Theater Studies at the University of Amsterdam, where he is working on technologies of vision and spectacle in the early nineteenth century. He is currently preparing a book on the concept of 'naturalness' in eighteenth-century French theater and drama, co-writing (with Stijn Bussels) a volume on spectacular culture and lifelike images in nineteenth-century Belgium, and co-organizing the conference *Waking the dead: sublime poetics and popular culture after the French Revolution* (Villa Medici, Rome, January 2011). His contribution to this volume was originally presented at the conference *The embodied myth in the dramma per musica*.

INDEX